AS Religious Studies

Sarah K. Tyler
Gordon Reid

Gopinder Kaur

Jon Mayled

Dominique Messent

Jennifer Smith

Published by:
Edexcel Limited
One90 High Holborn
London WC1V 7BH
www.edexcel.org.uk

Distributed by:
Pearson Education Limited
Edinburgh Gate
Harlow
Essex CM20 2JE

First published 2006

ISBN 1-84690-001-8
       978-184690-001-3

Dedication
This book is dedicated to Phil Tyler who, sadly, died during its production. He will be remembered always for the little things and the great.

Cover and book design by Rupert Purcell
Page make-up by Bob Vickers
Picture research by Susan Millership
Index by Joan Dearley
Commissioned by Bob Osborne
Project management by Jayne de Courcy and Will Burrows
Edited by Eva Fairnell
Production by Trudy Kimber
Printed and bound in Great Britain by CPI Bath Press

Picture credits
The Publishers would like to thank the following for permission to reproduce copyright material:
p3 © Mary Evans; p5 © TopFoto/HIP; p6 © 2003 Charles Walker/TopFoto; p8 © TopFoto; p15 © 2001 Topham Picturepoint/TopFoto; p16 © The British Museum/HIP/TopFoto; p17 © Lalla Ward; p18 © Mary Evans; p22 © 1999 Topham Picturepoint/TopFoto; p25 © Mary Evans; p28 © TopFoto; p35 © 2006/TopFoto/Carol; p37 © Volker Möhrke/CORBIS; p41 © 2001 Topham/AP; p43 © Alinari Archives/CORBIS; p44 © Russ Mackechnie; p46 © 2006 TopFoto/Photri; p47 ©Josef Polleross/The Image Works/TopFoto; p49 © TopFoto; p51 © Rick Wilking/Reuters/CORBIS; p54 © Roger-Viollet/TopFoto; p56 © Jean-Philippe Arles/Reuters/CORBIS; p60 © 2005 TopFoto/Fortean; p61 © Polak Matthew/CORBIS SYGMA; p62 © Historical Picture Archive/Corbis; p70 (top) © Ettore Ferrari/epa/CORBIS; p70 (bottom) © Kazuyoshi Nomachi/CORBIS; p72 © Bettmann/CORBIS; p76 © Historical Picture Archive/CORBIS; p83 © Mary Evans; p84 © Burstein Collection/CORBIS; p86 (top) © Christine Aldridge taken at the premiere of *Cinderella – An Original Opera* by Philip Tyler and Carlyon Viles (bottom) © CORBIS; p89 © Ross Taylor/CORBIS; P91 (top and bottom) © Bettmann/CORBIS; p96 ©Alinari/TopFoto; p102 © Rick Friedman/CORBIS; p106 © Kim Kulish/CORBIS; p109 © TopFoto; p110 © 2004 TopFoto/Image Works; pp112,115 © Bettmann/CORBIS; p116 © 2001 Topham Picturepoint/Touchstone Pictures/TopFoto; p117 © 2006 TopFoto; p119 © 2002 Topham Picturepoint/TopFoto; p121 © Namir Noor-Eldeen/Reuters/CORBIS; p122 © Russ Mackechnie Cover image © Aflo Foto Agency/Alamy

While every effort has been made to trace all copyright holders, if you have been overlooked, please contact the Publishers and they will be pleased to make the necessary arrangements at the first opportunity.

Contents

Introduction to Edexcel AS Religious Studies

About the exam

The AS exam revolves around two units – Unit 1: Foundations and Unit 2: Investigations. Unit 2 is a coursework unit while Unit 1 is assessed by a written exam. In this exam you will be required to answer three questions from a choice of eighteen, covering nine possible areas of study, of which you must study *at least* two. The nine areas of study are:

- Philosophy of Religion
- Ethics
- Buddhism
- Christianity
- Hinduism
- Judaism
- Sikhism
- New Testament.

Two questions will be set on each area of study.

About this book

The first four chapters of this book contain the content required by the specification for two areas of study: Philosophy of Religion and Ethics. Chapter 5 consists of exam guidance.

There are 'Test Yourself questions' at the end of sections within a chapter. These are denoted by this icon in the margin:

The questions – and sample answers – are on the accompanying CD-ROM.

About the CD-ROM

The CD-ROM contains the content for the other seven areas of study – Buddhism, Christianity, Hinduism, Judaism, Sikhism, and New Testament – as well as Philosophy of Religion and Ethics. There is also exam guidance for each area and general coursework guidance for Unit 2: Investigations.

The initial screen on the CD-ROM allows you to select any one of the nine areas of study. You can then decide whether to view the content on screen, go straight to the 'Test Yourself questions' or print off the whole module. (The print option is not available for Philosophy of Religion and Ethics as these are in the textbook.)

The CD-ROM also contains the full AS/A2 specification in printable form.

CHAPTER 1
Philosophical arguments about the existence of God

1.1 God and philosophy

Key Ideas

■ The nature of the God of classical theism as omnipotent, omniscient and perfectly good

■ The need to prove the existence of God

■ Types of philosophical reasoning and their attendant problems

The God of classical theism

The three main Western religious traditions, Judaism, Christianity and Islam, all hold to the central belief that God is one, hence they are **monotheistic** faiths. However God may reveal himself, he is indivisible; the Christian doctrine of the Trinity is not a violation of this central belief. The doctrine of the Trinity is the belief that God makes himself known in three distinct persons, the Father, Son and Holy Spirit, and yet remains wholly one. He is not three gods, but God manifests himself in creation, salvation and revelation in the three persons of the one Godhead.

For all the monotheistic faiths, God is the supreme reality or, as the 11th century theologian Anselm described him, 'that than which nothing greater can be conceived'. Such a being must, of necessity, possess all the perfections that there are to possess and cannot be exceeded in perfection by any other being, or this would be a contradiction of his supreme perfection.

The perfection of God has led to problems of how to express that perfection, and some philosophers have fallen back on the **via negativa**, speaking of God entirely in terms of what he is not, for example that he is not evil. However, this is not entirely satisfactory because it leaves us with no meaningful content to God, and believers clearly want to say something rather than nothing about him. This has led to many things being said about God in an attempt to capture his completeness and perfection, all of which are encapsulated in his personal nature. Richard Swinburne explains it as: 'By a person I mean an individual with basic powers (to act intentionally), purposes and beliefs' (*Is There a God?*, Oxford University Press, 1996). The primary attributes of the God of classical theism are his **omnipotence**,

Taking it further...

Anselm's ontological argument demonstrates that the existence of God is a necessary prerequisite of his being 'that than which nothing greater can be conceived'. This argument is covered at A2.

omniscience and **perfect goodness**. These attributes are essential to his role in creating and sustaining the world and serving as the ground to all human moral values.

Omnipotence

To be omnipotent means to be to able to do everything. However, it is reasonable to ask whether this means, in the case of God, literally everything or only those things (hardly a limited number) that are logically possible. If God can do literally everything, then he must be able to, for example, make a stone too heavy for him to lift, build a wall too high for him to climb over, make a square circle, create a thing that exists and does not exist at the same time, make 2 + 2 = 5 and change the past. Descartes maintained that God could do all these things and more, but centuries previously Aquinas had listed 20 things that God could not do. Certainly it would make little sense to say that God can do the logically impossible because these things themselves do not describe anything that makes sense. Aquinas defined as 'absolutely impossible' any thing where the 'predicate is altogether incompatible with the subject'. In the *Summa Theologica* (Resources for Christian Living, 1981) he wrote: 'Whatever implies contradiction does not come within the scope of divine omnipotence, because it cannot have the aspect of possibility. Hence it is more appropriate to say that such things cannot be done, than that God cannot do them.' Hence, to be omnipotent involves being able to do all things that are possible. For example, it is not considered a limit to God's powers that he cannot draw a square circle because it cannot be done.

So, God's omnipotence must include all those things that are logically and physically possible and that do not contradict his nature. Such a God can intervene in the world and act against what are commonly called 'laws of nature' and he does so on the grounds that he is the supreme creator on whom all things depend. **Classical theists** believe that God's creation of humanity and the universe was for a purpose, although he remains transcendent and exists above and beyond the limits of human experience. 'The God of the Bible stands above the world as its sovereign Lord, its Creator and its Saviour; but he appears in the world to set men tasks to do, speaking to men in demand, in promise, in healing and fulfilment' (John A. Hutchenson, *A Handbook of Christian Theology*, Fontana, 1960).

Throughout the Bible, God's action in the world is consistently illustrated by accounts of miraculous events in which God suspends the laws of nature to accomplish his purpose and guide the course of history. The biblical writers had no concept of natural law that determined how the universe operates, and so when God intervenes in the course of events it is never portrayed as a violation of natural laws. This certainly avoids the problem of why God would break his own rules when performing a miracle, because there are no rules to break or laws to violate.

'Belief in miracles exists where nature is regarded only as an object of arbitrariness... which nature uses only as an instrument of its own will and pleasure. Water divides or rolls itself together like a firm mass... the sun now stands still, now goes backward. And all these contradictions of nature happen for the welfare of Israel, purely at the command of Jehovah, who troubles himself about nothing but Israel' (Ludwig Feuerbach, *The Essence of Christianity*, Prometheus Books, 1989).

Omniscience

In the same way, if God is omniscient (all knowing), we need to establish the extent of God's all knowingness. Richard Swinburne suggests that God's omniscience means that whatever is true, God knows it: 'If it snowed on 1 January 10 million BC on the site of present-day New York, God knows that it snowed there and then… All God's beliefs are true, and God believes everything that is true' (*Is There a God?*, Oxford University Press, 1996). However, God is not required to know what it is logically impossible to know, or to know all fictions and false propositions, as some thinkers have suggested. Similarly, does God's omniscience mean that he must know what someone will freely do in the future? Because God is omnipotent, he has chosen to create free beings, which must impose a limit on his omniscience because it would be logically impossible for God to know in advance what free beings were going to do.

The Bible appears to support this view, for example, when God decides to destroy humanity in the Great Flood. In Genesis 6:6 the writers say: 'The Lord was sorry that he had made humankind on the earth and it grieved him to his heart. So the Lord said: "I will blot out from the earth the human beings I have created… for I am sorry that I have made them".' If God had known in advance that his creatures would behave so immorally that he would be obliged to destroy them, then surely he would not have created them in the first place?

This view depends, of course, on accepting that human agents do have at least some element of freewill in the sense that there are no external causes that determine how they will choose to act. It certainly seems that we have a sufficient degree of freedom and even the world itself is not fully determined. One explanation for the problem of natural evil may be that God gave to creation as well as to mankind the ability to make at least some choices for themselves.

Two major problems are raised by God's omniscience. The first is the classic problem of evil. If God knows of all past, present and future events of evil and suffering and has failed, and will continue to fail, to intervene to prevent their occurrence and, further, to prevent the occurrence of the consequences of those events, he faces some hard moral questioning. This further questions God's omnipotence because if he could have made a world in which evil and suffering did not occur, then it is reasonable to ask why he did not so, and, if he could not have made such a world, his sovereignty and power are compromised. Although the biblical writers seem to be comfortable with the view that God is, without contradiction, responsible for both good and evil, for example the great Flood, the sufferings of Job and the death of the first born, modern thinkers are less satisfied with this.

The second major problem is that of salvation. If God has chosen some people to be saved and others to suffer eternal damnation, then what difference does it make how we behave, what choices we make and what influence others attempt to have on us? How can we justify the moral goodness of those who do not believe in God, because what eschatological value can it have to them? If salvation is by faith and not works, does faith even have any meaning if God has determined that an individual should have faith?

Taking it further...

Freewill need not be limited to human beings, but also may apply to the natural order. Natural evil, events in the natural order that cause pain and suffering to humans, may be the consequence of the natural order exercising its divinely given freewill.

A 19th century print depicting God as a juggler, amusing himself with the worlds he has created

Anton Thorn argues why should anyone accept belief in an omniscient God when 'this notion cannot be integrated with the facts of reality'? (http://www.geocities.com/Athens/Sparta/1019/Omniscience.htm). Firstly, for an omniscient being, knowledge cannot be the result of the long processes that humans have to face to gain new knowledge. God's omniscience is therefore unearned knowledge and it is never the product of any mental effort. Thorn argues that such knowledge is at odds with every other concept of knowledge that we have and, hence, incomprehensible. Secondly, what purpose would exhaustive knowledge serve? If God is immortal, everlasting and eternal, what need does he have of such knowledge? The notion of a God who knows all things, however private, serves, Thorn claims, to benefit those who would seek domination over others through forcing them into certain behaviour patterns. He claims there is no real need for God to be omniscient.

Perfect goodness (omnibenevolence)

God's perfect goodness arises from him being omnipotent and omniscient and does not contradict or conflict with those attributes. The goodness of God is not a remote quality or attribute, but is expressed through his direct activity in the lives of his people. This is done both through the standards God sets and through how he responds to them in their attempts to live up to those standards. God himself is more than a model of goodness, he is perfectly good, although God's goodness is not the same as human goodness. If this is so, then nothing can give rise to our describing any of God's actions as cruel, vindictive or vengeful. J. S. Mill argued that a good God should not act differently to a good person, so we cannot justify apparently evil acts of God on the grounds that he is divine and so can act in mysteriously different ways.

One of the central questions in religious philosophy concerns the relationship between God and goodness. Does God create moral standards that he issues as commands, or does he command that which he already knows as good? This is known as the **Euthyphro Dilemma** (for a fuller discussion of this see section 3.2). This dilemma is difficult to solve, because religious believers tend to use God's commands as a means of deciding what is good but are aware that sometimes their relationship with God might call them to do something that they know rationally would be considered wrong.

The goodness of God, therefore, cannot be measured by human standards of goodness but is to be experienced within a relationship that is based in faith, not reason. God's goodness does not depend on circumstances or on him acting in an entirely predictable manner. If it did, then the believer would only be able to love and worship God when he was experiencing God's goodness in a consistent, unchanging way. The experience of many biblical characters shows that not to be the case: Job, Ezekiel, David, Paul, Stephen and Jesus himself, to name but a few. Despite their experiences, these characters, and others like them, accepted that God's goodness is ultimately incomprehensible but utterly reliable.

For the Israelites, God's goodness was experienced through his covenant relationship with them, first revealed in the giving of the Law, including the Ten Commandments (the Decalogue) at Sinai (Exodus 20:1–21). Nevertheless, God's goodness is not inflexible. Although he is angry when his people violate his standards, and because he is just he must judge, he does not do so hard-heartedly. The book of Hosea balances the thought of God's divine

Taking it further...

'Reason and morality normally go together but, just occasionally, it is possible for a love relationship with God to cause someone to do something which goes against society's accepted norms. It may call one of us to leave mother and father, brothers and sisters for a higher love… In the Christian life, lived as part of a love relationship with God, it is just possible that this relationship might call an individual to act against what appears to be rational, reasonable and understandable' (Peter Vardy, *And if it's True?*, Marshall Pickering, 1988).

wrath (which Israel's conduct deserved) against God's desire for them to repent and return to him. 'I will not execute my fierce wrath against them, I will not return to destroy Ephraim: for I am God and not man; the Holy one in your midst' (Hosea 9:11).

Philip Yancey uses the book of Hosea as an example of God's grace, his undeserved favour shown to sinful man. 'In a manner of speaking, grace solves a dilemma for God… On the one hand, God loves us; on the other hand, our behaviour repulses him. God yearns to see in people something of his own image reflected; at best he sees shattered fragments of that image. Still, God cannot – or will not – give up' (*What's So Amazing About Grace?*, Harper Collins, 1997).

The God who created the heavens and the earth, and who is perfectly good, is eager to forgive, and as '"my thoughts are not your thoughts, neither are your ways my ways", declares the Lord' (Isaiah 55:9), he can do what he likes and go to whatever lengths he chooses to be reconciled with his people.

For the New Testament writers, the ultimate demonstration of God's goodness is, of course, in the sending of Jesus. God takes the initiative to overcome the natural inclination to sin that is in all men, and provides the means of redemption in the new covenant promises in Jeremiah 31:31f: the covenant that will be written on men's hearts, not on tablets of stone. John 3:16 expresses it perfectly: 'For God so loved the world that he gave his only Son, so that all who believe in him should not perish but have eternal life'. God's willingness to sacrifice his son is the model of goodness and the saving act to which man is called by the New Testament writers to make a life-changing response, freeing him forever from the impossible task of measuring up to the perfect, unchangeable God.

God in Eastern religious tradition

Hinduism is commonly perceived as **polytheistic**; however, it is a monotheistic religion with one God (Brahman) assuming many forms and names. For example, Brahman as Nirguna has no attributes whereas as Saguna or Iswara he is manifested with attributes. The many different names for God can be found in hymns in the Rig Veda. For example: 'They call him Indra, Mitra, Varuna, Agni, and he is heavenly nobly-winged Garutman. To what is One, sages give many a title they call it Agni, Yama, Matarisvan' (Rig Veda Book 1, Hymn 164.46). Brahman is a mysterious being, occupying the highest place as the Creator, Ruler and Lord, without beginning or end, indestructible and indescribable.

Shiva, the Hindu God, performing the dance of creation

Thus the various forms and names of God that symbolise Brahman reflect different visions according to the many sages and seers. Hinduism is not **henotheistic**, where people believe in one god but are not concerned if he is the only god, because Brahman is one even though he has many names. Henotheism demands that there should be a competing deity against Brahman but this is not the case. Furthermore, even the different Avtars (reincarnations) are not considered independent of Iswara. Neither is Hinduism **pantheistic**, because there is no direct identification of God with the universe. Rather, God and the universe, belonging to the Absolute or Reality, are considered as distinct from each other in Hindu religious philosophy.

Buddhists do not believe in God but rather that by breaking the cycle of rebirth and achieving enlightenment it is possible to reach the state of Nirvana. This is not to be confused with Heaven but rather a state of eternal being, the end of suffering, where there are no desires and no individual. Although there is no omnipotent creator God, Mahayana Buddhists worship bodhisattvas. These are thousands of god-like figures who have gained enlightenment and could enter Nirvana but have chosen to stay in the world to help others. Tibetan Buddhists also worship gods. Manjushri is seen as a representation of the bodhisattvas and, along with Avalokiteshvra, represents the wisdom and compassion of Buddha. This is not limited, however, because, for example, the goddess Tara is worshipped for her compassion, which represents that of the Buddha. The Buddha himself (Siddhartha Guatama) is worshipped, but not as a god, rather as a human who gained enlightenment.

The problems of proving the existence of God

Islamic calligraphy is used to express the nature of God since pictorial images of God and his works are forbidden in Islam

Much of Western philosophy of religion is concerned with attempting to prove the existence of God, or at least to show that belief in God is logically coherent. This is a particular concern of Judaeo-Christian theism because the question of God's existence, or perhaps, more importantly, his non-existence, is not an issue for Islam. Denial of Allah (At Ta'teel) within Islam could include denying his perfection or his attributes (any of the 99 names), failing or refusing to worship him, or worshipping other gods or human beings alongside him (shirk). Claiming that the world can be explained without reference to Allah would also constitute At Ta'teel. Debates about the existence or otherwise of God are not tolerated within Islam as they are within Christianity, as they are considered blasphemous.

The problem of God's existence arises from the philosophical preoccupation with proof and evidence. It is not necessary for a teacher to prove her existence to her students because she is overwhelmingly obvious to them (probably sometimes disconcertingly so!). There are constant physical, empirical indications of the teacher's existence that students pick up through use of their physical senses: she can be seen, heard, touched and perceived as a set of sense data. The students have no reason to believe that they are deceived by any of these data and, although they may come to know other less overwhelmingly obvious things about the teacher, and may even anticipate them, the fact that their relationship is clearly being acted out in the physical world is the primary basis for their knowledge and understanding of her.

However, God cannot be known in this way. Although believers may claim that they hear God and speak to him, that they feel him in their lives in a vivid and real way, that experience can never be the same as their experience of another human being who exists in the spatiotemporal world.

The experience we access to reach conclusions about God is limited and the reasoning powers we have to draw conclusions on the basis of that evidence is limited because it is human. The evidence of our senses may not lead us towards a conclusive proof and relying on the testimony of others demands that we are convinced that their interpretation of the evidence is correct.

This has led to the development of formal proofs for the existence of God that employ logical processes in an attempt to demonstrate that the existence of God is at least highly probable, if not logically necessary. Proofs for the existence of God aim to demonstrate the reasonableness of belief in God, but there is no doubt that they are open to considerable criticism, as we shall see.

Belief in God may be understood in two ways: as **propositional**, i.e. the belief that there is an objective reality to which we ascribe the term God, and that we can make claims about him which themselves are objectively true, or as **non-propositional**, i.e. a trust in God that may be held even when evidence or experience would seem to point against it. This kind of faith must be based in some personal knowledge of God, and not simply in accepting facts about him. Basil Mitchell uses the *Parable of the Partisan and the Stranger* (cited in *The Philosophy of Religion*, edited by Basil Mitchell, Oxford University Press, 1971) to illustrate the nature of non-propositional faith.

> *In times of war a partisan meets a stranger who claims to be the leader of the resistance. He urges the partisan to have faith in him whatever the circumstances, even if he sees the stranger acting in ways that appear to contradict this claim. The partisan is committed to his belief in the stranger's integrity even when his friends think his is a fool to do so. When the stranger appears to be withholding help, or even acting contrary to the partisan's interests, he still believes that he is on his side, and has overwhelming reasons for doing so. The original encounter between the partisan and the stranger gave him sufficient confidence to hold on to his faith in the stranger even when the evidence counted against it.*

This parable demonstrates the problem of talking meaningfully about belief in God, because the believer has not allowed anything to count against his faith. None the less, despite the problems of proving God's existence, or proving that he has certain attributes, religious believers and philosophers have continued to pose formal proofs that meet many of the atheist's challenges.

Arguments for the existence of God

Most arguments for the existence of God fall into two categories, **a priori** arguments, which are entirely conceptual, and **a posteriori** arguments, which are essentially world based. The two arguments you need to address at AS both fall into this category, as they start from observations about the world and work from there towards the conclusion that God exists. In the first category, however, come the different forms of the **ontological argument**, which reasons from the definition of God to his necessary existence.

If God has necessary existence, it effectively means that he cannot not exist, i.e. it is impossible to conceive of him not existing. If all other beings are contingent, i.e. they may or may not exist, then God is the being on which they must necessarily depend for their own existence.

Arguments that appeal to the world as proof of God's existence generally fall into two categories: **cosmological** and **teleological**. The former appeals to

Taking it further...

Atheists may argue that as believers do not allow anything to count against their belief in God, then all arguments are flawed because the criticisms raised against them will not be allowed to carry any real weight. Atheists may claim that their conclusions are just as likely as theists' conclusions and there is no way of verifying or falsifying either of them.

Taking it further...

The psalmist wrote: 'The fool has said in his heart there is no God' (Psalm 14:1), effectively dismissing the need to prove the existence of God because it was foolishness to deny it. However, although God may have been overwhelmingly obvious to the biblical writers, the philosophical tradition of classical theism has consistently tackled the need to prove the existence of a being who is beyond time and space.

The need to explain the existence of the universe has preoccupied religious, scientific and philosophical thinkers throughout history

the existence of the world as demanding an explanation, the latter to features of the world such as order and purpose but also its fittingness for human life and its aesthetic (beautiful) appearance. Other arguments are also sometimes offered, including a moral argument that concludes that God is the necessary source of moral obligation, the existence of human consciousness and religious experience.

Richard Swinburne offers seven factors that he suggests lead to a cumulative argument for the existence of God:

- the very existence of the universe
- the fact that the universe is ordered
- the existence of consciousness
- human opportunities to do good
- the pattern of history
- the evidence of miracles
- religious experience.

Such a cumulative argument increases the probability of God's existence on the premise that the weaknesses of one argument are counterbalanced by the strengths of another.

The crucial question that needs to be asked of any argument for the existence of God is whether it lives up to the standards applied to other philosophical arguments. This means that it should be valid and its premises true. Inevitably, an argument will be appealing to some but not others, because the very nature of the subject of the proof leaves it open to questions of truth and validity.

Other attempts to establish the rationality of God's existence, i.e. not to prove it but to show that it is rational or reasonable to believe that he exists, have also been popular in Western theistic philosophy. For example, Pascal's Wager attempted to demonstrate that although the existence of God could not be proved, it was more prudent to gamble that God exists rather than risk the possibly disastrous consequences in the after life by gambling, incorrectly, that he does not! More recently, some thinkers, such as Alvin Plantinga, have argued that belief in God is a properly basic belief, it does not need to be justified by reference to any external source of proof but is non-foundational, although religious experience may count in its favour. Nevertheless, proofs have been offered because an explanation is needed for certain phenomena within the universe that are not self-explanatory and require an external explanation.

They appeal to reason and logic

It may be possible to show that the non-existence of God is logically impossible, i.e. that it is impossible to conceive of his non-existence. This could be claimed from an examination of the term 'God', which Anselm stated contained everything that was necessary to know about God, including the indisputable fact of his existence.

They may interpret evidence in terms of God rather than something else

Because the universe is religiously ambiguous it can be interpreted in religious or non-religious ways. Arguments for the existence of God seek to demonstrate that the most satisfactory way of interpreting the universe is by reference to God.

Principles of philosophical proof

Arguments for the existence of God should always be thought of in terms of proofs. 'A proof is an argument that starts from one or more premise, which are propositions taken for granted for the purpose of the argument, and argues to a conclusion' (Richard Swinburne, *The Existence of God*, Clarendon Press, 2005). Thus a proof can be represented as Premise (P) + Premise (P) = Conclusion (C). There need not be more than one premise, however, so a proof may simply be P = C or a conclusion may be reached by means of many premises.

A proof is offered as a statement that cannot be false, for example 4+4 = 8. Such a proof is logically necessary and it would be absurd to suggest alternative solutions. A logically necessary statement consists of a set of premises and a conclusion that cannot be disputed. These may include mathematical statements (as above) or tautologies, for example 'all humans are humans'. Other proofs, however, are only proofs in so far as they lead to conclusions that are only possible or probable. Evidence points towards a certain conclusion based on prior experience, or on similar instances, but it is still possible for there to be a different conclusion. For example:

- premise one, the sun rose today
- premise two, the sun rose yesterday
- conclusion, the sun will rise tomorrow.

Although it is highly probable that the sun will rise tomorrow, indeed it may be considered irrational to even suggest the possibility that it may not, it is not logically necessary that it will do so. For all we know, tomorrow may be the day that the natural order determines that the sun will not rise.

Proofs of this kind often work from a specific example to a more general conclusion. For example:

- premise one, Huw is Welsh
- premise two, Huw is a good singer
- conclusion, all Welsh men sing well.

The one instance of Huw's fine singing voice would not be sufficient to justify saying that all Welsh men sing well. If you encounter an increasing number of good Welsh singers, you may indeed increase the probability of an inherent singing ability in Welsh men, but it is not conclusive, neither is it necessarily true, that because Huw is Welsh he sings well, because 'singing well' and 'Welsh' are not a tautology. In other words, 'Welsh' does not mean 'sings well' in the way that 'circle' means 'round'.

Taking it further...

Francis Bacon illustrated the problem of induction with the example of chickens that have been fed and watered and kept in comfortable conditions throughout their life span. There is nothing in their previous experience that would lead them to anticipate that they were to be killed. Hence previous experience is not always a reliable guide to the future.

One of the major problems of philosophical reasoning is the problem of induction that, as the example above illustrates, makes an inference from the particular to the general. David Hume recognised this: 'All inferences from experience suppose, as their foundations, that the future will resemble the past… If there be any suspicion that the course of nature may change, all experience becomes useless and can give rise to no inference or conclusion' (*An Enquiry Concerning Human Understanding*, Oxford University Press, 1999). However, Hume maintained that it was still rational to make inductive inferences.

Probability measures the relative frequency or likelihood of an event taking place, or of circumstances unfolding in a particular way. It demands that we make judgments. If A and B are the case, how likely is it that C will follow? We consider the evidence available to us, and judge, or evaluate, whether the evidence points to a particular conclusion. In general, proofs may be:

- (a) a posteriori, synthetic and inductive
- (b) a priori, analytic and deductive.

A posteriori, synthetic and inductive proof

Such a proof is based on premises argued or drawn from experience but does not contain the conclusion within its premises, and so argues to a conclusion that is not logically necessary. The more evidence stating factors we employ, the greater the likelihood of the conclusion being correct, but it can always be disproved. We cannot conclusively prove it to be the case. For example:

- premise one, all events require a cause
- premise two, the universe is an event
- conclusion, God is the cause of the universe.

This proof is the basis of a **cosmological argument** and leads only to a probable conclusion because there is no analytical, logically necessary, a priori reason why God should be the cause of the universe and not anything else. Neither are the premises themselves logically necessary, there is no compelling reason to agree conclusively that all events require a cause. It is only on the basis of our regular experience that we assert that all events have a cause and experience can be deceptive, limited and open to many interpretations.

A priori, analytic and deductive proof

Such a proof is based on premises that are not drawn from or dependent upon experience, but which contain a logically necessary conclusion. We learn no more from the conclusion than we already knew from the premises, and the use of analytic terms means we are using terms that cannot be misinterpreted. They have a clear and distinct meaning. For example:

- premise one, God is that than which nothing greater can be conceived
- premise two, that than which nothing greater can be conceived must exist
- conclusion, God must exist.

This is known as the **ontological proof**. The ontological proof demands that if we accept this definition of God then we must accept that he possesses, analytically, existence, as he must necessarily possess all perfections, and existence, according to the ontological proof, is a perfection.

Strengths and weaknesses of proofs

Inductive reasoning is strong because it:

- relies on experience that may be universal, or at least may be testable
- is flexible, there is more than one possible conclusion
- does not demand that we accept definitions as fixed.

But it may be weak because:

- it relies on accepting the nature of the evidence
- it demands overwhelmingly good reasons for accepting that the conclusion is the most likely
- alternative conclusions may be just as convincing.

Deductive reasoning may be strong because:

- it does not depend on variable or misunderstood experience
- it accepts that words and definitions have fixed and agreed meanings
- there are no alternative conclusions.

But it may be considered weak because it:

- leads to apparently logically necessary conclusions
- depends on whether we accept the premises as analytically true
- can only say that if there is a God we might be able to make certain claims about him.

John Hick argued that **eschatological verification** could be the solution to establishing whether the atheist's or the theist's claims are valid. This means verification at the end of time, and he draws an analogy between two travellers who are heading down the same road. Neither knows where it leads but one believes that it leads to the Celestial City. He will be proved right or wrong when he gets to the end of the journey but in the meantime he has to live by faith. 'During the course of the journey… they entertain different expectations… about its ultimate destination. And yet when they do turn the last corner, it will be apparent that one of them has been right all the time, and the other wrong… their opposed interpretations of the road constituted genuinely rival assertions… whose status has the peculiar characteristic of being guaranteed retrospectively by a future crux' (John Hick, *Faith and Knowledge*, Fount, 1978).

Taking it further...

Arguments for the existence of God are strong or weak in terms of their form even before you consider their content. For example, if you consider that an inductive argument is relatively stronger than a deductive argument, because it is based on evidence, then it may be thought to be more secure even before the content of the proof is evaluated.

1.2 The design argument

Key Ideas

- Explaining order and design
- Aquinas's Fifth Way
- William Paley's analogical argument
- Arguments from probability and providence
- The aesthetic argument
- The anthropic principle
- Intelligent design

The design argument

'This proof always deserves to be mentioned with respect. It is the oldest, the clearest, and the most accordant with the common reason of mankind' (Immanuel Kant, *The Critique of Pure Reason* Cambridge University Press, 1997).

The **design argument**, often called the **teleological argument**, takes several forms. Coming from the Greek 'telos' meaning order or purpose, it may be concerned with the search for meaning or purpose in the world, usually starting from finding meaning and purpose in parts of the world and extrapolating from there to the whole, or it is concerned with the progress of the world and its parts towards an ultimate goal. This focuses on an interest in regularity.

The first form of the argument is an **analogical** argument, which depends on drawing an analogy between the world or its parts and objects of human design. The second form of the argument is the **inductive** argument, based on the observation that the universe demonstrates regular motion both in its parts and in the whole. To speak of regularity is to speak of a system that abides by laws or rules. If obedience to rules is evident in the universe it is reasonable to ask who or what put those rules in place.

Like the cosmological argument, the design argument goes back to Plato, who stated that the human body, with all its particles and elements, must owe its origin to 'the royal mind soul and mind in the nature of Zeus' (*Philebus*). The Roman thinker, Cicero, also offered a form of the argument in *De Natura Deorum*: 'What could be more clear or obvious when we look up to the sky and contemplate the heavens, than there is some divinity or intelligence.'

Taking it further...

Theology and religious philosophy often draw on the use of analogy. Because God is beyond direct human knowledge and comprehension, analogies are useful in making it possible to say something meaningful about God, while allowing that what is inferred about God from the analogy is greater than what can be said about the world.

Seeking explanations

The design argument has, of course, since undergone many formulations that have made it into a **theistic argument**, one that seeks to prove the existence of the God of classical theism. It suggests that certain aspects of the universe are so perfectly adapted to fulfil their function that they display evidence of being deliberately designed, and that such design can only be explained with reference to an intelligent, personal designer. Since the works of nature are far greater than the works of humanity, it must be an infinitely greater designer, God, who is suggested as the most likely explanation. The contemporary theistic philosopher, Richard Swinburne observes: 'So there is our universe. It is characterised by vast, all persuasive temporal order, the conformity of nature to formula, recorded in the scientific laws formulated by humans. It started off in such a way... as to lead to the evolution of animals and humans. These phenomena are clearly things too big for science to explain... Note that I am not postulating a "God of the gaps", a god merely to explain the things which science has not yet explained. I am postulating a God to explain what science explains; I do not deny that science explains, but I postulate God to explain why science explains' (*Is There a God?*, Oxford University Press, 1996).

The design argument considers a number of issues that are raised by the question 'Why is the universe as it is?' These issues are as follows.

- **Order**: regularities in the behaviour of objects and laws in the universe.
- **Benefit**: the universe is an orderly structure and provides all that is necessary for life.
- **Purpose**: objects within the universe appear to be working towards an end or purpose.
- **Suitability for human life**: the order exhibited by the universe provides the ideal environment for human life to exist.
- **Appearance**: the appearance of the universe, which could be said to exhibit beauty, suggests that it is intended for something more than basic survival.

Further, another approach could be to identify things about the world that could not be different without tremendous implications for human life:

- if the sun were just slightly further away or half as powerful
- if the axis of the earth were slightly different
- if the moon were larger or closer or further away
- if gravity were not such a weak force
- if DNA did not replicate
- if molecules were larger or smaller
- if there were 60 planets in our solar system
- if carbon did not exist
- if the speed of light were half what it is
- if genetic mutation did not happen
- if the rotation of the earth were one-tenth of what it is.

Taking it further...

Richard Swinburne's approach to the design argument appears to address the perennial problem of the relationship between science and religion. Atheist scientists often despair of religious believers who suggest that God is the only necessary explanation for the world and its features, but it is reasonable to offer an argument that unites the two disciplines: science offers insights and explanations that are valid and exciting, but they still need to be explained as they are not complete explanations. See section 1.3 on the **cosmological argument** for a discussion of complete explanations.

Taking it further...

The astronomer Fred Hoyle is said to have observed that the likelihood of the conditions necessary for life coming about by chance were akin to a hurricane sweeping through a scrap yard and assembling a Boeing 747.

These features could be explained as the result of one huge coincidence, but the design argument tries to show that the delicate balance of the universe is such that the probability of it coming about by chance is far too remote.

In seeking to explain these features, proponents of the design argument are committed to rejecting an apparently easy explanation: chance. The features of order and purpose, suitability for human life, even the providential nature of the universe, could all be explained as the result of one huge coincidence, akin to taking a million six-sided dice and with a single throw turning up a six on every one of them. The design argument seeks to demonstrate that the delicate balance of the universe is such that the probability of it coming about by chance is far too remote to be even a partial, let alone a complete, explanation.

There are many ways in which this has been expressed, but the following parable offered by Dave Hunt (*In Defence of the Faith*, Harvest House, 1996) is a useful starting point.

> Suppose two survivors of a shipwreck have drifted for days in a life raft across the South Pacific and at last are washed ashore on an island. Their great hope, of course, is that the island is inhabited so they can find food, medical attention, and a means of returning to their distant homes. Pushing their way into the jungle, they suddenly come upon an automated factory operating full tilt. Though no persona is visible, products are being manufactured, packaged, and labeled for shipping. One of the parties exclaims 'Praise God! The island is inhabited! Someone must have made and oversees this factory!' 'You're crazy', replies his companion. 'There's absolutely no reason to believe that this thing was designed and put together by some intelligent being. It just happened by chance over who knows how many billions of years.' The first man looks down at his feet and sees a watch with a broken wristband lying in the dirt. Again he exclaims, 'Look! A watch! This proves the island's inhabited!' 'You've got to be kidding', retorts his companion. 'That thing is just a conglomeration of atoms that happened to come together in that form by chance plus billions of years of random selection.'

The two characters in this parable represent sharply opposing positions: one believes that the evidence he sees leads to the only possible explanation that the island is inhabited by intelligent and purposeful beings, while his friend maintains that such an explanation goes way beyond the evidence, and is satisfied to say that it has come about by chance. Of course, the division need not be so sharp, as Swinburne observed. It is possible to recognise the claims of science with regard to evolution and modern cosmology, but still to find the need for God to explain those explanations. However, the burden of proof seems to rest with the theist to demonstrate that the universe demands in some way the existence of an intelligent, designing mind, which created and planned the universe for the benefit of all living things, and not just human beings, that inhabit it.

Aquinas's Fifth Way

In the first three of the Five Ways in the *Summa Theologica* (Resources for Christian Living, 1981), Aquinas rejected the possibility of an infinite regress of movers and causes to explain the existence of contingent, mutable beings, and concluded that a first mover and first cause, to which he gave the name God, was a necessary requisite of the universe. In the **Fifth Way** he observes that non-rational beings nevertheless act in a way that leads to the best result: he might have given as an example the annual migration of vast pods of grey whales from their subarctic feeding grounds off the Alaskan coast to their Mexican breeding grounds, a journey of some 20,000 km, taking up to 3 months. Aquinas maintained that since such behaviour patterns rarely change, and their end result is beneficial, there must be a purpose to them, and if non-rational beings can work towards such a goal, something must be directing them to do so. 'We see that things which lack knowledge, such as natural bodies, act for an end, and this is evident from their acting always in the same way, so as to obtain the best result. Hence it is plain that they achieve their end not fortuitously, but designedly. Now whatever lacks knowledge cannot move towards an end, unless it be directed by some being endowed with knowledge and intelligence and this being we call God.'

This form of the argument is based on the following premises.

- There is beneficial order in the universe, i.e. there are things in the universe that work towards an end or purpose.

- This beneficial order could not happen by chance.

- Many objects do not have the intelligence to work towards an end or purpose, i.e. the objects themselves cannot work towards an end or purpose.

- Therefore, they must be directed by something that does have intelligence.

- Therefore God exists as the explanation of beneficial order.

Aquinas's argument is influenced by the observation that the beneficial order in the universe cannot be adequately explained because the universe itself is not self-explanatory and does not exhibit intelligence in its own right. Although initially appealing, this argument could be considered unsound because the premises on which it is based are not necessary premises, and the conclusion is therefore not logically necessary. Who establishes that there is beneficial order in the universe? How do we argue from that to the conclusion that God has designed it?

It is clear that the design argument, in this form and others, is highly **empirical.** By this, we mean that it draws its premises from observation of nature and the world that is based on our experience. It is highly accessible, requiring the observer to note nothing more than the world in which he or she already lives. It is, therefore, an a posteriori argument.

See section 1.1 for an explanation of the different principles on which philosophical proofs work, and for the terms a posteriori and inductive.

St Thomas Aquinas

William Paley

William Paley's analogy of the watch has become the classic form of the analogical argument: 'In crossing a heath, suppose I pitched my foot against a stone, and were asked how the stone came to be there, I might possibly answer, that, for anything I knew to the contrary, it had lain there for ever; not would it, perhaps, be very easy to show the absurdity of this answer. But suppose I found a watch upon the ground, and it should be inquired how the watch happened to be in that place, I should hardly think of the answer which I had before given – that, for anything I knew, the watch might always have been there. Yet why should not this answer serve for the watch as well as for the stone? For this reason... that when we come to inspect the watch we perceive... that its several parts are framed and put together for a purpose' (cited in *The Existence of God*, edited by John Hick, Macmillan, 1964).

For Paley, the world was like a machine that was made up of intricate parts, all of which worked towards an end for the benefit of the whole and all the small adaptations in nature were, for Paley, proof of a providential designing intelligence. Just as the discovery of a watch could not be explained by saying it had always been there, the order evident in the universe also demands an explanation. The watch serves as an analogy for the world: it demonstrates purpose, design and *telos* (an end or ultimate function). All parts of the watch unite to fulfil that function and this unity cannot be explained by chance. 'When we come to inspect the watch, we perceive that its several parts are framed and put together for a purpose, that they are so formed and adjusted as to produce motion, and that motion so regulated as to point out the hour of the day.'

The intricate mechanisms of a watch suggest purposeful and intelligent design

Paley was aware that 30 years previously, David Hume had offered a resounding criticism of the analogical form of the design argument. He was therefore careful to cover many of the criticisms that Hume had raised, suggesting that the analogy could serve only to demonstrate that there was a designer, and not anything about the nature of the designer. He did not commit himself to suggesting that the world was perfect or that it was completely within the grasp of human reason to understand. Hence Paley claims that, even if the watch goes wrong or shows evidence of bad design (the problem of evil), we could still deduce that it had been designed. Perhaps most of all, Paley was concerned to avoid the criticism of anthropomorphism by noting that everything said about the watch applied to the world, but that, in the case of the world, its 'contrivances surpass the contrivances of art, in the complexity, subtlety, and curiosity of the mechanism' (cited in *The Existence of God*, edited by John Hick, Macmillan, 1964).

Working on the principle of like causes produce like effects, Paley concludes that what is true of human design must also be true of the world, and what is true of human designers can also be said of God, although God too is, of course, far greater than a human designer in all his designing power. Richard Swinburne claims: 'The analogy of animals to complex machines seems to me correct, and its conclusion justified' (*Is There a God?*, Oxford University Press, 1996).

Paley is highly critical of the suggestions that the watch might have taken on the form it has by chance, or by some impersonal operating agency, such as a principle of order or the laws of metallic nature, or even that the appearance of design was in some way a trick to persuade mankind that it had been designed. Above all he objects to the criticism that it is impossible to come to conclusions about design on the basis of the limited information available: 'He knows enough for his argument; he knows the utility of the end: he knows the subserviency and adaptation of the means to the end.

These points being known, his ignorance of other points, his doubts concerning other points, affect not the certainty of his reasoning. The consciousness of knowing little need not beget a distrust of that which he does know.'

Paley goes on to show how intricate animals and humans are, leading to the conclusion that God must have been their maker. He famously used the example of the eye and the arm that appear to have design, and clearly have a purpose. In keeping with scientists and naturalists of the 18th century, he was struck forcibly by the intricacy of human bodies and their component parts and, interestingly, the invention of the microscope probably did much to increase an awareness of this complexity.

Criticisms of the analogical argument

Paley could be thought to have made a fundamental problem by using the analogy of the works of human contrivance because we know about a watch and about its maker, therefore it is easy to reach the conclusion that it is designed. The same cannot be said about nature and its apparent order. Furthermore, it is worth asking why Paley did not think that the stone needed an explanation because stones too are complex and could easily have been designed by someone for a purpose. Above all, Paley makes an assumption about the universe and its apparent order because he has observed the universe and its operation and, along with many others, chosen to call it order. However, to say that the universe is patterned on order is to say nothing more than the universe is patterned on the universe.

The well-known atheist and biologist Richard Dawkins has addressed the problems of these assumptions many times. While he agrees that it is unlikely that life in the universe came about by a single chance, there is no reason, he suggests, that it could not have come about through a series of chances, by a series of very small randomly generated steps, each one increasing the likelihood of the next. He challenges too the assumption made by humans that the universe has a purpose. The notion of purpose, he suggests, is a human conceit, because we are purpose driven and, as a result, look at the world through 'purpose-coloured spectacles'. We assume purpose, but, he suggests, there is none. Purpose lies within not outside human beings. In *The Root of all Evil?* (Channel Four, 2006), Richard Dawkins poses the question of why it is necessary to have religious faith in order to find something important and significant in life. 'We are so grotesquely lucky to be here', he claims. Although his choice of terminology is not philosophically helpful, his point is valid. The combination of factors, biological, geographical, ancestral, social and the like, which result, in Dawkins' words, 'in a me or you' are highly improbable. We may as easily, more easily in fact, have not existed than existed. This is enough, he claims, for us to value life as intrinsically special, there is no need to ask for more.

Dawkins is resistant to any attempts to suggest that natural selection can be interpreted as the way in which an intelligent designer plans and gives purpose to his creation. He expresses it thus: 'A true Watchmaker has foresight; he designs his cogs and springs, and plans their interconnections, with a future purpose in his mind's eye. Natural selection, the blind, unconscious, automatic process which Darwin discovered, and which we now

Taking it further...

In a good analogical argument, the characteristics cited as shared characteristics must be truly shared.

Richard Dawkins

know is the explanation for the existence and apparently purposeful form of all life, has no purpose in mind. It has no mind and no mind's eye. It does not plan for the future. It has no vision, no foresight, no sight at all. If it can be said to play the role of the watchmaker in nature, it is the blind watchmaker' (*The Blind Watchmaker*, Longman Scientific and Technical, 1986).

David Hume

David Hume

David Hume criticised the analogical form of the argument in both *An Enquiry Concerning Human Understanding* (Oxford University Press, 1999) and *Dialogues Concerning Natural Religion* (Oxford Paperbacks, 1998). Crucially, he argues that the analogy on which Paley's form of the argument depends is unsound, because it argues from that which we know to that of which we are ignorant. How can we legitimately draw an analogy between that which we know to be limited and imperfect to that which we claim is unlimited and perfect? Furthermore, it is not clear whether the analogy is intended to refer to parts of the universe or the universe as a whole. While we might agree that parts of the universe appear to have a purpose, it is difficult to argue the case for the universe as a whole having such purpose: if so, what is it and how do we discern it?

From a philosophical point of view Hume also observed that we cannot assume that like effects infer like causes. Hume identified the problem of induction in this respect. We infer a designer when we see design because custom has taught us that this is a legitimate connection to make. In most, if not all, cases where there is design there is a designer, but the problem of induction demands that we ask why, rationally, we infer this association. Like effects may infer like causes in 99 out of 100 cases, but not necessarily in 100 out of 100 cases.

Although Paley later attempted to redress this problem, Hume argued that to draw an analogy between the universe and the works of man was highly dangerous to the theist because it led inevitably to **anthropomorphism.** The analogy meant God's qualities and characteristics were so closely identified with those of man in order to make it work that it removed from him the divine distinctiveness that the believer surely wants to preserve. If God is to be compared with a human designer then it serves only to emphasise his limitedness, changeability and fallibility, and in no way serves to support the view that a single deity of infinite capacity designed and created the universe with a benevolent interest in his creatures. The implications of this criticism are important, because comparison with a human agent would surely imply that God is non-moral, limited and fallible, and that his creation is conceivably 'only the first rude essay of some infant deity, who afterward abandoned it, ashamed of his lame performance … it is the production of old age in some superannuated deity, and ever since his death has run on from the first impulse and active force which he gave it' (David Hume, *Dialogues Concerning Natural Religion*, Oxford Paperbacks, 1998).

Hume's general objection was regarding in what ways the world is like the products of human design, because there is really only a tenuous connection between nature and human works. In reality, humans can hardly begin to produce anything that compares with the marvels of nature. The argument depends on ensuring that we draw not direct but indirect comparisons based simply on the principle of means to an end. Hume argued that the better analogy was with a vegetable or an animal, and this organic model may be thought to be more compatible with the findings of science, which suggest that the universe is in a permanent state of development and decay, not of unchangeable order. The universe is not like a machine, nor does it function like one. Hence the analogy is not as strong as it may have first seemed.

In any case, the presence of order could be explained in many ways without reference to God. Because the universe is religiously ambiguous it cannot be assumed that God is the only explanation for its features. While there may be grounds for saying that the designer was very powerful and highly intelligent, it is a significant further step to say that the designer is all-powerful and morally perfect. Whether the argument succeeds or fails depends entirely on how an individual judges the evidence. Some may maintain that there is insufficient evidence for claiming that there is design in the universe at all, still less that it can only be explained with reference to God. The evidence can legitimately be explained in several ways and there is no way of establishing which is the correct one until we can conceivably reach some eschatological destiny.

The **Epicurean hypothesis** suggests that, in any quantum interaction, all possible states are actualised in some universe or other, with universes constantly diversifying. The resulting parallel universes have no contact with each other, and each observer observes only one universe. However, all universes are equally as real as all the others. Given the possible combinations it is not surprising that at least one produces intelligent life, but this is the product of chance rather than design. This is akin to the argument that if an infinite number of monkeys were all put together in a room each with a typewriter, one of them would produce the works of Shakespeare. According to this principle, again, no special explanation is demanded for the universe.

Perhaps one of the biggest problems of the analogical argument is that it seeks to explain the totality of the universe despite our lack of experience of it. Furthermore, the universe is unique and cannot be reasonably compared with anything. The argument therefore attempts to draw conclusions based on very limited knowledge and experience or genuine points of comparison.

The problem of evil and suffering

Evil and suffering could be said to deal a significant blow to the argument and we can legitimately question the idea that the universe is a particularly harmonious and beautiful place. John Stuart Mill wrote: 'Next to the greatness of these cosmic forces, the quality which most forcibly strikes everyone who does not avert his eyes from it is their perfect and absolute recklessness. They go straight to their end, without regarding what or whom they crush on their road' (cited in *The Existence of God*, edited by John Hick, Macmillan, 1964). John Stuart Mill argued that the most we can claim is that the designer of the universe might be benevolent but must be seriously limited in power to allow such suffering. Mill, pessimistically, drew the conclusion: 'If the Maker of the world can do all that he will, he wills misery and there is no escaping that conclusion.' Furthermore, Charles Darwin commented: 'I cannot persuade myself that a beneficent and omnipotent God would have designedly created the Ichneumonidae with the express intention of their feeding within the living bodies of Caterpillars, or that a cat should play with mice' (http://www.talkorigins.org/faqs/ce/3/part10.html).

> **Taking it further...**
>
> The second law of thermodynamics observes that the universe is in a process of decay or **entropy**.

David Hume and John Stuart Mill effectively offer a version of the problem of evil, seeing it as an absence of order. This is sometimes called the **dysteleological argument**, a form of the argument for poor design. Examples of poor design, which may simply be inefficient rather than causing evil and suffering, include:

- the pointless existence of the appendix in humans, which can lead to fatal appendicitis
- the existence of unnecessary wings in flightless birds such as ostriches
- portions of DNA that do not appear to serve any purpose
- congenital and genetic disorders such as Huntington's Disease
- the common malformation of the human spinal column that leads to many painful and recurring conditions
- photosynthetic plants, which reflect green light even though the sun's peak output is at this wavelength, whereas a more optimal system of photosynthesis would use the entire solar spectrum, resulting in black plants.

The argument from probability

Richard Swinburne approached the argument from the **angle of probability**, suggesting that the evidence of design and order in the universe increases the probability of the existence of God. Swinburne's argument is based on the remarkable degree and extent of order in the universe. Given the size of the universe, how does it behave in such a coherently ordered way. To explain regularities simply in terms of other regularities would lead to an infinite chain that offers no explanation.

We could accept them as 'brute facts' and so essentially unexplainable, but this is not ultimately satisfactory. Swinburne acknowledges that the most general regularities of the universe can be explained by science, but that it is reasonable to postulate another source: 'All the regularity in nature would be due to the action of a postulated god, making mature, as it were, performing a great symphony in the way in which a man produced from his throat a regular series of notes' (*The Existence of God*, Clarendon Press, 2005). He makes a number of key observations about the universe: its fittingness for human life, its scope for humans to share in God's creative activity, and to make significant choices: 'God being omnipotent is able to produce a world orderly in these respects. And he has a good reason to choose to do so: a world containing human persons is a good thing… God being perfectly good, is generous. He wants to share' (*The Existence of God*, Clarendon Press, 2005). Furthermore, Swinburne observes seven features of the universe which, he argues, increase the probability of the universe being designed:

- the very existence of the universe
- the fact that the universe is ordered
- the existence of consciousness
- human opportunities to do good
- the pattern of history
- the evidence of miracles
- religious experience.

Taking it further…

This is also an issue in the cosmological argument. See section 1.3 for a discussion of how an infinite series can never offer an explanation for anything.

Along similar lines, Swinburne argues that God is the best explanation for the design that is evident in the universe, and points not only to the order and purpose that it displays but to the **providential** nature of the universe: it contains within it everything that it necessary for survival, and natural laws function within the universe making it a place where humans can develop. He maintains that it is a universe in which man is designed to occupy the highest position and that natural laws function within the universe making it a place where man can meaningfully contribute to its development and maintenance. This kind of universe is, he maintains, the kind of universe that God would have a reason to create, and not just for humans either but for animals too. The higher animals can reason and plan, observes Swinburne, and are enabled to do so by the predictability of the most obvious aspects of the natural world.

Overall the argument is one from probability: there is a probability that God exists that is considered greater than the probability that he does not exist. Such a God does not come under the control of the laws of nature and he must be the only designing God because other gods would simply be unnecessary.

Problematically, however, Swinburne presumes that the universe exists for the sake of humanity, which is compatible with a theistic view of the world and may be supported by a traditional reading of the creation narratives. However, it would surely be possible for any creature to claim that the universe existed for its benefit if it was able to survive in it, even an earthworm. At the time when dinosaurs ruled the earth, they could have reasonably claimed that it was designed for their benefit. Given that they were wiped out over a comparatively short time, perhaps the same fate awaits humans, to be replaced by another species that will consider itself to be the reason for the design of the universe.

Furthermore, to hold that there is a high degree of probability that God exists demands that we concede that other probabilities also exist, even the probability of another divine being. F. R. Tennant responds to this, however, with the observation that when people view the universe they cannot accept that it came about by chance, and are more inclined to accept the probability of God, on psychological grounds as much as any other.

The aesthetic argument

Another form of the argument is the **aesthetic form**, which observes that the universe possesses a natural beauty that goes beyond that which is necessary to live. This aspect of the universe, it is argued, shows the handicraft of God. Some of that beauty is part of order: the beautiful patterns of the stars, for example, or the changing colours of the seasons. Our appreciation of it not only reflects our attraction to that which is aesthetically pleasing, but also our dislike of chaos. Chaos is ugly and we seek to impose order upon it if it does not occur naturally. But beauty can also be found in things that are not part of the natural world but which humankind appreciates, although they have no part to play in the survival of the species. Art, music, literature and culture all contribute to the way we perceive the world as a beneficial, appealing and attractive place, although we would be able to live without them. F. R. Tennant observes: 'Nature is not just beautiful

Taking it further...

Richard Swinburne employs the principle of Ockham's Razor: 'do not multiply causes or reasons or beings unnecessarily'.

Taking it further...

Richard Swinburne's approach to the argument ties in closely with his view on miracles (as evidence of the providential nature of God) and the problem of evil (evil and suffering as part of the necessary design of a world that God would want to create). See section 2.1 for a discussion of his views on these topics.

in places; it is saturated with beauty – on the telescopic and microscopic scale. Our scientific knowledge brings us no nearer to understanding the beauty of music. From an intelligibility point of view, beauty seems to be superfluous and to have little survival value' (*Philosophical Theology*, 1930).

This aspect of the universe has long appealed to religious writers and thinkers concerned with a wider audience than the educated philosopher. The 19th century Jesuit poet Gerard Manley Hopkins (*The Major Works*, Oxford University Press, 2002) wrote of how the beauty of the universe is besmirched by man, and yet rises up again to reveal God's glory.

A beautiful winter's day – an advocate of the aesthetic argument would say that such natural beauty goes beyond that which is necessary to live and that is therefore crafted by God

> *The world is charged with the grandeur of God*
> *It will flame out, like shining from shook foil...*
> *And all is seared with trade, bleared, smeared with toil...*
> *And for all this, nature is never spent;*
> *There lives the dearest freshness, deep down things...*

In 1886 Carl Boberg wrote:

> *O Lord my God, when I in awesome wonder*
> *Consider all the works thy hands have made,*
> *I see the stars, I hear the rolling thunder,*
> *Thy power throughout the universe displayed.*

Tennant's argument postulated that this view of the world was also to be considered superior to others in that it catered for moral and spiritual dimensions. He made five key observations about the universe:

- the universe is intelligible and not chaotic
- the significance of the evolutionary system is that it underpins direction and progress
- the universe is absolutely suitable to sustain life
- the created universe exhibits standards and values of aesthetic value
- humanity possesses an awareness of moral worth and works in harmony with nature.

Like Richard Swinburne's argument from probability, Tennant offers a cumulative argument, suggesting that once these aspects have been identified the existence of a divine designer becomes more probable than not. He suggested that when humans see the universe they cannot accept that it is the outcome of random activity.

The problem of evil and suffering of course poses a serious challenge to this form of the argument as well, although it may be possible to argue reasonably that what constitutes beauty is a matter of human perspective. To argue that any aspects of the world lack beauty and therefore count against the existence of God reflects only what humans believe that a loving and omnipotent God should have created, and that to question the value of any aspects of creation is impertinent because God is not bound by human conceptions of perfection or adequate design. What may appear inelegant, inefficient or imperfect to humans may be perfectly fulfilling its purpose as far as God is concerned. But if one takes this line of reasoning to its logical conclusion, then we are able to say nothing at all about God. Some would maintain that the minimum standard God should be held to is what a reasonably competent group of intelligent humans could design. If God's designs fall short of this, then perfection has no meaning when applied to God and his creation and, if we accept the principle that the ways of God are mysterious, then nothing is incompatible with his designing of the universe, his love or his power, to the extent that God could be pure evil and yet still compatible with classical theism, surely an absurdity.

The anthropic principle

Having established the probability of God's existence, Tennant extended the argument to include observations and ideas that come from evolutionary theories in the form of the **anthropic principle**, which proposes that the reason and purpose for the universe is the support of human life: 'As we look out into the Universe and identify the many accidents of physics and astronomy that have worked together to our benefit, it almost seems as if the Universe must in some sense have known that we were coming' (Freeman Dyson, cited in *The Anthropic Cosmological Principle*, by J. Barrow and F. J. Tipler, Oxford University Press, 1986). In this line of reasoning, speculation about the vast, perhaps infinite, range of possible conditions in which life could not exist is compared with the speculated improbability of achieving conditions in which life does exist, and then interpreted as indicating a fine-tuned universe specifically designed so that human life is possible.

The anthropic principle demonstrates that, contrary to what might be suggested, the design argument need not reject the principles of evolution in order to postulate a designing God. However, theistic supporters of evolution argue that scientific principles alone are not sufficient to explain how evolution led to the perfectly balanced natural order that prevails. Again, Tennant writes: 'The fitness of the world to be the home of living beings depends on certain primary conditions – astronomical, thermal, chemical, and so on, and on the coincidence of qualities, apparently not casually connected to each other. The unique assembly of unique properties on so vast a scale makes the organic world comparable to a single organism… The world is compatible with a single throw of the dice and common sense is not foolish in suspecting the dice to have been loaded' (F. R. Tennant, cited in *The Puzzle of God*, Peter Vardy, Fount, 1999).

According to this perspective, scientific explanations of the universe are compatible with the design argument because evolution or a cosmic explosion can be seen to be the means which the designer has employed to bring the universe to this point. Furthermore, it could be claimed that the order of the universe is beyond chance, in other words the odds on it coming about by chance are so high as to render it virtually impossible. Evolution could then be part of God's plan for the world. Although many Victorian Christians found their faith to be seriously challenged by Darwin, in the late 19th century Archbishop Temple claimed: 'The doctrine of evolution leaves the argument for an intelligent Creator and Governor of the earth stronger than it was before.' Indeed, it is possible to argue that the laws that govern natural selection were brought about by God because they were the laws that would ensure that eventually humans and animals would evolve. Richard Swinburne maintains: 'The very success of science in showing us how deeply orderly the natural world is, provides strong grounds for believing that there is an even deeper cause of that order' (*Is There a God?*, Oxford University Press, 1996).

Taking it further...

Tennant employs the catch phrase of the evolutionists but turns it to his advantage: 'The survival of the fittest presupposes the arrival of the fit.'

Order is improbable

It is possible to criticise this view, however, with the observation that unless the universe did contain exactly the right conditions for life and if there were no natural laws there would be no humans or animals, and we would not be here to comment upon how improbable it all is! In other words, of course we perceive order in the universe, there could be nothing else or we would not be here to perceive it. Order is not improbable, and we should not approach it as if it were extraordinary. Akin to this idea is that of A. J. Ayer, who claimed that to speak of a designed universe is meaningless because unless we could say what the world would be like without design we cannot reach the conclusion that this world is designed. Furthermore, the universe would look the same to us whether it was designed or not. In *Language, Truth and Logic* (Penguin, 1936), Ayer claims that to suggest that God is proven by the evidence of regularity in nature is to say that 'God exists' and 'Certain types of phenomena occur in certain sequences', which, he presumes, is not what the 'religious man would admit that this was all he intended to assert in asserting the existence of God'.

To argue that it is remarkable that the conditions necessary for life exist is an argument about facts that cannot be denied. If things were different then they would be different, but because they are not different is there any point to the argument? The sun cannot support life on several other planets and at some point in the future it will not be able to support life on this plant. Does this prove anything about design, good or bad? Many of the factors that guarantee life on this planet did not exist in the past and will not exist in the future, just as there was a time when there was no life on this planet and there will be a time when no life exists here in the future.

Nevertheless, Cressy Morrison (*Man Does Not Stand Alone*, World's Work, 1962) observed:

> Suppose you put ten pennies, marked from one to ten, into your pocket and give them a good shuffle. Now try to take them out in sequence from one to ten, putting back the coin each time and shaking them all again. Mathematically we know that your chance of first drawing number one is one in ten; of drawing one and two in succession, one in 100; of drawing one, two and three in succession, one in 1000, and so on; your chance of drawing them all, from number one to number ten in succession, would reach the unbelievable figure of one in ten billion. By the same reasoning, so many exacting conditions are necessary for life on the earth that they could not possibly exist in proper relationship by chance. The earth rotates on its axis 1000 miles an hour at the equator; if it turned at 100 miles an hour, our days and nights would be ten times as long as now, and the hot sun would likely burn up our vegetation each long day while in the long night any surviving sprout might well freeze.

Problematically, however, Morrison raises the following. The earth with life on it is here and so the odds are 1/1 of its existing. As we are here, it is 100% certain that it can happen! Furthermore, if an individual had 20 billion years to pull ten numbered coins from his pocket, the odds of him drawing out the coins in sequence at least once are very good.

Taking it further...

A counter-argument to the anthropic principle is that one could manipulate statistics to define any number of natural situations that are extremely improbable but that have happened nevertheless. Critics suggest that a key problem is that improbable conditions are identified after the event, so they cannot be checked by experiment regarding the actual degree of their improbability.

But, for many thinkers, the amount of order in the universe needs an explanation because it would appear to be far more than is necessary for human survival. Furthermore, Richard Swinburne observes that we do not simply perceive order rather than disorder but that we should be amazed by the fact that there is order rather than disorder. Just because we are there to observe it does not make it less improbable. He illustrates this with the following parable (*Is There a God?*, Oxford University Press, 1996).

> *Suppose that a madman kidnaps a victim and shuts him in a room with a card-shuffling machine. The machine shuffles ten packs of cards simultaneously and then draws a card from each pack and exhibits simultaneously the ten cards. The kidnapper tells the victim that he will shortly set the machine to work and it will exhibit its first draw, but that unless the draw consists of an ace of hearts from each pack, the machine will simultaneously set off an explosion which will kill the victim, in consequence of which he will not see which cards the machine drew. The machine is set to work, and to the amazement and relief of the victim the machine exhibits an ace of hearts drawn from each pack.*

Swinburne claims that it would not be adequate for the victim to claim that there is no explanation required why the ten aces appeared, because if they had not he would not be there. It is not legitimate to say that the cards came up as they did because the victim survived! 'True, every draw, every arrangement of matter, is equally improbable a priori – that is, if chance alone dictates what is drawn. But if a person is arranging things, he has reason to produce some arrangements rather than others' (*Is There a God?*, Oxford University Press, 1996).

The design argument and modern science

Darwin's theory of evolution appeared to destroy completely the concept of goal-orientated design and the beauty of the world as the work of God. Natural selection could answer all the questions raised by complexities in nature, and effectively removed the mystery of the life and its origins. Nevertheless, of course, many Christians are not committed to a literal understanding of the biblical literature and are fully able to accept natural selection. However, it may be argued that it does not fully account for morality, or for the ability of humans to create things of artistic beauty. Natural and human beauty, both physical and 'inner' beauty, can be explained scientifically, however, as they serve a vital function in sexual selection of partners who appear to be the best mates.

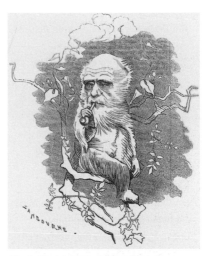

Charles Darwin's The Origin of Species was published in 1859. It provoked an outraged response from the Church of England because it contradicted the belief in divine creation. This cartoon published in Punch satirises Darwin's theory by depicting him as a tree climbing anthropoid

Many scientists would argue that it is not helpful to infer a supernatural explanation for the universe because it precludes continuing to explore the possibility of other, non-theistic, explanations. Richard Dawkins consistently reinforces this point (all from *Does God Believe in Atheists?*, John Blanchard, Evangelical Press, 2000). 'Religion is no longer a serious candidate in the field of explanation. It is completely superseded by science.' 'What has theology ever said that is of the smallest use to anybody? The achievements of theologians don't do anything, don't affect anything, don't achieve anything, don't even mean anything. What makes you think that theology is a subject at all?' 'Faith is the great cop-out, the excuse to avoid the need to think and to evaluate evidence.'

Invoking God as an explanation is sometimes called the **God of the gaps** approach, which in turn is challenged by the view that because so much natural phenomena previously explained by God is now explained by science or reason alone, theistic or divine explanations for any natural phenomenon become less plausible.

Recently, the theory of **intelligent design** has proposed that certain features of the universe and of living things are best explained by an intelligent cause, not an undirected process such as natural selection. Some say that intelligent design is a scientific theory that stands on equal footing with, or is superior to, current scientific theories regarding the origin of life. Intelligent design deliberately does not try to identify or name the intelligent cause, merely stating that one or more must exist, although many proponents of intelligent design believe that it is the God of classical theism. This has largely been rejected by the scientific community and in *Kitzmiller v. Dover Area School District* (2005), United States District Judge John E. Jones III ruled that intelligent design is not science and is essentially religious in nature. Proponents of intelligent design claim that it should be taught in the science classroom as an alternative to the science of evolution. Arguably, however, intelligent design is a confidence trick, because evolution is already considered by many to be consistent with a belief in an intelligent designer of the universe and so is not necessarily contradictory or competitive. Furthermore, a key strategy of the intelligent design movement is in convincing the general public that there is a debate among scientists about whether life evolved, seeking to convince the public, politicians and cultural leaders that schools should expose and evaluate the controversy. However, there is arguably no such controversy; the scientific consensus is that life evolved.

Intelligent design is proposed mainly by Christian apologists at the Discovery Institute (Washington, Seattle) and their allies, who feel science threatens their biblical-based view of reality.

The key principle of intelligent design is that of **irreducible complexity**, the argument that in the universe there are biological processes that are so complex they cannot be broken down into smaller functioning systems. This was proposed by Michael Behe in his book *Darwin's Black Box* (Free Press, 1996): 'A single system which is composed of several interacting parts that contribute to the basic function, and where the removal of any one of the parts causes the system to effectively cease functioning.' Intelligent design also includes features associated with the anthropic principle, the fine tuning argument, identifying features of the universe that make life possible and that cannot apparently have come about by chance. Essentially, intelligent design has re-awoken interest in the issues arising from questions about the features of the universe, but does not appear to have contributed to the scope of the debate.

The success of the argument

The design argument has clearly stood the test of time in many ways, although it hinges on several assumptions that it would be reasonable to question. Should it be valid, then it can prove the existence of a sentient, designing intelligence, but this is not the same as an eternal, omnipotent deity. Although Hume wrote, 'A purpose, an intention, a design strikes

Taking it further...

The Discovery Institute's web page makes the following claim: 'Discovery Institute's mission is to make a positive vision of the future practical. The Institute discovers and promotes ideas in the common sense tradition of representative government, the free market and individual liberty. Our mission is promoted through books, reports, legislative testimony, articles, public conferences and debates, plus media coverage and the Institute's own publications and Internet website' (http://www.discovery.org).

everywhere the most careless, the most stupid thinker; and no man can be so hardened in absurd systems as at all times to reject it' (*Dialogues Concerning Natural Religion*, Oxford Paperbacks, 1998), he was aware of many of the argument's serious weaknesses. It is true that a chaotic universe for us would be non-intelligible, and the intelligibility of the universe is one of its most attractive features, and it is reasonable to ask why we have such a universe rather than any other. However, all that it succeeds in proving is that the universe is very probably ordered, but no more than that. Above all, the argument cannot prove that there is design, only that to us there appears to be design.

1.3 The cosmological argument

Key Ideas

- The need to explain the existence of the universe

- Pre-Thomistic approaches to the cosmological argument

- Aquinas and the Five Ways

- Leibniz, Russell and Copleston, and David Hume's criticisms of the argument

- The continuing value of the argument

The need for explanation

The **cosmological argument** refers to a collection of arguments that have been continually improved and developed. They are arguments from **natural theology**, which holds that humanity does not know God through reason, but through the work of God in creation, which is accessible to all humans.

The cosmological argument in all its forms responds to man's instinctive awareness that the existence of the universe is not explicable without reference to causes and factors outside itself. It cannot be self-causing because it is contingent and only the existence of a first, necessary cause and mover explains the origin of an otherwise 'brute fact'. The argument assumes that the universe has not always been in existence, and for it to come into being an external agent was necessary. That external agent is itself beyond being affected by anything and the question, 'Who made that agent?' is considered irrelevant. Cosmological arguments essentially contain three elements: there exist things the non-existence of which is a possibility; the existence of such beings needs to be explained; the explanation of these beings lies in something that is self-caused and totally independent.

Taking it further...

The word 'cosmological' comes from the Greek for 'order' but in the case of these arguments refers to the order that derives from the *whole* of creation: the universe.

Proponents of the argument identify the external agent as God, a supremely perfect and self-sufficient being. The cosmological argument, therefore, and its sister, the **design** or **teleological argument**, is concerned with finding an explanation for the universe. Both arguments look to the universe and find that it is not self-explanatory, and it demands that we ask questions about its origin, nature and purpose. The cosmological argument essentially deals with questions that logically precede those of the design argument because they are concerned with asking why the universe exists at all, rather than why it possesses the features it does. Furthermore, the cosmological argument is based on the sense that life is not random or accidental. If God is the reason why there is a universe, then we are free to believe that the universe, and the people in the universe, are here for a good reason rather than no reason at all.

Such questions might include the following.

- Why is there something rather than nothing?
- Why does the universe possess the form it does, and not some other form?
- How can the series of events that culminate in the universe be explained?
- Must a chain of movers have a first cause or is an infinite regress of causes a sufficient explanation for the universe?
- What kind of cause or agency is necessary for the universe to come into being?

The success of the cosmological argument will depend entirely on our willingness to ask these questions and to seek an answer to them, and we should not take for granted that everyone is so inclined. It was over this question that F. C. Copleston and Bertrand Russell famously debated in 1947, Russell doubting whether it was even meaningful, let alone important, to argue the case for a cause of the universe, and, having established that for him it was 'a question that has no meaning', declared to Copleston, 'What do you say – shall we pass on to some other issue?' For Copleston this was an unsatisfactory response and he wrote in *Aquinas* (Penguin, 1961): 'If one does not wish to embark on the path which leads to the affirmation of a transcendent being, however the latter may be described... one has to deny the reality of the problem, assert that things "just are"; and that the existential problem is a pseudo-problem. And if one refuses even to sit down at the chessboard and make a move, one cannot, of course, be checkmated.'

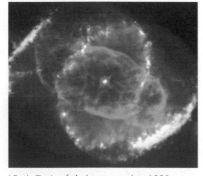

'Cat's Eye' nebula in space – since 1990, images taken by the Hubble telescope have provided a wealth of new information about the universe

Richard Swinburne is a great contemporary supporter of the quest for explanation reflected in the cosmological argument. He writes: 'The human quest for explanation inevitably and rightly seeks for the ultimate explanation of everything observable – that object or objects on which everything else depends for its existence and properties... A may be explained by B, and B by C, but in the end there will be some one object on whom all other objects depend. We will have to acknowledge something as ultimate – the great metaphysical issue is what that is' (*Is There a God?*, Oxford University Press, 1996).

Proponents of the cosmological argument are not satisfied with finding partial explanations for the universe, but seek a complete explanation or, what Gottfried Leibniz called, a 'sufficient reason'. It is over this need for a complete explanation that supporters and opponents of the argument are crucially divided, as Russell and Copleston discussed (cited in *The Existence of God*, edited by John Hick, Macmillan, 1964):

> Russell: *'But when is an explanation adequate? Suppose I am about to make a flame with a match. You may say that the adequate explanation of that is that I rub it on the box.'*

> Copleston: *'Well, for practical purposes – but theoretically, that is only a partial explanation. An adequate explanation must ultimately be a total explanation, to which nothing further can be added.'*

The cosmological argument reaches the conclusion that God is the ultimate, complete and adequate explanation for the universe, and possesses in himself all the necessary characteristics to be that complete explanation.

Although the cosmological argument is essentially a posteriori, it does depend on the **ontological argument** having proven that God is analytically a necessary being. The ontological argument, proposed by Anselm in the 11th century, is based on a definition of God as 'That than which nothing greater can be conceived', the supremely perfect being. Anselm maintained that if God fulfilled this definition, then he must exist, because a supremely perfect being had to exist or it would not be perfect. Hence, God's existence is necessary: he cannot not exist. The cosmological argument also proposes that God exists necessarily, although it argues to this conclusion from experience, not from reason as the ontological argument concluded. Potentially, though, any argument that aims to prove the necessary existence of God is a priori rather than a posteriori, because we cannot argue from experience of the world to the logical necessity of God.

For Richard Swinburne, as for Aquinas before him, God is the simplest explanation: 'Theism claims that every other object which exists is caused to exist and kept in existence by just one substance, God... There could in this respect be no simpler explanation than one which postulated only one cause. Theism is simpler than polytheism. And theism postulates for its one cause, a person, infinite degrees of those properties which are essential to persons... infinite power... infinite knowledge... and infinite freedom' (*Is There a God?*, Oxford University Press, 1996).

Pre-Christian applications of the argument

The cosmological argument is not just a Christian attempt to prove the existence of the classical theistic deity. Plato and Aristotle postulated the need for a craftsman for the universe and both began their arguments with the fact of motion which, they argued, needs a prior agency to motivate it. This mover would, itself, need no further mover, because it would be a prime mover, which is a self-actualising, necessary being. Neither Aristotle nor Plato understood how the universe could exist without such a mover.

Plato identified other different types of motion or change, for example round an axis, from place to place, growth and decay, as well as the power of something to move other objects when it is moved by something else, and the power of something to move itself as well as other objects. He argued that the power to produce motion is logically prior to the power to receive it and pass it on, so there must be a first cause, itself uncaused, that originates that movement. He believed that this had to be a soul, not physical and of a

Taking it further...

The principle that the simplest explanation is the most satisfactory, and the most likely, is known as Ockham's Razor, sometimes expressed by the recommendation 'Do not multiply entities unnecessarily'. In other words, if a simple, single, self-sufficient explanation can be found, there is nothing to be gained philosophically, or intellectually, in pursuing other explanations.

higher order than the human soul. However, he did not consider this mover to be a creator, rather the source of the activity that there is in the world, which itself existed eternally.

Aristotle took this further by separating the prime mover from the material universe, arguing that it could not fit into an ordinary chain of physical, material causes. Hence, the prime mover is:

- an intelligence that activates the world by its presence
- non-spatial and eternal
- good and perfect.

Aristotle argued that all things are encouraged towards the ultimate good, whose effects could be felt and offered something of a model for other beings to follow.

Aristotle's argument was seen as a rational basis for monotheism, and an Islamic form of the argument, the **kalam argument**, was developed by al-Kindi (*c.* 870) and al-Ghazali (1058–1111) as follows:

- premise one, whatever comes into being must have a cause
- premise two, the universe came into being
- premise three, the universe must have a cause
- premise four, if the universe has a cause of its existence is must be God
- conclusion, God exists.

The principle is that if something is not its own reason for existing, then it must have been caused by something else, and that by something else again. Only when we arrive at a self-causing, necessary being can we say we have reached the end of the chain of causes and effects. Supporters of the kalam cosmological argument claim that it is impossible that the universe has an infinite past, which might appear to be a logical alternative to a first cause of its existence. In support of this, modern advocates often appeal to modern science, specifically to the Big Bang theory, which has identified the need for a first cause or a singularity at the root of the existence of the universe. Arguably, it only takes one more step to propose that God is the first cause of the Big Bang.

The kalam argument has recently been revived by William Lane Craig, who proposed an argument that runs:

- everything that comes into existence must have a cause of its existence
- the universe came into existence
- the universe must therefore have a cause of its existence
- no scientific explanation (physical laws) can provide a sufficient explanation for the origin of the universe, thus the explanation must lie in a personal agent
- an actual infinite cannot exist
- a temporal series of events that has no beginning is an actual infinite
- therefore a temporal series of events without a beginning cannot exist
- if something has a finite past, its existence has been caused
- the universe has a finite past

Taking it further...

The difficulty inherent in the kalam argument is that it postulates a cause that comes into existence without having a cause itself, but arguably there is no reason why there may not be such a cause, only that science has not yet discovered it.

Taking it further...

The argument of William Lane Craig depends on the claim that it is logically unsound to propose an infinite series because to have arrived at the present moment we would have had to have travelled an infinite length of time and so would still not be at the present time.

- therefore the universe has been caused
- space and time originated with the universe and also have a finite past, so the cause of the universe existence must itself be beyond space and time
- if the cause of the universe is beyond space and time, no scientific explanation can sufficiently explain the origin of the universe
- if no scientific explanation can explain the origin of the universe, the cause must be personal, not physical.

Some schools of quantum mechanics hold that the existence of particles is a matter of probability. Indeed, empty space swarms with ephemeral particles that wink in and out of existence with no apparent cause (whether they have a hidden cause or not is a matter of debate). The universe itself may be explained by this quantum fluctuation, thus removing the necessity for God as the first premise. Hence we might say that, at a realist level, subatomic particles pass in to and out of existence without any known cause.

Aquinas and the Five Ways

The most famous Christian application of the argument was offered by Thomas Aquinas (1225–1274) in the *Summa Theologica* (Resources for Christian Living, 1981). He proposed **Five Ways** that he believed 'demonstrated' the existence of God, although in reality it is unlikely that he thought an atheist would be convinced by them. The first three are cosmological arguments, the fourth is a form of an ontological or even a moral argument, and the fifth is a teleological argument. The first four ways propose similar arguments: that everything depends on something else in a constant regression until a beginning is reached, which is God. Each of the proofs starts from a general feature of the world and argues that there could not be a world unless there was also the ultimate reality of God.

The First Way: from motion

It is certain, and evident to our senses that in the world some things are in motion. Now whatever is moved is moved by another... It is therefore impossible that in the same respect and in the same way a thing should be both mover and moved... If that by which it is moved be itself moved, then this also must needs be moved by another... But this cannot go on to infinity, because then there would be no first mover, and, subsequently, no other mover... Therefore it is necessary to arrive at a first mover, moved by no other; and this everyone understands to be God. (Thomas Aquinas, *Summa Theologica, Third Article, Whether God Exists?*, cited in *The Existence of God*, edited by John Hick, Macmillan, 1964.)

This argument can be set out in the form of premises (P1, etc.) and a conclusion.

- P1: nothing can move itself, since nothing can be both mover and moved, yet things are evidently in motion.
- P2: an infinite chain of movers that has no beginning can have no successive or ultimate movers.
- Conclusion: there must therefore be a first mover that causes motion in all things, and this we call God.

Taking it further...

The First Way is also called the **kinetological way**, from the word 'kine' meaning motion.

Aquinas called motion 'the reduction of something from potentiality to actuality'. For example, fire, which is actually hot, changes wood, which is potentially hot, to a state of being actually hot. Motion, therefore, is a change of state, and not just movement in time and space from one place to another. Things have motion when they go through change in location, quantity or quality, such as leaves rotting to become compost, or a human being growing old. The world is constantly in process and the changes that are part of that process are the result of some prior changes and states of affairs. However, that motion and change require an explanation because we know that nothing can be both in potentiality and actuality in the same respect; in other words, nothing can be simultaneously hot and cold, and something cannot be simultaneously in motion and motionless. Something is required to bring about the change from hot to cold and vice versa and it must be something upon that which is changed is dependent. Aquinas argues that God is the initiator of change and motion in all things.

Aquinas maintained that when two objects, A and B, come into a relationship with each other, one affects the other and brings about a transfer of effect. Say a ball travels towards a second ball and when it strikes the second ball it is set in motion from the first. To do this, what ball A does to ball B, has already been done to A. In other words, we are faced with a communication or transfer of essences. Movement in A communicates or transfers to B, empowering it to motion.

The Second Way: from cause

The second way is from the nature of efficient cause. In the world of sensible things we find there is an order of efficient causes. There is no case known (neither is it, indeed, possible) in which a thing is found to be the efficient cause of itself; for so it would be prior to itself, which is impossible... Therefore it is necessary to admit to a first efficient cause, to which everyone gives the name of God (John Hick, *The Existence of God*, Macmillan, 1964).

This follows the same lines of reasoning as the First Way.

- The world is a series of events.
- All events are caused and nothing can be its own cause (a logical impossibility).
- There must be a first cause (God) on which all other causes depend.
- An infinite chain of causes is rejected because in an infinite chain there can be no first cause.
- Therefore there must be a cause of the whole sequence.
- God is therefore the first cause of all that exists.

In the Second Way, Aquinas observes that there is something different about God. While all other beings are caused, God is not. Furthermore, God is not just the first cause in a chain of causes that are otherwise just like him, he is one on whom all subsequent causes and effects are dependent. As with the First Way, Aquinas again rejected an infinite chain of causes but insisted that without a first cause there could be no subsequent causes and so in effect, without a first cause, there would be nothing at all. Furthermore, the implication is that Aquinas is not just looking for a first cause in a temporal or linear chain but one that maintains the existence of all effects that derive from that first cause: the dependency of the effects on the first cause does not cease once they have come into being.

Taking it further...

The Second Way is also called the **aetiological way**, because it seeks to explain things from their origins.

Richard Swinburne distinguishes between different ways in which objects or beings cause events. **Inanimate causation** occurs when something that has the power to act under certain conditions does so. He uses the example of dynamite causing an explosion. However, **intentional causation** provides the reason why the dynamite was set off, say, perhaps, that a terrorist had ignited it. Intentional causation is personal and is motivated by beliefs and purposes. It is this model that he believes is fundamental to theistic thinking about the world in relation to humans.

Richard Swinburne observes: 'We know very well that if we ceased to form purposes and to try to execute them that nothing would happen; we would cease to eat and talk and write and walk as we do. What we try to achieve makes all the difference to what happens' (*Is There a God?*, Oxford University Press, 1996).

We could set Aquinas's arguments out so far as follows.

- P1: the universe exists and is in a constant state of flux.
- P2: everything in existence has a cause and that which is in a state of motion must be moved.
- P3: causes come before their effects; that which is moved cannot move itself.
- P4: a chain of causes and effects, movers and moved cannot regress to infinity.
- P5: there must therefore be a first cause and first mover that is not in itself an effect.
- P6: this first cause/mover is dependent on nothing else to come into existence.
- P7: this first, self-causing cause/self-moving mover, is God.
- Conclusion: God exists.

The Third Way: from necessity and contingency

The third way is taken from possibility and necessity… We find in nature things that are possible to be and not to be, since they are found to be generated, and to be corrupted, and consequently, it is possible for them to be and not to be… Therefore if everything can not-be then at one time there was nothing in existence… [and] it would have been impossible for anything to have begun to exist and thus even now nothing would be in existence, which is absurd… Therefore we cannot but admit the existence of some being having of itself its own necessity, and not receiving it from another, but rather causing in others their necessity. This all men speak of as God (John Hick, *The Existence of God*, Macmillan, 1964).

Hence we can say the following.

- Everything we can point to is dependent upon factors beyond itself and thus is contingent. While they exist, their non-existence is always possible and realisable.
- Therefore, the presence of such contingent items can only be explained by reference to those factors that themselves depend on other factors.
- These factors demand an ultimate explanation in the form of a necessary being (God) dependent on nothing outside himself.

We cannot postulate an infinite series of contingent causes because all the possibilities that can affect any contingent item or being will have been realised before we have reached the present, including the non-existence of all contingent things.

God's necessary existence is thus established *de re*. The very nature of things in the universe demands that God exists necessarily and not contingently. F. C. Copleston defines such a being as one that must, and cannot not, exist.

This is perhaps the most interesting of the Ways and depends on the view that the world (or the collection of things that depend on one another for their existence) might not have been: there is no reason why it had to exist, anymore than human beings as a species or as individual people had to exist. The world would fundamentally be no different if the author of this book did not exist, and this is the real test of contingency. Such beings and items in the universe are capable of existing or not existing (i.e. are contingent) and it is impossible that all beings should be capable of existing or not existing or there would be no impetus for the existence of anything. Copleston maintained that if we do not postulate the existence of a necessary being 'we do not explain the presence here and now of beings capable of existing or not existing. Therefore we must affirm the existence of a being which is absolutely necessary and completely independent' (cited in *The Existence of God*, edited by John Hick, Macmillan, 1964).

Overall, we see that Aquinas's form of the argument has attempted to demonstrate that whether we think of the world as a process or a sequence of events or a collection of things, it would still need to be explained.

Sufficient reason and complete explanation

In 1710 Gottfried Leibniz explained the cosmological argument in the form of the **principle of sufficient reason**: 'Suppose the book of the elements of geometry to have been eternal, one copy having been written down from an earlier one. It is evident that even though a reason can be given for the present book out of a past one, we should never come to a full reason. What is true of the books is also true of the states of the world. If you suppose the world eternal, you will suppose nothing but a succession of states, and will not find in any of them a sufficient reason' (*Theodicy*, Open Court Publications, 1988).

Leibniz's argument is that even if the universe had always been in existence it would still require an explanation, or a sufficient reason for its existence, because we need to establish why there is something rather than nothing. However, the universe is a finite and specific thing, and as it stands it needs to be explained. By going backwards in time forever we will never arrive at such a complete explanation. Leibniz identified that even if we are sure that the universe has always existed, there is nothing within the universe to show why it exists: it is not self-explanatory, so the reason for its existence must lie outside of it. At the heart of the argument is the premise that there must be a cause for the whole that explains the whole, and unless this is accepted as a meaningful and purposeful exercise the argument will fail. Furthermore, Leibniz's form of the argument pushes us to find an explanation that lies beyond those that are immediately evident and explains not just how things came into existence but why. After all, we cannot

Taking it further...

Significantly, the cosmological argument shows that even an infinite chain would demand an explanation so cannot be the explanation for all other events or causes.

explain our existence by referring to parents alone, or even to their decision to conceive.

Interestingly, none of the cosmological arguments arrive at an answer to the question, 'Why did God create the world?' The medieval scholars, in line with Christian tradition, claimed that God created the world out of nothing more than his abundant love because God does not need the world. He is complete and perfect without it, so there is no other reason for God to create than as an expression of his perfect love.

Undeniably, a key element to the cosmological argument is the rejection of **infinite regress** as unable to provide logically a complete explanation. After all, if we were satisfied with the explanation that all effects and causes, movements and mover, could be traced back infinitely in time without ever needing, factually or logically, to arrive at a first cause we would never, it seems, arrive at an explanation. This is because the argument identifies the dependency between cause, movements and events. In the sense that we would not expect a railway train consisting of an infinite number of carriages, the last pulled along by the second last, the second last by the third last, and so on, to move anywhere without an engine, in an infinite series of causes and effects there is nothing to support them. God is like an engine: not just another truck, but a machine that has the power to move without requiring something else to act upon it. God is different from the other causes, the other things in motion, in the way that the engine is different from the carriages: it has a different nature that enables it to affect the carriages. It acts upon them so that they move; their potential is fulfilled.

An infinite chain of railway carriages can go nowhere without an engine

F. C. Copleston supported Aquinas's rejection of infinite regress on the grounds that an infinite chain of contingent beings could only ever consist of contingent beings, which would never be able to bring itself into existence. The most an eternal series of contingent beings can do is maintain an eternal presence of contingent beings, it cannot explain how they came into being in the first place. 'You see, I don't believe that the infinity of the series of the events – I mean a horizontal series, so to speak – if such an infinity could be proved, would be in the slightest degree relevant to the situation. If you add up chocolates you get chocolates after all and not a sheep. If you add up chocolates to infinity, you presumably get an infinite number of chocolates. So if you add up contingent beings to infinity you still get contingent beings, not a necessary being. An infinite series of contingent beings will be, to my way of thinking, as unable to cause itself as one contingent being' (cited in *The Existence of God*, edited by John Hick, Macmillan, 1964).

Copleston himself had reformulated the cosmological argument along the following lines.

- P1: some things exist that do not contain within them the reason for their own existence.
- P2: the world consists of the totality of such objects, none of which contain the reason for their existence.
- P3: thus the explanation for the existence of everything in the universe must lie outside it.
- Conclusion: this explanation must be a self-explanatory being that contains the reason for its own existence.

More recently, Richard Swinburne has argued that the real need for an explanation lies in the fact that it is more likely that there be nothing rather than something. 'It is extraordinary that there should exist anything at all. Surely the most natural state of affairs is simply nothing: no universe, no God, nothing. But there is something. And so many things. May be chance could have thrown up the odd electron. But so many particles! Not everything will have an explanation. But… the whole progress of science and all other intellectual enquiry demands that we postulate the smallest number of brute facts. If we can explain the many bits of the universe by one simple being which keeps them in existence, we should do so – even if inevitably we cannot explain the existence of that simple being' (*Is There a God?*, Oxford University Press, 1996).

The supposition that the universe had a beginning, which is the corner stone of the cosmological argument, is surprisingly supported in many ways by the findings of modern science. The Big Bang theory, although typically seen as offering a challenge to religious interpretations of the universe, proposes a finite history of the universe: a beginning point, not an infinite regress of events. Furthermore, if the universe has an infinite history then an infinite number of years must have already passed to arrive at the present, which is nonsense.

Criticisms of the cosmological argument

Despite the popularity of the cosmological argument, it has come under sustained criticism not only from philosophy but from modern science. Arguing from motion is, perhaps, particularly vulnerable because it postulates a stable form of order arising from motion, while the second law of thermodynamics or the **principle of entropy** states that everything eventually collapses into chaos or decay. Furthermore, Newton's first law of motion, the law of inertia, states that an object will continue at rest or in motion in a straight line unless directly affected by some other body that assumes that we cannot explain ultimate motion.

Arguing from motion (change of state) or cause is open to challenge by the **theory of evolution**, which maintains that creatures already contain the necessary qualities to accommodate changes in their situation not because they respond to that change but because they are already inherently fit for that new state and change as a result of an 'accident', not an observable principle of cause and effect. When applied to the universe as a whole it is reasonable to ask what we mean when we talk of it, or anything else, beginning to exist. If we attempt to answer this question by making statements about the empirical world that cannot be empirically investigated, have we proposed anything meaningful at all?

Furthermore, we can only draw conclusions about the origin of the universe on the basis of the knowledge we have at any given time, so how do we know when we have every arrived at a conclusion?

Atheist and scientist Richard Dawkins is not dismayed by the limitations of science in this respect. However, he wholeheartedly objects to offering mythological explanations when it seems that science does not yet have the full answer. Such explanations he dismisses as intellectually degrading non-

Taking it further...

The danger here is that the cosmological argument attempts to offer a non-scientific explanation that is then interpreted as being in competition with scientific (non-theistic) explanations, and purports that it is the only logical explanation possible.

explanations that frustrate the possibility of finding out the real truth. If science does not provide the answer so far, he argues, we must do better science. Significantly, Dawkins does not dismiss the importance of the questions that are a catalyst for the cosmological argument. He maintains that they are vital questions, so vital that to assume they are solved by a divine explanation is beyond reason.

The cosmological argument could be criticised for presuming a principle of shared essences. We say whatever is moved is moved by something already moving, and what is caused is caused by that which is already caused, but is this necessarily the case? After all, as has been variously suggested, a king does not need to be crowned by a monarch, dead men do not commit murders, a surgeon who amputates limbs need not be limbless, and a farmer who fattens his livestock need not himself be fat!

The dependency of the cosmological argument on rejecting infinite regress may also not be so decisive as the various forms have suggested if we ask whether an infinite regress is chronological or logical. A chronological series of causes and effects, even if infinite, would still need an explanation, but nevertheless we can conceive of the infinity of such a series, for example an infinite number of dominoes falling in an infinite line. However, a logical regress cannot go back to infinity. For example, the logical series of thunder and lightening, which appear as two separate events, are actually simultaneous to their cause, which is an electrical discharge between earth and sky.

It is hugely significant that Aquinas concludes that God is the first mover, cause and necessary being, because the logic of the premise does not demand that God be a necessary conclusion. All it need imply is a first mover or cause, and by no means demands that it be the God of classical theism. Even if it seemed that he is the best explanation for the origin of the universe that is not the same as proving that he still exists.

Neither does causation necessarily involve creation, an on-going, personal process that involves the continual activity of God. The language of Aquinas's arguments does not rule out more than one possible mover, cause or necessary being, so it is only by adding to his premises his pre-existing belief in a single supremely powerful God that his conclusion becomes the only apparently logical one to draw. However, the principle of Ockham's Razor rules out the unnecessary multiplication of entities. Where God suffices as the simplest explanation, why postulate further explanations? Furthermore, it may be suggested that Aquinas's arguments serve only to postulate that the world is made up of contingent items and beings rather than that God's existence is either factually or logically necessary.

Essentially, to arrive at the existence of God from the premises of the cosmological argument involves an inductive leap, which takes us further than the premises legitimately allow us to go.

David Hume's challenges to the cosmological argument

David Hume proposed the classic criticisms of the cosmological argument in *Dialogues Concerning Natural Religion* (Oxford Paperbacks, 1998), which essentially revolve around three issues.

Newton's first law of inertia dictates that these balls need to be started by an external force for motion to occur. Like the universe, they cannot have an infinite regressive movement without a first cause

Taking it further...

If the cosmological argument does not prove the continued existence of God, then we are left with a form of **Deism**. Deism involves the belief in the existence of God, on purely rational grounds, without any reliance on revealed religion or religious authority.

- Why presume the need for a cause?
- Why look for an explanation for the whole?
- Is the concept of a necessary being meaningful?

Hume, like Bertrand Russell after him, argued that the notion of a necessary being is an inconsistent one because there is no being the non-existence of which is inconceivable. Even if there was such a being, why should it be God? He argued: 'Any particle of matter, it is said, may be conceived to be annihilated, and any form may be conceived to be altered. Such an annihilation or alteration is not therefore impossible. But it seems a great partiality not to perceive that the same argument extends equally to the Deity, so far as we have any conception of him.' Even if it were reasonable to postulate a necessary being, why should it be the God of classical theism? Aquinas is guilty of an inductive leap of logic in moving from the need for a necessary being to identifying it as God when nothing in the premises of the argument leads logically to that conclusion. Obviously, proponents of the argument believe that they have overwhelmingly good reasons why it should be God rather than anything else, but Hume argued: 'Why may not the material universe be the necessarily existent being, according to this pretended explication of necessity? We dare not affirm that we know all the qualities of matter; and for ought we can determine, it may contain some qualities which, were they known, would make its non-existence appear as great a contradiction as that twice two is five.' Indeed, if the material universe were the necessarily existent being, it would open the way for **pantheism**. This is the view that God is everything and everything is God and hence the world is either identical with God or in some way an expression of his nature. Similarly, it is the view that everything that exists constitutes a unity that is in some sense divine.

Hume is playing Devil's advocate here. He knows that the nature of the universe is such that it would be virtually impossible to claim that it possessed some essential necessity, but his point is why should we be able to say that God, unknowable and inconceivable, possesses qualities that make his non-existence logically impossible? Furthermore, any perceived truth of the claim that there is a God cannot be assumed in order to establish the verisimilitude of an argument that is supposed to prove his existence.

Hume further observes that the argument begins with a concept familiar to us, the universe, but claims to be able to reach conclusions about things that are outside our experience. This criticism applies to all arguments from natural theology or that attempt to argue from some facet of human experience to God, and yet proponents of the argument claim that there is sufficient evidence in the natural world to point irrefutably to the existence of God. Surely this is a matter of perception and of pre-existing belief? The nature of the world is religiously ambiguous and there is nothing about it that demands belief in God. The theist chooses to interpret the world in the light of the existence of God; he is not logically compelled to do so.

Furthermore, why do we need to find a cause for the whole chain if we can explain each item in the chain? Hume wrote: 'Did I show you the particular causes of each individual in a collection of twenty particles of matter, I should think it very unreasonable should you afterwards ask me what was the cause of the whole twenty. This sufficiently explained in explaining the cause of the parts' (in *An Enquiry Concerning Human Understanding*, Oxford University Press, 1999).

Taking it further...

Scientific theories of everything, or **unified field theories,** have been attempted in cosmology and biology so, to some degree, we can establish that theories of the parts can be related to the whole.

Hume's criticism is effectively arguing that partial explanations should be quite sufficient and that it is somehow gratuitous to seek an explanation for the whole if we are able to explain the parts. Linking together of individual causes and effects into a whole is merely arbitrary, Hume maintained, and makes no difference to the nature of things. Nevertheless, there are clearly instances when it is more logical to ask for the explanation of the whole rather than the parts. Robert Gardener-Sharpe observed that in the instance of a cake cut into 20 slices, it would be more unreasonable to ask for an explanation of the 20 slices than the whole cake. In such a case an explanation of the whole serves to explain the parts. Furthermore, if we explain each individual component of a computer, have we explained the whole? This perhaps gives way to the **design argument**, which emphasises the significance of the parts to the whole, as in Paley's analogy of the watch (see section 1.2 for a discussion of Paley's argument). Nevertheless, it is reasonable to argue that, in the case of the universe, while its individual parts may come and go out of existence, the universe has existed eternally.

Even if specific instances of things in the universe require an explanation, why should this be the case for the universe as a whole? Nor can we work from the specific to the general. This is a well-worn criticism that Bertrand Russell famously exploited in his dialogue with F. C. Copleston by means of *a reductio ad absurdum:* 'Every man who exists has a mother, and it seems to me your argument is that therefore the human race must have a mother, but obviously the human race hasn't a mother – that's a different logical sphere' (cited in *The Existence of God*, edited by John Hick, Macmillan, 1964). Copleston replied that to postulate a mother for the whole of humanity is to turn the human race, an empirical concept, into an abstract one. In the case of human beings, individuals are satisfactorily explained and the whole of humanity it not reasonably considered as a whole in terms of origin.

Of course, Russell's overwhelming objection was why does anything need an explanation? Russell claimed that some things are 'just there' and require no explanation and the universe was such a case. It is a 'brute fact'. Interestingly, Russell did not dismiss the quest for an explanation *per se*, but he maintained that it was a fallacy to assume that you would arrive at one: 'A man may look for gold without assuming that there's gold everywhere; if he finds gold, good luck, if he doesn't, he's had bad luck.'

Russell's objection is essentially that of the existentialist, which runs as follows.

- Existentialist: why should there be anything?
- Theist: but you cannot deny that there is.
- Existentialist: yes, but to admit that something does exist is not to admit that it must exist.

Russell's argument too is based on the view that in reality the world is no more than a totality of its parts, which may or may not legitimately be assumed to take a certain shape or pattern when viewed together. If not, it may reasonably be suggested that the universe is an 'intelligible brute fact', or at least this possibility should not be excluded from an attempt to explain it. Certainly, Russell could be forced to acknowledge that scientists are concerned with explaining the universe, even at the time of his debate with Copleston, but it would be easy for this to open up another issue: if it is reasonable to seek an explanation for the universe, why is it not reasonable to do so for God? The cosmological argument constantly faces this problem: why is it reasonable to say that God is different from everything else and does not need to be explained?

The value of the argument

Despite the many criticisms that have been raised against the argument, its strength as an a posteriori argument that draws on evidence that is universally available and that in itself cannot be challenged gives the argument lasting appeal. The ultimate result of the cosmological argument is that it provides a way of explaining the universe, although it cannot offer any guarantees that the explanation is the correct one. Although John Hick maintained that, 'The atheistic option that the universe is "just there" is the more economical option' (*Philosophy of Religion*, Prentice Hall, 1993), Richard Swinburne disagrees, arguing that 'God is simpler than anything we can imagine and gives a simple explanation for the system' (*Is There a God?*, Oxford University Press, 1996). Problematically, however, the argument relies on a medieval view of the universe that has long been superseded, and at least the scientist needs to be convinced that God as an ultimate or complete explanation is compatible with modern understandings.

Nevertheless, the proponent of the argument will ask whether questions about the universe can ever be separated from questions about God. Herbert McCabe observed: 'The question is: is there an unanswered question about the existence of the world? Can we be puzzled by the existence of the world instead of nothing? I can be and am; and this is to be puzzled about God' (*A Modern Cosmological Argument*, New Blackfriars, Vol. 61, 1980).

However, although it is perfectly reasonable and legitimate to propose as a hypothesis that there is a God who created the universe, the argument will only work if it reduces the number of unanswered questions. Ultimately, the argument cannot explain God, only postulate God as an explanation, and if we are not satisfied with the idea of God as a being who himself requires no explanation, the argument will fail.

CHAPTER 2
Problems in the philosophy of religion

2.1 The problem of evil

Key Ideas

- The nature of evil and suffering

- The theological and philosophical problems of evil and suffering

- The need to solve the problem

- Traditional theodicies: Augustine and Irenaeus

- Modern approaches: process theodicy and freewill

The nature of evil and suffering

The terrible extent of human suffering in the world and the evil actions that often cause it provide, perhaps more than anything else, the reasons why many people find it difficult to believe in a loving God. The problem of evil is, according to the 18th century atheist David Hume, 'the rock of atheism'.

Evil and **suffering** were defined by John Hick in *Philosophy of Religion* (Prentice Hall, 1993) as: 'physical pain, mental suffering and moral wickedness. The last is one of the causes of the first two, for an enormous amount of human pain arises from people's inhumanity. This pain includes such major scourges as poverty, oppression and persecution, war and all the injustice, indignity and inequalities that have occurred throughout history.'

Natural evil is the apparent malfunctioning of the natural world, which produces diseases, earthquakes, volcanoes, famines and floods. 'Natural evil is the evil that originates independently of human actions, in disease… in earthquakes, storms, droughts, tornadoes', writes John Hick in *Evil and the God of Love* (Fontana, 1968).

Moral evil arises as the result of human actions that are morally wrong, such as murder, war and cruelty. 'Moral evil I understand as including all evil caused deliberately by humans doing what they ought not to do, or allowed to occur by humans negligently failing to do what they ought to do, and also the evil constituted by such deliberate actions or negligent failure', writes Richard Swinburne in *Is There A God?* (Oxford University Press, 1996).

Evil produces suffering, which often appears to be unjust. The innocent seem to suffer most. Evil may also include animal suffering; psychological,

Plymouth, the capital of Montserrat, was destroyed and two-thirds of the island's population was forced to flee abroad due to a volcano erupting

emotional and mental suffering; the evil of contingency (that things corrupt and die); and the question of whether death itself is an evil. Different types of evil sometimes overlap, for example the natural evil of famine caused by drought can be worsened by the moral evil of civil unrest and corruption in countries struggling to get aid.

Does evil exist?

There would be no problem with evil if it could be proved that evil does not exist or that our perception of evil is wrong in some way. There are several ways to consider this:

● There is no evil

Monists claim that the universe is a single, harmonious unity that is good, and so evil is a mere illusion in our minds. Evil causes a feeling of suffering only because we cannot see the whole picture. If we could see the whole picture, we would realise that evil is an illusion. Evil is not something that God has deliberately created. Evil is simply the absence of good, like an eye that is blind.

This raises problems because it seems to contradict our own experience of the world in which there is obviously evil and suffering. Nor does it really explain why a loving God would allow humanity to suffer from an illusion. It trivialises evil and suffering: if evil is only an illusion, why should we bother to try to avoid it?

● There is no God

For **atheists**, evil is convincing evidence that God does not exist because, they claim, a loving God would not have created a universe so full of evil and suffering: 'I cannot imagine any omnipotent sentient being sufficiently cruel to create the world we inhabit' (Iris Murdoch, *A Severed Head*, Chatto, 1961). The atheistic argument is that it is just as rational to reject belief in God as it is to believe that an all-loving and all-powerful creator would be responsible for the evil and suffering that characterises the world.

● Our view of evil is distorted

In **Hindu** and **Buddhist** thought, evil is an illusion brought about by human greed and selfishness. Under the doctrines of karma and rebirth, all suffering is the result of evil committed in a previous life. Suffering is not from God, nor is God responsible for it, the actions (karma) of a person in one life affects that person in the next. Evil and suffering can therefore be overcome by a person achieving good karma by becoming more and more detached from the world.

● The reality of evil

For the **monotheistic** religions, there is no suggestion that evil is an illusion of the human mind. The scriptures tell of the mixture of good and evil in human experience and record sorrow, suffering and human wickedness. Evil is seen as utterly bad and entirely real. The writers of the Bible did not attempt to underestimate the reality of evil and suffering. The Psalmist writes in the most graphic detail of his personal suffering: 'Save me, O God, for the waters have come up to my neck. I sink in the miry depths, where there is no foothold. I have come into the deep waters; the floods engulf me. I am worn out calling for help; my throat is parched. My eyes fail, looking for my God' (Psalms 69:1–3). One of the most often cited biblical narratives is that of Job, who suffered at the hands of Satan but with God's permission, raising difficult questions about the nature of innocent suffering and God's role in human pain. Similarly, in the New Testament suffering is a crucial part of the

Taking it further...

Benedict Spinoza claimed that we consider things in terms of how useful they are to us and we miss their true value. We assume that there are norms to which humans, animals and natural objects conform, and so we regard anything that does not fit into the norm to be defective. Spinoza argued that, if we looked at the universe objectively, without putting ourselves first, we would see that everything has a unique value: 'All things are necessarily what they are, and in Nature, there is no good and evil' (*Ethics*, Wordsworth Editions, 2001).

Taking it further...

G. Leibniz believed that this world was the best of all possible worlds, because God, in his infinite wisdom and goodness, could not have made it any other way (*Theodicy*, Open Court Publications). Therefore evil must be an illusion: it cannot have any reality in such a world. Mary Baker Eddy, the founder of the Christian Science Movement, argued that evil is in the mind. She suggested that evil has no reality and that when sufferers realise that there is no reality to their pain, they can do nothing other than stop suffering (*Science and Health with Key to the Scriptures*, The Writings of Mary Baker Eddy, 2000).

ministry of Jesus. God becomes human in order to take on human sin through genuine suffering and death.

One way of approaching this problem is the dualist notion, such as that of **Zoroastrianism**, which assumes that the universe is a battlefield on which the Principle of Good and the Principle of Evil fight for supremacy until the end of time. God is the source of perfect good and is in conflict with the powers of darkness, which may be understood as Satan or the Devil. Paul writes of the spiritual struggle in which believers engage: 'For our struggle is not against enemies of blood and flesh, but against the rulers, against the authorities, against the cosmic powers of this present darkness, against the spiritual forces of evil in the heavenly places' (Ephesians 6:12). The writer of Revelation graphically describes the final, eschatological battle over evil that will last until Satan, the final enemy, is destroyed: 'The great dragon was hurled down – that ancient serpent called the devil, or Satan, who leads the whole world astray' (Revelation 12:9).

Michelangelo's Last Judgement

The challenge of evil

Evil presents the ultimate challenge to belief in the existence of God. This is because it is a problem that cannot be solved: even if evil ceased to exist there would still be the question of why so much evil has already happened. In fact some may claim that no amount of peace can ever make up for all the suffering that humanity has experienced. Therefore there can be no religious justification for evil: it is unacceptable.

The problem for **theism** (belief in a loving and powerful God) is that if God is all-knowing and perfectly loving he must want to abolish all evil and suffering, and if God is all-powerful then he must be able to abolish all evil and suffering. However, evil and suffering exist; therefore God cannot be all-knowing, perfectly loving and all-powerful. Augustine expressed the problem as: 'Either God cannot abolish evil or he will not: if he cannot then he is not all-powerful, if he will not, then he is not all good' (Augustine of Hippo, *Confessions*, Oxford Paperbacks, 1998). In the *Summa Theologica*, Aquinas similarly wrote: 'If one of two contraries be infinite, the other would be altogether destroyed. But the name God means that he is infinite goodness. If, therefore, God existed, there would be no evil discoverable; but there is evil in the world. Therefore God does not exist' (cited in *The Existence of God*, edited by John Hick, Macmillan, 1964). Neither Augustine nor Aquinas believed that the existence of evil disproved the existence of God, but they did recognise the problem that it raises. The challenge is expressed by contemporary thinker Richard Swinburne as: 'There is a problem about why God allows evil, and if the theist does not have (in a cool moment) a satisfactory answer to it, then his belief in God is less than rational, and there is no reason why the atheist should share it' (*Is There A God?*, Oxford University Press, 1996).

This dilemma of evil presents four distinctive problems:

- a **theological** problem, which challenges the nature of God
- a **philosophical** problem, which requires the believer to accept conflicting claims
- a **diverse** problem, that evil comes in many forms that demand different explanations
- a **challenging** problem, that the existence of evil and suffering is an objective reality.

Taking it further...

This was most famously stated by Dostoevsky in *The Brothers Karamazov* (Dover Giant Thrift Editions, 2005). Having seen a child being tortured by her parents, Ivan asks his religious brother Alyosha: 'Imagine that you are charged with building the edifice of human destiny whose ultimate aim is to bring people happiness, to give them peace and contentment at last, but that in order to achieve this it is essential and unavoidable to torture to death only one little speck of creation… that same little child beating her breasts with her little fists and imagine that this edifice has to be erected on her unexpiated tears. Would you consent to be the architect under those conditions?'

The inconsistent triad

J. L. Mackie discussed in his paper *Evil and Omnipotence* (Mind, 1955) that the three propositions comprising the problem of evil (shown below) form an **inconsistent triad**: the conjunction of any two entails the negation of the third. However, believers in the God of classical theism say that only a solution to the problem of evil that in some way demonstrates the compatibility of the propositions, and does not reject or disregard any of them, can be said to be a true theodicy. Mackie argues that, 'From these it follows that a good omnipotent thing eliminates evil completely, and the propositions that a good omnipotent thing exists and that evil exists are incompatible' (*Evil and Omnipotence*, Mind, 1955).

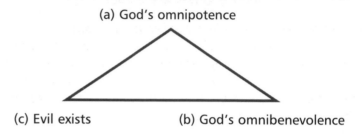

(a) God's omnipotence

(c) Evil exists   (b) God's omnibenevolence

Note how each corner of the triad represents a claim that religious believers have to accept as a part of their faith, i.e. God's omnipotence and omnibenevolence, or it would be counter-intuitive for them to reject, i.e. evil exists.

The problem of evil can be examined further.

- God has created the universe out of nothing (ex nihilo) and is totally responsible for it. If he is all-powerful, then he can do anything that is logically possible. This means he could create a world free from evil and suffering.

- God is omniscient and knows everything in the universe. He must, therefore, know how to stop evil and suffering.

- He is omnibenevolent and, in his love, would wish to end all evil and suffering. No all-loving God would choose his creation to suffer for no reason.

- God is omnipotent and could therefore stop all evil and suffering.

- Evil and suffering do exist, so either God is not omnipotent or omnibenevolent or he does not exist.

The famous atheist David Hume concluded that because the qualities of omnipotence, omnibenevolence and evil cannot exist simultaneously but evil does exist, then the God of classical theism cannot exist.

11 September 2001: 9/11

Few people who saw the television coverage and pictures in newspapers will forget the effect the tragic events of 9/11 had on the city of New York, USA. It was a truly global disaster in so far as surely no one could fail to feel empathy and sorrow for those who had suffered or lost loved ones on that day. Perhaps more than anything in living memory since the Holocaust, 9/11 posed horrifyingly challenging questions regarding the problem of evil. How could God allow so many people to suffer so much, particularly if the tragedy was, as some claimed, executed in the name of religion?

The impact of 9/11 was felt around the world

New York resident Russ Mackechnie saw the events unfold as he made his way to work on the morning of 9/11. He wrote a personal account called *One Man's 9/11*, from which the following is an extract.

> *My express bus from Brooklyn arrived near Battery Park and started north on Church Street, its normal route. When we came up out of the Brooklyn Battery Tunnel at about 8:55 a.m., several passengers noticed the burning upper floors of the north tower, 1WTC, which apparently had been hit by the first plane only moments before we emerged from the tunnel. Our driver suggested that we might make better time on foot, so I hopped off the bus and began to walk north on Church, all the while gazing in horror at the flames and billowing smoke from the north tower, just two blocks north and one block west of me.*
>
> *When I reached Liberty Plaza Park I pulled out the camera and started to take pictures, then I walked a block north to the intersection of Cortlandt Street and Worth, now virtually beneath the towers, to get a better view. It was here that I witnessed the most horrifying, for me, images of the day: three or four people leaping to their deaths from the upper floors of the north tower. I will never forget it…*
>
> *There was no subway or bus service, and cell phones were inoperable – nothing left to do but walk out of Manhattan… St Paul's Chapel was untouched by the devastation whirling all around it. I'd be tempted to call it a miracle were I not absolutely certain that a universe with a God of any kind could never have countenanced what I saw that day.*

The nature of God

God is not perfectly good

If God is not perfectly good, as the problem of evil may lead us to suggest, then he is, at least in this sense, morally imperfect. Supporters of this view argue that, if this is so, then God is not a being worthy of worship, in fact is not worthy of the title 'God'.

This has led, quite recently, to the development of a kind of 'protest theodicy', for example God's apparent failure to act during the Holocaust seems to suggest he is not all-loving. In a BBC interview (*The Trial of God*, 1979), writer Elie Wiesel said: 'In a wartime concentration camp, three rabbis put God on trial for the suffering of the Jews. They found him guilty. They added that the only counsel they could have called to speak on God's behalf would have been Satan.'

However, this logical argument only works if we think of God's goodness as being of the same nature as human goodness. In fact, it can be argued that God's goodness is a very different concept from human goodness.

God is not all-powerful

In this view, God is incapable of destroying evil because he lacks the power to do so. The dualist view suggests that there are two co-eternal sides, good and evil, that are in conflict in the universe, and that God, in this sense, represents the good side of good. This view limits God's power and he is not the powerful, almighty sovereign of the universe. He cannot, therefore,

---

Taking it further...

Russ Mackechnie concludes his account (*One Man's 9/11*) with these powerful words: 'In less than two hours, Aquinas's proofs of God [were] blasted, seared, choked with acrid smoke, and snuffed out forever, along with the more than 3000 lives now reduced to powder in the rubble of Ground Zero.' Aquinas's proofs of God are found in the *Summa Theologica*, and include Five Ways, which he maintained proved decisively the existence of God against the atheist's opposing claims, including the problem of evil (*The Existence of God*, edited by John Hick, Macmillan 1964).

Taking it further...

Supporters of protest theodicy even cite the scriptures, for example how God commands Abraham to kill his only son, Isaac (Genesis 22), and the death of the Egyptian firstborn at the time of Moses (Exodus 12). In fact there are many biblical instances of defiant protest against God.

'I form the light and create darkness, I bring prosperity and create disaster; I, the Lord, do all these things' (Isaiah 45:7).

'We are consumed by your anger and terrified by your indignation… our days pass away under your wrath; we finish our years with a moan' (Psalm 90:7–9).

control events, but only lead them towards good. Nor can he control nature: 'If cancerous cells have developed in your body, God cannot lure them to leave voluntarily' (David Griffin, *Encountering Evil*, edited by Stephen Davis, Westminster/John Knox, 2001).

This view of God does not coincide easily with the God of classical theism because there is no guarantee that good will overcome evil and it questions whether he is a being worthy of worship. However, it may be easier for believers to accept that God is not in control of the universe than accept that he may not be all-loving. In *Testing God* (Channel 4, 2000), Jocelyn Bell Burnell, an astronomer at Cambridge University and a Quaker, explained that it was this assumption of classical theism which she felt most able to abandon: 'I haven't the guts to relax the idea of a loving God,' she explains, 'I need a loving God. But if we relax the view that God is in control of the universe, the problem goes away.'

God is not all-loving

It often seems to people who are not religious that there is no event that would make a religious person admit there was a case for suggesting that 'God does not really love us' (Anthony Flew, *Theology and Falsification*, SCM, 1955). Flew argues that the biggest challenge that a believer faces is allowing that the existence of suffering (or other reasons to deny the existence of God) is a real problem that demands an answer. It is not enough to say, 'We don't really understand how God works' and carry on believing in the same way. If we say, 'God's love is not like human love, so we can't expect him to intervene where there is suffering' this is simply qualifying God's love rather than providing a good reason why he should not intervene.

Does evil have a purpose?

Apart from the classical theodicies (solutions to the problem of evil) which we shall explore later, several arguments can be proposed that suggest God uses what humans regard as evil and suffering for a purpose.

Evil is a punishment

A popular response to the problem of evil is that God uses evil and suffering to punish those who do not do as he asks. Many people, including religious believers, often feel that their sufferings are deliberately sent by God, asking, 'What have I done to deserve this?' The Bible does seem, to some extent, to support this view: 'The Lord will send on you curses, confusion and rebuke in everything you put your hand to, until you are destroyed and come to sudden ruin because of the evil you have done in forsaking him' (Deuteronomy 28:20).

Similarly in Islam, all natural phenomena are understood to be expressions of God's will and disasters can be tests of fortitude and faith as well as expressions of God's displeasure. The *Daily Telegraph* on 16 January 2005 reported that, in the wake of the tsunami disaster, Islamic television and newspapers were full of speculation that the tsunami was an act of God, punishing the people of the countries affected. As recorded on *Tsunami: Where was God?* (Channel Four, 2005), Mark Dowd visited Aceh, a strict

Taking it further...

Basil Mitchell, in his *Parable of the Partisan and the Strange* (cited in *The Philosophy of Religion*, edited by Basil Mitchell, Oxford University Press, 1971), observed that theists should 'face the full force of the conflict', i.e. not avoid the problem of suffering but confront it, without allowing it to count decisively against their belief. But they should not use 'vacuous formulae' such as 'It's God's will', which are neither explanations nor justifications.

The Asian tsunami of 26 December 2004 raised the question, 'Where was God?' for many people

Muslim province in Indonesia, which bore the brunt of the tsunami, and discovered that for many of its victims there was no question of asking, 'Why did this happen?' Rather, Muslims of all ages, even children aged under 10, were sure in their hearts that it was a punishment from God that they fully deserved. The overwhelming sense was that God's actions were in keeping with his nature, not opposed to it, and that he was fully entitled to have acted in such a way. The problem of evil and suffering as it appears to Christian theists is not, it seems, shared by Muslim theists.

However, the Bible also offers passages that disagree with this view, people seem to suffer even though they have done nothing wrong and God's love is seen to be for all people: 'He causes the sun to rise on the evil and the good' (Matthew 5:45). Furthermore, when Job challenged God about why he was suffering, refusing to accept that it was a punishment, God confirmed his sense that there was no direct relationship between Job's sins (if any) and his sufferings, but asserted his right to allow him to suffer simply because he is God, the creator: 'Where were you when I laid the foundations of the earth? Tell me if you have understanding?' (Job 38:4)

Evil is a test

This view maintains God uses evil and suffering in order to test human qualities and give humans the opportunity to show love, courage and other noble traits. Such testing builds character and helps humans to become better and closer to God: 'though now for a little while you may have had to suffer grief in all kinds of trials. These have come so your faith… may result in praise, glory and honour' (1 Peter 1:6–7). Interestingly, this view is also part of the Muslim understanding of the problem of suffering. In *Tsunami: Where was God?* (Channel Four, 2005) one young man who had lost 30 members of his family told Mark Dowd that he felt closer to God after the disaster than he had done before. Others claimed that the natural order as created by God was such that humans were not spoiled but expected to be tried and tested by their struggles with the environment.

However, others argue that not everyone benefits from this kind of test. For many people, suffering is little more than torture.

Evil is inevitable

In this view, God is not responsible for evil and suffering, it is simply that this world, with all its imperfections, is the best possible world. If there were no evil there could be no good, and growth and achievement only happen by overcoming difficulties. Moreover, in the end, everything will be perfected in God's love: 'He will wipe every tear from their eyes. There will be no more death or mourning or crying or pain, for the old order of things has passed away' (Revelation 21:4).

Evil allows God's love to be displayed

The scriptures are full of references to the love of God, revealing that he is a personal God who loves his creation and humanity in particular. He is not a distant God, but one who cares for those who suffer and enables people to bring good out of evil. In the Christian faith, God becomes incarnate (human), and makes himself vulnerable to evil and suffering, through Jesus Christ.

Taking it further...

Hinduism and Buddhism teaching considers everything to be impermanent and that humans and all living things are part of the cycle of birth, life, death and destruction. The world is in a permanent state of flux and imbalance and it is an illusion to think that humans are masters over nature: instead, humanity should live alongside nature. Karma is the principle of cause and effect, which states that all acts or deeds leave their influence on a person's future transmigration. In other words, the current situation of a human being is the consequence of the person's actions and thoughts in current and past lives. God is not to blame for such disasters and they must be accepted as part of the cycle of life and death. Significantly, it seems, therefore, that the problem of evil and suffering is a distinctively Judaeo-Christian problem.

Refugees fleeing drought and tribal fighting

Solving the problem: the Augustinian theodicy

Aquinas argued that God allows evil to exist as part of his greater plan of love. In such a case, there is no logical contradiction in God still being regarded as all-loving and all-powerful because he has a reason for evil to exist. Such an approach has led religious thinkers to evolve **theodicies** explaining what God's reason is. Theodicies are arguments that suggest God is right to allow the existence of evil and suffering because, in some way or another, they are necessary and essential.

In his works *Confessions* (Oxford Paperbacks, 1998) and *City of God* (Penguin Books, 2004), Augustine (354–430 CE) argued that the universe is good, that it is the creation of a good God for a good purpose. The Bible shows God creating a world that was perfectly good and free from defect: 'God saw all that he had made, and it was very good' (Genesis 1:31). Augustine believed that there were higher and lower goods, in huge number and variety, but that everything was, in its own way, good. Evil itself is not a thing or a substance and God did not create it. Evil is the going wrong of something that is, in itself, good, for example the evil of sickness is a physical lack of good health. Consequently Augustine called evil a **privation of good**.

However, how did evil come about? Augustine believed that evil did not come from God, nor did it exist in its own right. Evil comes when those beings that had freewill, angels and humans, turned their back on God, the supreme good, and settled for lesser goods. In other words, they cease to be what they were created to be. This caused the Fall and the biblical narrative of Adam and Eve highlights the disobedience of humanity and its consequences: 'But God did say, "You must not eat fruit from the tree that is in the middle of the garden, and you must not touch it, or you will die." "You will not surely die", the serpent said to the woman. "For God knows that when you eat of it your eyes will be opened and you will be like God, knowing good and evil"' (Genesis 3:3–5). As a consequence the state of perfection was ruined by human sin and the delicate balance of the world was destroyed. Natural evil came through the loss of order in nature and moral evil from the knowledge of good and evil that humanity had discovered through disobedience. Augustine believed that the sin of Adam was passed on to all humans ('seminally present'). This is called **original sin**. As a result, humanity could no long remain in Paradise: 'So the Lord God banished him from the Garden of Eden to work the ground from which he had been taken' (Genesis 3:23).

Augustine believed that God is right not to intervene to put a stop to suffering, because the punishment is justice for human sin and God is a just God. He said that, at the end of time, those who followed God would have eternal life and those who rejected God would suffer eternal torment. In *On Free Choice of the Will* (Hackett Publishing, 1993), he wrote: 'since there is happiness for those who do not sin, the universe is perfect; and it is no less perfect if there is misery for sinners… the penalty of sin corrects the dishonour of sin'. However, Augustine concluded that, if God were simply just, then everyone would receive their rightful punishment in Hell. However, in his infinite love and grace, he sent his son, Jesus Christ, to die so that those who believed and accepted him could be saved and have eternal life: 'Nevertheless, death reigned from the time of Adam… grace might reign through righteousness to bring eternal life through Jesus Christ' (Romans 5:14,21).

Taking it further...

The term theodicy was first used by Gottfried Leibniz (*Theodicy*, Open Court Publications, 1988) and comes from the Greek 'theos', god, and 'dike', righteous. A theodicy (literally 'righteous God') is the name given to an attempt to justify the existence of a loving God in the face of evil. A theodicy must not qualify God, deny the reality of evil or suggest that the only option is to give up faith, but it must offer a convincing reason why a better state of affairs prevails by God not removing evil than if he did.

Taking it further...

Augustine said that both forms of evil were a punishment and that all humans have brought suffering upon themselves because they are all 'in the loins of Adam'. For Augustine, all humans are as guilty and deserving of punishment as Adam. In *De Genesi Ad Litteram* he wrote: 'All evil is either sin or the punishment for sin.' However, Augustine's view that every human was seminally present in Adam is not biologically accurate and, consequently, all of humanity cannot be guilty of Adam's sin. This means that God is unjust in allowing humans to be punished for someone else's sin.

Evaluation of Augustine's theodicy

The Augustinian theodicy clears God of any responsibility for the existence of evil: the responsibility lies with the angels and humanity. But this view has been criticised by Friedrich Schleiermacher (1768–1834). In his book *The Christian Faith* (T&TC, 1999) he argued that it was a logical contradiction to say that a perfectly created world had gone wrong, because this would mean that evil had come out of nothing. If God really is a being of absolute power, then he must have created the universe exactly as he wished it to be, without evil of any kind. Angels and humans would have no trace of evil in them and, because they exist in a perfect universe, would never have used their freewill to choose evil, just as Jesus Christ chose only to do good.

A further criticism of the theodicy is that, if the world was perfect and there was no knowledge of good and evil, how could there be the freedom to obey or disobey God, because good and evil were unknown? If humans chose to disobey God, then knowledge of good and evil must have already existed. God's love may be the key to this issue. God wishes to have a loving relationship with humanity, but genuine love involves both sides having the freedom to choose: to accept or reject the love of the other. Therefore humans had the freedom (given to them by God) to reject him. God has to take the risk that humans will not reject his love but cannot blame them for it if they do. In *Philosophy of Religion* (Hodder and Stoughton, 1999) Peter Cole writes: 'Without freedom we could not share in God's goodness by freely loving Him. Nevertheless, the creation of free creatures involved the risk that persons would misuse their freedom and reject the good, and this is what happened.'

The Augustinian theodicy can also be criticised at a scientific level. Augustine's view that the world was made perfect and damaged by humans is contrary to the theory of evolution, which asserts that the universe began as chaos and has been developing, not diminishing, continually. Moreover, it seems unlikely that humans were once perfect but are not any more. Scientific evidence suggests that humans evolved from lower forms of life that had only limited moral awareness. Suffering is essential to survival: things must die in order that others might eat and live. God must bear the responsibility of this, and yet to call it evil calls into question the whole natural order, implying that God should have created the world quite differently. However, if we allow that natural order, like humanity, was created with freedom, then it is reasonable to argue that natural evil is the way the earth demonstrates its own God-given freedom.

Although Augustine said that evil was not a thing but a privation of good, many religious believers argue that evil is a very real entity in the form of Satan. At the same time, the existence of Hell as a place of eternal punishment seems to contradict the existence of an all-loving God. Eternal punishment serves no useful purpose. If Hell was part of the design of the universe, then did God know that the world would go wrong and allow it to happen? This suggests an angry, malicious God who knows what people are going to do before they do it and punishes them as a result. It begs the question as to whether humans have freewill at all.

Nonetheless, the Augustinian theodicy offers a classical theistic response to the problem of evil that is consistent with classical theistic belief and so is appealing to conservative theists. The blame for the existence of evil and suffering is placed firmly on the shoulders of humans exercising their God-

Taking it further...

The essence of Friedrich Schleiermacher's argument (*The Christian Faith*, T&TC, 1999) is that either the universe was not perfect to start with or God made it go wrong. If either of these is the case, then it is God who is to blame for the existence of evil. In *Philosophy of Religion* (Prentice Hall, 1993), John Hick observed: 'a flawless creation would never go wrong and that if the creation does in fact go wrong the ultimate responsibility must be with its creator'.

The Garden of Earthly Delights (detail): Hieronymus Bosch used demonic images to portray human evil

given freedom, liberating God from direct responsibility. If freewill is seen to be inherently good, then humans are better off being free, despite the inevitability of their exercising that freedom to choose to disobey God. His choice of creating humans capable of choosing evil is legitimised by the freedom of their response to choose the good, including accepting salvation through Jesus.

Solving the problem: the Irenaean theodicy

In his work *Against Heresies* (Newman Press, 1992), Irenaeus (130–202 CE) argued that the world was the way it was because God had a plan and a purpose to provide humanity with the opportunity to develop the qualities necessary to become perfect. He referred to humanity as **children of God**. According to Irenaeus, there were two stages in the creation of the human race. Firstly, humans were made in the 'image of God' (Genesis 1:26), i.e. brought into existence as intelligent but immature beings with the capacity of moral and spiritual perfection. Secondly, humans would grow into the 'likeness of God' (Genesis 1:26) by developing, over a long period of time, into perfect moral and spiritual beings.

Irenaeus maintained that God could not have created humans in complete perfection, because attaining the likeness of God needed the willing co-operation of human individuals. This meant God had to give them freewill, the only means by which humans can willingly co-operate or act without coercion. Therefore, God did not make a perfect world because evil has a valuable part to play in God's plans for humanity. Freedom requires the possibility of choosing good instead of evil, and therefore God has to allow evil and suffering to occur. Irenaeus (*Against Heresies*, Newman Press, 1992) claimed: 'How, if we had no knowledge of the contrary, could we have instruction in that which is good?' Humanity is given evil in order to enable them to develop the characteristics needed for perfection, such as courage, generosity, kindness and love. This view has biblical support as Paul observed: 'We also rejoice in our sufferings because we know that suffering produces perseverance; and perseverance, character; and character, hope' (Romans 5:3). Furthermore, Paul saw this as valuable for humans because: 'I consider that our present sufferings are not worth comparing with the glory that will be revealed in us. The creation waits in eager expectation for the sons of God to be revealed' (Romans 8:18–19).

God created the natural order to include the possibility of good as well as evil and suffering. He then stood back to allow humans to use their freewill for good or evil. He cannot intervene or that freedom is lost. Humans have to make responsible choices in real situations. Irenaeus concluded by suggesting that, eventually, evil and suffering will be overcome and humanity will develop into God's perfect likeness and will live in Heaven, where all suffering will end forever and God's plan will be complete.

Modern scholars have developed Irenaeus's ideas further. John Hick has highlighted the importance of humans being allowed by God to develop for themselves. He suggested that if God had made humanity perfectly, then this would have been the goodness of robots, which would automatically love God without thought or question. He said that such love would be valueless and that, if God wanted humans to be genuinely loving, he was right to let them have the freedom to develop this love for themselves. In *Evil and the God of Love* (Fontana, 1968), John Hick wrote that the value of this world was: 'to be judged, not primarily by the quantity of pleasure and pain occurring in it at any particular moment, but by its fitness for its primary purpose, the purpose of soul-making'.

Hick observed that, to achieve this, God had to create human beings at an **epistemic** distance from himself. This is a distance in dimension or knowledge that means God must not be so close that humans would have no choice but to believe and obey him. God allows humans to choose freely. Furthermore, the world has to be imperfect because if it were a paradise in which there were no evil and suffering, humans would not be free to choose because only good could actually happen.

The only other option would be for God to interfere constantly in the world in order to protect humans from harm. If this were to happen, then humans simply could not develop. Instead, nature would have to work by special rules instead of general laws. For example, if someone fell from an aeroplane God would have to suspend the law of gravity in order to ensure the person was not harmed. But then would people on the ground float upwards without gravity to keep them on land? If God changed the rules of nature all the time, there could be no science, no order, no need to be kind or loving: we would not know what would happen next. Life would be like a dream where we simply drifted aimlessly from one thing to the next. This prompted John Hick to write in *Philosophy of Religion* (Prentice Hall, 1993): 'God's purpose was not to construct a paradise whose inhabitants would experience a maximum of pleasure and a minimum of pain. The world is seen, instead, as a place of "soul making" or person making in which free beings, grappling with the tasks and challenges of their existence in a common environment, may become "children of God" and "heirs of eternal life".'

Is this the best possible world?

Supporters of Irenaean theodicy argue that this world is the best of all possible worlds because it offers an environment in which humans are able to develop the finest characteristics of life. There are general laws of nature that allow the operation of science and discovery, and there are dangers, difficulties and problems to overcome and pain, sorrow and suffering to experience. In other words, it is a 'vale of soul making'.

Finally, Irenaeus argued that a heavenly afterlife was necessary for humans in order to achieve perfection: no one would be left out and all would achieve ultimate perfection. He believed that humans could not achieve perfection in their lifetime and that suffering did not always produce good qualities. Sometimes suffering leads to fear, resentment and the worsening of character. Yet all the suffering that people felt would, in the end, be justified and ultimate perfection would be found in the afterlife.

Evaluation of the Irenaean theodicy

Although Irenaean theodicy allows room for the theory of evolution and avoids some of the problems associated with Augustinian theodicy, particularly the notion that evil seemed to come from nowhere, it still has a number of significant weaknesses.

Taking it further...

A **counterfactual hypothesis** is the view that God can continually make everything good. However, if this were the case, humanity would have no opportunity to experience the benefits of their genuinely free opportunities to do good.

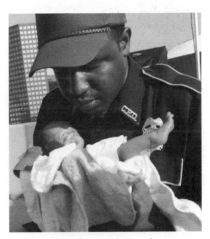

Suffering allows the opportunity to know compassion

Taking it further...

Peter Cole observes that the Irenaean theodicy: 'has an element of "greater goods". For instance, some moral goods are responses to evils and hence could not exist without them, e.g. courage, compassion, forgiveness. Sometimes this is referred to as a "second order good". The moral goods are those that result from alleviating, resisting and overcoming evil and involve intelligent and informed responses to evils. This could be seen as a necessary part of the soul-making process' (*Philosophy of Religion*, Hodder and Stoughton, 1999).

- If we need an afterlife to achieve perfection, would it not have been easier for God to give us longer earthly lives?

- Philosophers have argued that the challenges of the world do not always result in genuine human development, and often seem to produce nothing but great misery and suffering. Moreover, it does not justify the actual extent of human suffering, for example the Holocaust. Does the world really need such extremes of suffering to produce good?

- The Irenaean theodicy attempts to justify natural evil with the view that suffering is, in some sense, a good thing and that without suffering humans cannot develop good qualities. Yet this seems to ignore the fact that many people develop good qualities without suffering and that many who have suffered a great deal are made worse by their experiences. In fact, Jesus Christ seemed to go out of his way to ease peoples' sufferings: 'He has sent me to proclaim freedom for the prisoners and recovery of sight for the blind, to release the oppressed, to proclaim the year of the Lord's favour' (Luke 4:18–19).

- Many apparently evil people are mentally disturbed and cannot be held totally responsible for their actions.

- Why is the process of human development taking so long? Could God speed it up and prevent more suffering?

- Evil seems to be a random occurrence and many people feel that there is no apparent reason why some people suffer and others do not, especially regarding suffering of children.

Richard Swinburne

Modern philosopher Richard Swinburne is a staunch supporter of a form of the Irenaean theodicy, arguing that a world that includes suffering is the best possible world for humans. God had a choice what kind of world to create, and his choice to create one in which humans could meaningfully contribute through their free responses to the imperfect world in which they were placed was the best possible choice. He argues, for example, that although God could have made a world in which the cure for cancer was prayer, to have done so would be to take away from humans the opportunity to be involved in discovering the cure for themselves. This responsibility and opportunity is far better for humans than to be in a toy world in which whatever they did would make little difference because God was controlling it in order to ensure that the good would always prevail. Instead, humans are given the opportunity to grow in power, freedom and knowledge, and to make a difference to their own lives and the lives of others in the present and the future. Although the price may sometimes be high, it is a price worth paying and points more fully to the existence of a loving God than a world in which humans could make no appreciable difference.

Solving the problem: process theodicy

Process theodicy arose from the views of A. N. Whitehead and was developed by David Griffin in his book *God, Power and Evil: A Process Theodicy* (Westminster, 1976). It is a radical theodicy that suggests that God is not omnipotent. He did not create the universe because the universe is an uncreated process of which God is himself a part. God is, therefore, part of the universe and is bound by natural laws. In this sense, it is not a true theodicy because it demands a qualification of God's nature. However, for those who do not feel compelled to preserve the classical theistic God with all his attributes, the approach usefully frees God from the responsibility of evil whilst allowing him to be involved with the world and human activity.

According to process theodicy, the ultimate reality is continuous creativity: new things happen all the time as part of the universal process and from one thing stems another with endless possibilities. Every happening is momentary and creates new happenings in a never-ending process. When the process produces harmony, there is good. When the process produces discord, there is evil. Evil is, therefore, inevitable in the overall process. Process theology argues that the reality of God is not fixed and that God himself is still developing. From this point of view, God is 'dipolar': he has two 'poles', one mental and one physical. The physical pole is the material world itself, which acts almost as God's 'body'. God is partly distinct and partly immersed in the world, just as we are in our bodies. As a result, any suffering in creation, which is constantly changing, is also undergone by God, and creation itself is seen as co-operation between God and all other beings.

God's role in creation was to start off the evolutionary process, which, eventually, led to the development of humans. But God does not have total control and humans are free to ignore him. David Griffin observed in *God, Power and Evil: A Process Theodicy* (Westminster, 1976): 'God does not refrain from controlling the creatures simply because it is better for God to use persuasion, but because it is necessarily the case that God cannot completely control the creatures.' God suffers when evil happens because, like everything else, he is part of the universe. Whitehead described God as the: 'fellow sufferer who understands'.

God cannot stop evil because he does not have the power to change the natural process. However, in a sense, he bears some responsibility for it because he started off the evolutionary process knowing that he would not be able to control it. David Griffin claimed in *God, Power and Evil: A Process Theodicy* (Westminster, 1976) that: 'God is responsible for evil in the sense of having urged the creation forward to those states in which discordant feelings could be felt with greater intensity.' God seeks to maximise the harmony in the universe and tries to ensure that the overall good outweighs the evil. He helps people to live in the best way, by what Hick called 'persuasion and lure' but he cannot control them. In *Philosophy of Religion* (Prentice Hall, 1993), John Hick observed: 'the reality of evil in the world is the measure of the extent to which God's will is, in fact, thwarted. God offers the best possibility for each occasion as it creates itself, but the successive occasions are free not to conform to the divine plan.'

God need not have created the world, he could have left the original chaos undisturbed instead of forming it into an ordered universe. God, therefore, bears a great responsibility for the good and the evil that have occurred. However, in process theodicy, God's actions are justified because, as Hick observes: 'God's goodness is vindicated in that the risk-taking venture in the evolution of the universe was calculated to produce, and has produced, a sufficient quality and quantity of good to outweigh all the evil' (*Philosophy of Religion*, Prentice Hall, 1993).

Criticisms of process theodicy

Some philosophers have doubted whether process theodicy really is a theodicy at all. It has a number of significant weaknesses.

Taking it further...

The claim that God is omnipotent is equivalent to the claim that God possesses the logical limits of power. If this is the case, Whitehead argued that no being could be omnipotent. But, given any system of thought in which God is portrayed as having something less than perfect power, at least one version of the traditional problem of evil will not arise within it. However, Hartshorne and Griffin argued that while God possesses the greatest possible power, that power is not sufficient to bring about a world containing no instances of evil. This is because:

- a being of maximal power has no possible superior and therefore possesses power at the logical limit

- as Griffin claims, it is a 'metaphysical truth' that in any conceivable world there must be a number of beings that have power so that, at least partially, they can determine their own activities and the activity of others

- if there is a being that possesses the logical limit of power, all the power that there is to possess, any other beings would possess no power at all.

Thus, if the second point is the case, then the notion of a being which possesses all the power is not coherently conceivable.

- It is elitist: many suffer but only a few gain any benefit.

- It denies that God is all-powerful. He also seems to lack the all-loving qualities of the God of classical theism. He seems to allow the majority to suffer at the expense of the minority. John Hick argued: 'The God of process theodicy is… the God of the elite, or the great and successful among humankind… This is not the God of those millions who have been crippled by malnutrition and have suffered and died under oppression and exploitation, plague and famine, flood and earthquake' (*Evil and the God of Love*, Fontana, 1968).

- It does not explain the nature of God in order to justify the existence of evil. He seems to permit what is morally unacceptable, namely the death and suffering of millions. It produces a few apparently marvellous human beings, at the cost of millions who have had nothing but a desperate struggle to survive.

- It brings into question whether such a limited God is a being worthy of worship.

- There is no promise of heaven; there is no certainty that the innocent will be rewarded. Yet David Griffin believed that the justification for good would be found in the examples of human existence in this life, even if it all ends in a nuclear holocaust: 'No matter how bad the future actually turns out to be, it will not cancel out the worthwhileness of the human goodness enjoyed during the previous thousands of years' (*God, Power and Evil: A Process Theodicy*, Westminster, 1976).

- While it may be the case that the good has outweighed the evil, this is not much comfort to those who have actually suffered. Hick observes (*Evil and the God of Love*, Fontana, 1968): 'However, the starving and the oppressed, the victims of Auschwitz… can hardly be expected to share the process God's point of view, or to regard such a God as worthy of their worship and praise'. God is responsible for 'risking the vast dead-weight of human suffering and the virulent power of human wickedness, for the sake of the morally and spiritually successful, in whom God rejoices'.

Solving the problem: freewill defences

The notion of **freewill**, the belief that humans can only develop fully if they are free to choose how to act, is a crucial key to solving the problem of evil. The notion of freewill is important in Augustinian and Irenaean theodicy and some modern philosophers have developed it into a kind of theodicy in its own right, arguing that the world is the logically necessary environment for humans to develop because it provides an opportunity for people to exercise their freedom to make real choices that produce both good and evil. In *The Existence of God* (Clarendon Press, 2005), Richard Swinburne argued that without such choices people would not be free. God allows these free choices and does not intervene, even if the evil is excessive, because to do so would limit human freedom and take away the need for humans to be responsible: 'The less he allows men to bring about large scale horrors, the less freedom and responsibility he gives them.' Swinburne argues that even death is necessary because if humans were immortal they would have infinite chances to get things right and might never develop. Life has to be limited if humans are to take their responsibilities seriously. There can be no second chance because if there is always another chance there is no incentive for moral development.

Sixty thousand civilian prisoners were found at the Bergen-Belsen concentration camp, 1945

Swinburne also said that natural evil was necessary so that humans could have knowledge of evil and how to avoid it, for example not building near a volcano. In other words, the world needs to contain natural laws that include death, despite the suffering they may cause: 'If men are to have knowledge of the evil which will result from their actions or negligence, laws of nature must operate regularly: and that means that there will be victims of the system' (*Is There a God?*, Oxford University Press, 1996).

Moreover, humanity cannot argue that certain evils are unacceptable because, as John Hick pointed out in *Evil and the God of Love* (Fontana, 1968), if we say that some evils are too great, then we begin to go down the scale of evils until even the slightest suffering becomes too much. For instance, if we say that cancer is too severe, then what about heart disease, a cold, or a headache? Hick suggested that we must either demand a world with no evil and suffering in it at all, or accept what we have now. The alternative Hick says: 'would approximate to a prolonged dream in which our experience arranges itself according to our desires'.

Criticisms of freewill defences

The freewill defence has several weaknesses.

- It leaves unresolved the issue of a loving God allowing evil and suffering to occur.

- Not everyone, for example the enslaved and oppressed, has the chance to exercise freewill.

- People still reject God whether they have suffered or not. Could God have created people who would always freely choose him? In *Evil and Omnipotence* (Mind, 1955) J. L. Mackie wrote: 'God was not, then, faced with a choice between making innocent automata and making beings who, in acting freely, would sometimes go wrong: there was open to him the obviously better possibility of making beings who would act freely but always go right. Clearly, his failure to avail himself of this possibility is inconsistent with his being both omnipotent and wholly good.'

- However, Hick argued that, in such a case, humans would not be truly free, because God would always know they would choose good: their actions would have been decided before they were actually made, even if they believed they were acting freely.

Conclusion

Evil and suffering are major arguments against the existence of God. For non-believers, it strengthens their point of view. Religious believers, in turn, find it difficult to explain beyond saying that God has a purpose that we cannot understand. The problem raises all sorts of issues about the nature of life and death and whether the suffering of life is worthwhile. More than this, it challenges the power of God. There are no easy answers, as Richard Swinburne acknowledges in his work *Is There a God?* (Oxford University Press, 1996): 'A generous God will seek to give us great responsibility for ourselves, each other, and the world, and thus a share in his own creative activity of determining what sort of world it is to be. And he will seek to make our lives valuable, of great use to ourselves and to each other. The problem is that God cannot give us these goods in full measure without allowing much evil on the way.'

Taking it further...

In a sense, humans cannot have it both ways. If we value being able to make up our own minds and making our own decisions in life, then we must accept that some wrong decisions will cause harm. We cannot both be free and have a world in which wrong choices do no harm: that is the price we have to pay in a world where freedom of choice is possible.

Taking it further...

In *Two Cheers for Secularism* (Pilkington Press, 1998), John Mortimer warned against the danger of seeing freewill as simply a choice that everyone has between right and wrong: 'The standard explanation is that we are given freewill which enables us to choose between good and evil. This may be very satisfactory for the concentration camp guards and assassins who can choose whether or not to commit their crimes; but the innocent men, women and children whom they march into the gas ovens, or whose throats they slit, have no freewill to exercise the matter.'

2.2 Miracles

Key Ideas

- The problem of defining a miracle

- Types and accounts of miracles

- The reliability and verifiability of miracles

- Do miracles prove the existence of God?

Taking it further...

'It is possible to define the term in either purely physical and nonreligious terms, as a breach or suspension of natural law, or in religious terms, as an unusual and striking event that evokes and mediates a vivid awareness of God' (John Hick, *Philosophy of Religion*, Prentice Hall, 1993).

'The laws of nature never cause anything; they are merely our assessment of how things normally happen, and the person who believes in God claims that they describe what God normally causes to happen' (John Blanchard, *Why Believe the Bible?*, Evangelical Press, 2004).

The sick seeking a miracle at Lourdes

The concept of miracle

Paul Tillich in *Systematic Theology* (Nisbet, 1953), defines a miracle as '...an event which is astonishing, unusual, shaking, without contradicting the rational structure of reality... an event which points to the mystery of being'. The traditional understanding of miracles is that they are divine acts of God that cannot be explained in any other way. They are a religious experience with the power to convert people and affirm their religious belief. Thousands of testimonies abound from witnesses throughout the ages who have claimed to have experienced miracles in their own lives. Although these claims have been examined by scholars, doctors and theologians, no certain conclusion has been reached. Miracles capture the imagination of the religious and non-religious alike, all seeking to discover whether miracles happen and, as a result, discovering whether or not God exists.

What is a miracle?

A miracle is: 'The unexpected and unusual manifestations of the presence and power of God' (M. Cook, *Miracles: Cambridge Studies on their Philosophy and History*, Mowbray, 1965). Scholars throughout the centuries have been divided in their views on the definition of a miracle, although there is broad agreement that a miracle must contain three basic attributes:

- the event must be against regular experience, sometimes referred to as breaking the laws of nature (this will be discussed further)
- the event has a purpose and significance
- it is possible to ascribe religious significance to the event.

'A miracle occurs when the world is not left to itself, when something distinct from the natural order as a whole intrudes into it' (J. L. Mackie, *The Miracle of Theism*, Oxford University Press, 1982).

Thomas Aquinas

Thomas Aquinas proposed a traditional definition of miracle in the *Summa Theologica*, suggesting that miracles were: 'Those things... which are done by divine power apart from the order generally followed in things' (cited in *The Existence of God*, edited by John Hick, Macmillan, 1964). Aquinas proposed three categories of miracles.

- Events done by God that nature could never do, for example stopping the sun (Joshua 10:13). Such events are logically impossible, or a physical or natural impossibility.

- Events done by God that nature could do but not in that order, for example exorcisms (Mark 1:31). These events are not impossible but are highly unexpected.

- Events done by God that nature can do but God does without the use of natural laws, for example healing by forgiving sins (Mark 2:5). Such events take place in the natural order of things but the means by which God brings them about warrants the designation miracle.

Aquinas's definition is not without its difficulties, however. What Aquinas is suggesting is an interventionist God, who only acts on certain, almost random, occasions. Brian Davies, in *Introduction to the Philosophy of Religion* (Oxford University Press, 1993), argues that to talk about God 'intervening' suggests that he is normally just a spectator in human affairs who watches us struggle and suffer. This seems contrary to the classical theistic view, which says that God is a loving father who is always interacting with his creation.

Moreover, Aquinas's argument is based on the idea that God breaks natural laws. The problem here is that we may not actually know all the natural laws, nor how they operate. We cannot, therefore, tell if a natural law has been broken or not. In the same way, if a natural law is broken this may be no more than saying that something happened that we did not understand or expect. What we call natural laws are effectively no more than descriptions of things that have occurred frequently enough for it to be rational to believe that they will happen in that way all the time. For example, we consider it a law of nature for the sun to rise tomorrow because it has happened that way every day of our lives. It is not irrational to believe that it will do so, but we have to allow for the (very low) probability that it will not. It would not, strictly speaking, be breaking a natural law if the sun did not rise because we cannot say decisively what the action of the sun will be in the future; we can only say what has definitely happened in the past.

Richard Swinburne

Richard Swinburne claims that the laws of nature are reasonably predictable and that, if an apparently 'impossible' event happens, then it is fair to call it a miracle. He gave examples of such events recorded in the Bible and in Christian history: 'the resurrection from the dead in full health of a man whose heart has not been beating for twenty four hours and who was dead also by other currently used criteria; water turning into wine without the assistance of chemical apparatus or catalysts; a man getting better from polio in a minute' (Richard Swinburne, *Miracles*, Macmillan, 1989). He suggests that while people actually do recover from illness and some are even resuscitated from death, what actually determines if an event is a miracle is the way and the timescale in which it occurs. Miracles take place outside the normal conditions in which such cures usually happen.

Miracles as fortuitous coincidences

In *Thinking about God* (Oxford University Press, 1985), Brian Davies argues that miracles are: 'unexpected and fortuitous events in the light of which we are disposed to give thanks to God'. Yet such a view presents the problem of how to determine whether or not an event is truly a miracle. Perhaps the

Taking it further...

We could illustrate the idea of an interventionist God with the picture of a father standing on the sidelines watching his son play rugby. When his child is knocked to the ground and appears to be injured, the father rushes onto the pitch to give aid, but whilst all is going well, he just stands and watches. There is also no compulsion upon him to hurry onto the pitch, even at the moment of crisis. He may refrain from doing so for any number of reasons, not least because his son might be deeply embarrassed! This is contrary to the classical theistic view, which says that God, as a loving father, constantly interacts with his creation, not just occasionally or when he feels he has no other option. God does not need to take his children's possible embarrassment at his intervention into account.

Taking it further...

Some scientists suggest that within nature a certain number of unexpected or random actions may occur, and modern philosophers, such as Anthony Flew have argued that it is logically impossible that the balance of evidence should ever favour the occurrence of a miracle. 'The idea of a miraculous event introduces a sense of arbitrariness and unpredictability into an understanding of the world' (Mel Thompson, *Philosophy of Religion*, Hodder and Stoughton, 1997) biblical miracles, such as the parting of the Red Sea, could be interpreted as natural occurrences that happened so fortuitously that the people saw them as miracles performed by God. However, what about many of the testimonies concerning miracles today: are they also simply 'fortuitous events'? For instance, what are we to make of the many testimonies from survivors of the Asian tsunami in 2005 about how they were apparently saved by the miraculous intervention of God? And there are similar stories from some of the survivors of the 9/11 World Trade Centre terrorist attack. In addition, there are many miracles reported in the media: are they truly acts of God? Consider this headline from *The Observer* newspaper printed on 24 November 1995: 'Priests in Bethlehem proclaim a miracle as "tears" appear on the painted face of Christ in the church built over his birthplace.' Also in 1995, on 22 September *The Daily Telegraph* reported on the so-called 'miracle of Nandi' where marble idols in several different Hindu temples were seen to drink the milk offered to them by believers.

In his work *The Miraculous* (in *Religion and Understanding*, Oxford University Press, 1967), R. F. Holland suggested that a miracle is nothing more than an extraordinary coincidence that is seen in a religious way. He uses the example of a small boy who is stuck on a railway line. The driver of the express train, who cannot see the boy, unexpectedly faints and falls onto the brake lever bringing the train to a halt, saving the boy. His mother claims that a miracle has taken place even after she has been told what led up to the event. According to Holland: 'A coincidence can be taken religiously as a sign and called a miracle.'

The problem with Holland's interpretation is that it makes a miracle dependent on personal interpretation and this will vary from person to person. If one person says an action is a miracle and another says it is not, how are we to judge? Mel Thompson in *Philosophy of Religion* (Hodder and Stoughton, 1997) makes a similar point: 'In July 1995, a Roman Catholic priest suffered a severe stroke and was not expected to live. A fellow priest took the 300 year old mummified hand of an English martyr and placed it on his forehead while he was in hospital. The hand... has long been regarded as being able to bring about miracles. The priest recovered.' There is no evidence to suggest the recovery was anything other than a coincidence.

Miracles and the Bible

If miracles are indeed divine acts of God, then we must define what we mean by God. For this purpose, God is the title given to the supreme being in the universe. He is the creator and sustainer of the universe and all things depend upon him for their continued existence. He has created the universe, and humanity, for a purpose and he is wholly good, wishing only good for his creatures.

In the Bible, God also reveals himself to his people through miracles, events in which he suspends the laws of nature (the way in which events regularly occur) in order to accomplish his divine purpose for the universe. However, it must be remembered that biblical writers had no concept of the natural laws and so when God is seen to intervene it is interpreted in terms of God acting out of divine love and providence for his people. Although there may be opportunities for the glory of God to be revealed through events that appear to suspend or go against nature, the primary response of the observers is to praise God for his providential care for them.

The miracles of Jesus

The New Testament speaks about miracles in two different ways. Firstly, they are shown as God's mighty power; secondly they are shown as signs. In the biblical accounts faith is required in order to understand the miracles. Such faith enables believers to see God's work in these acts: they are signs of God's power and love. The miracles of Jesus point to who he is and what he teaches. They help a believer understand Jesus's nature. But only those with faith will see and understand the miracles in this way. For example, Jesus heals the daughter of the Canaanite woman because of her great faith: 'Woman, you have great faith! Your request is granted' (Matthew 15:28). Similarly, when Jesus heals the leper: 'Rise and go; your faith has made you well' (Luke 17:19).

The miracles of Jesus were signs that he was from God and that God's kingdom was being established in the world. They were signposts telling the people to respond and change their lives and believe: 'The miracles I do in my Father's name speak for me... even though you do not believe me, believe the miracles, that you may know and understand that the Father is in me, and I in the Father' (John 10: 25,38).

However, the miracles of Jesus present problems for both philosophers and religious believers. It would surely have been impractical for Jesus to heal every sick person he met, but this raises the question of how he chose who to heal. In the same way, why does God seem to intervene is some people's lives and not others? Furthermore, given the state of medicine at the time of the New Testament, how do we know what was actually wrong with the people Jesus healed: were they really sick or possessed by demons? There is a similar issue today with those believers who claim to be cured by religious healers such as Benny Hinn or by visiting shrines such as Lourdes: why are these people cured and not others? The answer may lie in the religious significance of miracles.

Science, reason and morality

Until the 18th century, most people believed that God regularly intervened in the world. However, during the Enlightenment a more rational, scientific and mathematical way of understanding the world developed and miracles were investigated in a new way. Science and rationality gave a superior role to reason in human thinking, along with the view that what was true could be proved by the senses and by experience. In an article in *Dialogue* (1998), Peter Atkins observed: 'Everything in the universe can be explained in terms of physical science.' Science offers a mechanistic view of the universe: it runs according to scientific principles and natural law, and these can be established and determined by empirical investigation. Knowledge of the universe, claim many scientists, can be found without reference to religion: 'God is the last resort of feeble minds masquerading as truth. Science... respects nobility of the human spirit' (Peter Atkins, *Dialogue*, 1998).

From the scientific viewpoint, that which can not be categorised in a scientific manner is considered to be untrue and false. This is a problem for testimonies concerning miracles. The laws of nature are considered to be reliable and unchanging, and reports of miracles seem to deny this understanding of how the world worked. As a result there was a reaction against miracles, with claims that they went against science and reason.

Taking it further...

In the Christian tradition, the Bible is the story of the on-going personal relationship between God and his people. The human race is at the heart of God's creative work and the universe is **anthropocentric**, centred on the needs of humanity.

Taking it further...

At times Jesus seemed reluctant to perform miracles. He did not want to do them just for people to be amazed. He wanted people to believe in him because of what he taught, rather than for what he did: '"Unless you people see miraculous signs and wonders" Jesus told him, "you will never believe"' (John 4:48).

Taking it further...

In *The Life of Jesus Critically Examined* (Fortress Press, 1972), D. F. Strauss used the term 'myth' to cover all the miracles in the gospels. He argued that the miracle stories were not proof of the power of God, but were the way in which the people of that time tried to understand what they could not explain. A century later Rudolph Bultmann observed that: 'It is impossible to use electric light and the wireless, and to avail ourselves of modern medical and surgical discoveries and at the same time to believe in the New Testament world of spirits and demons' (cited in *The New Dictionary of Theology*, edited by S. Ferguson and D. Wright, IVP, 1988). He claimed that the modern reader must **demythologise** the biblical text to extract the meaning that its writers intended to convey, but which, to the modern mind, was obscured by concerns about 'what really happened'.

St Januarius with phials of liquified blood

Religious believers take the opposite view, saying that it is God, not science, that provides the ultimate explanation. However, Keith Ward observes that God is the 'terminus' (end) of the quest for intelligibility, a rational complete explanation for events that are otherwise inexplicable. Inevitably, there are accounts of miracles today that cannot be explained by science or medicine. More than 70 miracle cures at Lourdes have been ratified by the Vatican, thousands of miracles have been declared by leaders of international miracle crusades and, perhaps more significantly, thousands more by individuals healed at prayer meetings or in private with no witnesses to support their testimony.

The moral dimension

Peter Vardy, in *The Puzzle of God* (Fount, 1999), questioned miracles on moral grounds: 'A God who intervenes at Lourdes to cure an old man of cancer but does not act to save starving millions in Ethiopia – such a God needs, at least, to face some hard moral questioning.' Other modern philosophers agree, for example, Maurice Wiles wrote: 'It seems strange that no miraculous intervention prevented Auschwitz or Hiroshima. The purposes apparently forwarded for some of the miracles acclaimed in the Christian tradition seem trivial by comparison' (*God's Action in the World*, SCM, 1986). This leads to the moral criticism that certain miracles seem to be incompatible with the notion of the love and justice of God. God appears to help some people through miracles, but not others. If he is indeed all loving and just, he should treat everyone equally. For example, he saved the Jews in the Exodus yet he did not save the millions of Jews who died in the Holocaust. On the other hand, the miracles of the Bible are clearly selective and a broader purpose lies behind them, as Jesus claimed: 'Believe me when I say that I am in the Father and the Father is in me; or at least believe on the evidence of the miracles themselves' (John 14:11).

The religious significance of miracles

In *The Concept of Miracle* (Macmillan, 1970), Richard Swinburne argues that there must be a reason for God to act in a miraculous way and that a miracle must, therefore, have a deep religious significance: 'If a god intervened in the natural order to make a feather land here rather than there for no deep, ultimate purpose, or to upset a child's box of toys just for spite, these events would not naturally be described as miracles.' However, some miracles appear to be almost without an obvious purpose or significance. For example, in St Clare's Basilica in Naples, Italy, people regularly gather to see the 'miracle' of the dried blood of St Januarius, who died in 305 CE, liquefying before their eyes. In this ceremony, which has been carried out since 1337, the bishop holds the reliquary that contains the dried blood of the saint. The bishop gently turns the vessel over and over until, eventually, the blood liquefies. He then holds it up to the crowd and declares, 'The miracle has happened!' Legend has it that if the blood fails to liquefy disaster will follow, and this has come true on five occasions.

There have been many reported miraculous appearances by the Virgin Mary. One of the most famous of these appearances happened in 1917, when the Virgin Mary visited three children in the town of Fatima, Portugal. On each occasion the Virgin warned of wars and persecution to come and said that she would perform a miracle. On 13 October 1917, a crowd of 70,000 apparently witnessed the sun grow large, then small and move in the sky.

There are equally baffling 'miracles' in other world faiths. In *The Daily Express* in June 1997 there was a story called 'The Miracle Tomato of Huddersfield'. A young Muslim girl, Sehilgal Shasta Aslam, cut open a tomato and found that its veins spelt out the Shahada in Arabic. In the weeks that followed Muslims from all over the country came to see the miraculous tomato.

On 21 September 1995 a miraculous phenomenon spread through the Hindu faith as Hindu statues in temples around the world appeared to drink milk offered to them by devotees. The 'Great Hindu Milk Miracle', as it became known, was witnessed by thousands of devotees not only in India but also in London where, at the Vishwa Temple, 10,000 people saw the statues drinking milk from cups and spoons.

Hindu statue drinking milk

John Locke

In his essay *A Discourse of Miracles* (Black, 1958), John Locke argued the case that the definition of a miracle must be seen in the broader context of who performs it and who sees it. Locke claimed that miracles must act as a witness to a person's mission from God and this must be acknowledged by the observers: 'Miracles must testify to truths relating to the glory of God and the great concern of men.' For Locke, proof that an act is a miracle depends on knowing that the person who performs it is sent by God as his messenger: 'he who comes with a message from God to be delivered to the world, cannot be refused belief if he vouches his mission by a miracle, because his credentials have a right to it'.

Gareth Moore

In *Believing in God: A Philosophical Essay* (T & T Clark, 1988), Gareth Moore argues that talking of God performing miracles is pointless because God is not a person. Moore said that when it is claimed that God performed a miracle it is actually the same as saying no one performed the miracle: 'Think of the shrine at Lourdes where, it is claimed, people are sometimes miraculously cured of their diseases... How are such claims investigated and what is taken to establish that a recovery is indeed miraculous? Much of the investigation is concerned with ruling out possible causes for the cure, showing what has not caused it; and it is certainly not proved to be a miracle by the discovery for the cure and its subsequent identification as God.' Moore used the example of a small boy trapped on a mountain. A huge boulder is rolling towards him but suddenly stops and hovers in the air above his head. There is no reason found for this: it is a miracle. However, this does not mean that God held the boulder up. It is a miracle simply because there is no reason for the boulder to hover in the air: that is the miracle.

Is the evidence for miracles reliable?

In his classic essay *Of Miracles*, in *An Enquiry Concerning Human Understanding* (Oxford University Press, 1975), David Hume defines a miracle as: 'A transgression of a law of nature by a particular volition of the Deity.' He approached the issue of the existence of miracles by concentrating on experience, observation, evidence and probability. He argued that a miracle was not simply an extraordinary event, but one that violates the laws of nature. Most importantly, he claimed that it was not reasonable to believe in the existence of miracles because the evidence was totally unreliable. He based his argument on the fact that the laws of nature have been seen to

Taking it further...

Part one of Hume's essay *Of Miracles* (in *An Enquiry Concerning Human Understanding*, Oxford University Press, 1975) was concerned with *a priori* arguments: those arguments that can be said to be true or false without reference to actual experience. In part two, Hume looked at *a posteriori* arguments: arguments based on personal experience.

The parting of the Red Sea could be described as a violation of natural law

work regularly over thousands of years. A miracle that contradicts these laws of nature would need to outweigh all the evidence that had established that law in the first place.

His argument is an exercise in logic and runs:

- miracles are violations of the laws of nature
- firm and unalterable experience has established these laws of nature
- improbable events need witnesses of greater reliability than witnesses for more probable events
- miracles are improbable events
- therefore miracles need very strong evidence from witnesses
- witnesses to miracles are invariably unreliable and their testimonies cannot be trusted
- therefore, miracles do not occur.

Hume gave four reasons why, in his view, there was insufficient evidence for miracles. In the first, he challenged the testimonies of miraculous occurrences on the grounds that there were not enough reliable witnesses: 'There is not to be found in all history, any miracle attested by a sufficient number of men, of such unquestioned good sense, education and learning, as to secure us against all delusion.'

Secondly, he argued that human nature was such that it tended to believe the unbelievable, particularly religious believers, who were always looking for miracles: 'The passion of surprise and wonder, arising from miracles... gives a tendency towards belief of those events... a religionist may be an enthusiast and imagines he sees what has no reality.'

Thirdly, Hume observed that miracle stories tended to come from what he saw as unreliable places: 'It forms a strong presumption against all supernatural and miraculous relations that they are observed chiefly to abound amongst ignorant and barbarous nations.' By this, Hume meant nations that had not been touched by the spirit of secular, rational Enlightenment thinking, despite the fact that at this time most accounts of miracles derived from France, Spain and Italy.

Finally, Hume was sceptical of the fact that miracles played an important part in many different religions, carried out, apparently, by different gods. He said that if all religions reported miracles, then these claims, in effect, cancelled each other out: 'In matters of religion, whatever is different is contrary... every miracle, therefore, pretended to have been wrought in any of these religions... destroys the credit of those miracles.'

The Islamic scholar, Illiyaas Ali, observes that this fourth observation of Hume's forms an **inconsistent triad** (cited in *AS Philosophy of Religion Workbook*, Sarah K. Tyler and Gordon Reid, Philip Allan, 2004):

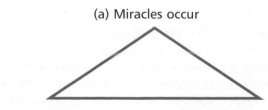

(a) Miracles occur

(c) Religions claim exclusivity   (b) Miracles are claimed in all religions

If (a) is accepted as true, then either (b) or (c) can be true, but not both, if the occurrence of miracles in any religious tradition is to establish that religion as exclusively true. However, the three claims can be true if the occurrence of miracles within a variety of religions is independent of claims made by any religion to have exclusive possession of the truth.

Evaluation of Hume's critique

Hume's definition of miracle as 'the violation of a law of nature' (*Of Miracles*, in *An Enquiry Concerning Human Understanding*, Oxford University Press, 1975), is problematic. Hume believed that the laws of nature were firm and unalterable and therefore could not be violated and, consequently, there could be no such thing as a miracle: 'Nothing is esteemed a miracle, if it ever happens in the common course of nature.' However, if Hume's view of natural laws is true, we would have to disregard many recent scientific advances because, in the past, they would have been seen as violation of natural law. What, for example, would stone age man have made of space rockets?

Hume's language is very ambiguous. He does not say what he means by 'unalterable' in relation to the laws of nature, which are, after all, descriptive and not prescriptive and likely to change as our understanding increases. Indeed, Hume's argument is open to widely differing interpretations; he seems to suggest that the improbability of an event leads to the logical conclusion that it did not happen. However, to religious believers the opposite is the case; the very improbability of the event makes it all the more likely that God did perform it. Hume remains unclear on other aspects of his argument. He does not, for instance, say what would constitute a sufficient number of witnesses, or what 'unquestioned good sense, education and learning' in a witness, actually means.

Hume suggests that only religious believers see miracles and implies that, because of this, their testimonies are unreliable. Yet why should religious believers be more unreliable than anyone else? In fact, some religious believers would argue that every event and action in the world is directly dependent on God and therefore he has no need to intervene, because he is already involved. However, other believers tend to take the view that God has put a set of natural laws into place to give humans a consistent environment; yet God can still leave himself the opportunity to interrupt the working of his natural laws if he chooses. Finally, Hume argues that is it not possible for God to perform miracles for people in different religions and that, as a consequence, the testimonies of miracles from different religions cancel each other out. But why should this be so? If there is a God, is he only supposed to perform miracles for Christians? Richard Swinburne writes: 'Evidence for a miracle wrought in one religion is only evidence against the occurrence of a miracle wrought in another religion if the two miracles, if they happen, should be incompatible with each other' (*Is There a God?*, Oxford University Press, 1996).

Overall, Hume avoids tricky problems with his arguments by appealing to common sense, and this leads to a range of inconsistencies and conclusions because he refuses to admit the possibility of miracles occurring. Hume famously rejected the accounts of miracles that had been experienced at the grave of Abbe Paris, a well-known Jesuit. There were a number of miracles, all witnessed by credible and reputable people, but Hume rejected them all, saying: 'and what do we have to oppose such a cloud of witnesses but the absolute impossibility or miraculous nature of the events to which they relate?' (*An Enquiry Concerning Human Understanding*, Oxford University Press, 1975)

Taking it further...

'We might say (though rather oddly) that until someone walked on the moon, people were regularly observed not to walk on the moon. And people, in time, have come to do what earlier generations would rightly have taken to be impossible on the basis of their experience' (Brian Davies, *An Introduction to the Philosophy of Religion*, 2nd edition, Oxford University Press, 1993).

Taking it further...

Hume's logic was sometimes faulty because he used examples of miraculous testimonies to prove his point and then contradicted himself. In one instance, Hume spoke of the Cardinal de Retz, who fled into Spain to avoid religious persecution and sought refuge in Saragossa Cathedral. There he met the doorman who, for many years, had had only one leg but had now, miraculously, got two. The miracle was witnessed by the canons of the church and by the entire population of Saragossa. However, Hume refused to accept these testimonies and rejected the miracle even though it had been witnessed by a large number of reputable people.

However, Richard Swinburne argued that there are three types of historical evidence that can be used to support miracles:

- our memories
- the testimony of others
- the physical traces left behind by the event in question.

He claims that our knowledge of scientific laws actually comes from these three types of evidence. Therefore, if the evidence is not sufficient to establish the occurrence of a miracle then neither is it sufficient to establish the certainty of a natural law. Swinburne suggested that it is possible that the best explanation for an event is that it is indeed a miracle. He said that the evidence in favour of a miracle must be considered properly, not simply dismissed because it may not be scientific, and that Hume was wrong simply to assume that miracles cannot occur.

Furthermore, Swinburne argues that it is reasonable to adopt principles of testimony and credulity in such cases: the assumption that people tell the truth and it is therefore reasonable to believe them. More significantly, he also argues that it is consistent with the nature of a loving God to perform miracles as a response to his peoples' 'special pleading'. In the way that a loving parent will sometimes bend the rules, so will God if he is to be more than a system of rules. But he will not bend the rules too often so that people still have a sufficient degree of responsibility for and control over their actions.

Do miracles prove the existence of God?

There is no certain answer regarding whether miracles actually occur; nor is there an agreed definition on what a miracle actually is. As we have seen, ordinary events can be seen as miracles and today many religious believers consider the possibility that the gospel miracles may not have happened in the way they were described. And there is always the possibility of a natural explanation. Indeed, it is even possible that miracles are the work of unseen beings or aliens, or the result of undiscovered powers within the human mind. For those who have religious faith, miracles are completely consistent with the existence of God. Swinburne suggests that miracles are one of the ways through which God would choose to relate to his people: 'If there is a God, one might well expect him to make his presence known to man, not merely through the over-all pattern of the universe in which he placed them, but by dealing more intimately and personally with them' (*Is There a God?*, Oxford University Press, 1996).

Equally, for those who do not believe in the existence of God, it is impossible for miracles to occur. As Peter Atkins observed: 'There is a sharp contrast between the impenetrable prose of theological comprehension, which is largely pretentious gobbledegook and the sharp, limpid explanations of science' (*Dialogue*, 1998).

In a very real sense, then, miracles prove nothing convincingly. They neither prove nor disprove the existence of God. Neither does science. Perhaps the most that can be said is that a miracle is an event that is interpreted within the context of religious belief and faith as an act of God. It may, or may not, be a violation of a natural law, but it is understood by believers to have religious significance and to be, in some way, the result of God's direct action in the world.

Taking it further...

The principle of Ockham's razor could be applied here. This principle argues that the simplest explanation for an unusual event is generally the most philosophically viable explanation. There is no reason why, when all other issues have been considered, that the simplest explanation for an unexpected event is that it is, in fact, a miracle.

Taking it further...

'The question of miracles is not a scientific question at all, but a theological one. If God exists, and determines the laws of nature, he himself is not subject to them and can override them whenever he chooses to do so' (John Blanchard, *Why Believe the Bible?*, Evangelical Press, 2004).

CHAPTER 3
Ethical concepts

3.1 Introducing ethics

Key Ideas

- The need to identify what is good and to distinguish between ethics and morality

- Meta-ethics and the meaning of ethical language

- Ethical theories as a means of solving ethical dilemmas

- Applied ethics: moral issues arising from human choice and behaviour

What is ethics?

Broadly speaking, **ethics**, or moral philosophy, is the attempt to formulate codes and principles for human behaviour that help answer the question 'How should we live?'. Attempts to do this go back to Greek philosophers such as Protagoras, a conservative Sophist, who valued moral codes as a useful means of setting out customs and conventions that made social life possible. Protagoras was a **relativist** in this sense; he did not advocate a universal code of morals that would be applicable all the time, but rather the idea that morality derives from its social and cultural setting. Other approaches to morality are **absolutist**; they identify moral codes that are claimed to be universal, i.e. there is never an occasion on which they do not apply. This is the key problem of ethics: is it possible to arrive at a moral code that is always applicable? Is it more appropriate to allow moral codes to emerge from societies? Societies are inevitably very different, not just around the world but within small communities, such as religious groups, and amongst those concerned with particular moral issues, such as abortion and genetic engineering.

The terms ethics and morality are often used interchangeably, but can still be thought of as having distinct meanings. One way of making that distinction may be to think of ethics as dealing with what we think of as acceptable in a social sense: such as offering a seat to a pregnant woman, keeping confidences, fulfilling your job to the best of your ability, while morality is concerned with issues of life and death: such as abortion, euthanasia, sexual behaviour, organ transplantation. Ethical and moral issues are diverse and you cannot begin to consider them all, but it is clear that they do affect human beings every day, even if it is simply a question of whether to use an out-of-date train ticket or more significant issues, such as whether to marry or end a marriage. Alternatively, we could understand ethics as offering many subgroups of morality, for example business ethics and medical ethics.

A key factor is whether ethical views are subjective or objective, i.e. whether they are based on personal preference or external facts. If a moral opinion is independent of external facts then it is essentially internal, is to do with how we feel about an ethical issue and is therefore **subjective**. An **objective** fact, however, is related to how things actually are in the real world, which would be the case irrespective of how we feel or even whether we exist at all, and so is true for everyone. If moral values are objective then they are similarly true for everyone. Whether morality deals in facts or opinions is a crucial issue for ethical debate and the key to this is whether we can place goodness in an objective category, as it is clearly open to so many different interpretations.

Meta-ethics

Meta-ethics is the branch of ethics that is concerned with the meaning of ethical language. Ethical language is simply the way in which we express ethical opinions and judgements. If morality is objective, then it is **cognitive**. Cognitive language deals with making propositions about things that can be known and so can be held to be true or false.

If morality is subjective, then it is **non-cognitive**, and deals with matters that are not simply resolved by establishing whether they are true or false. This is a non-propositional view, which understands language as serving some function other than that of making claims about what is true or false.

If you witness a boy smashing car windscreens and report it to the police, then you are reporting a fact, but if you tell them that you thought the boy was wrong to be doing so, you would be reporting your feelings about it and this would not be a fact. Presumably the boy doing the smashing did not consider his actions to be wrong, so it is a subjective, not an objective, matter, even if more people share your opinion than his.

Meta-ethics is important because before we can begin to establish what constitutes good or bad moral or ethical behaviour we need to consider whether we can say an action, intention or outcome is good, bad, right, wrong, moral or immoral. A primary consideration is whether ethical language can be said to have any meaning at all.

If we are unclear regarding the meaning of basic ethical terms such as these, then how can we begin to make authoritative, or at least convincing, claims about the morality of particular actions? The statement 'killing is wrong' is complicated because we are immediately faced with a vast range of different situations in which not everyone would agree that killing was wrong, such as in war, self-defence or even capital punishment, but if we are not even sure about what we mean by 'wrong' then ethical debate will be fraught with difficulties.

Furthermore, the word 'good' has many meanings and most of them are not used in a moral context. You could say that your computer is 'good' because it fulfils the task that it was purchased to fulfil, but you are not ascribing moral status to it, because a computer is not a moral agent, it is not capable of making moral decisions or acting in morally good or bad ways. Similarly, we use the word 'ought' in different contexts: 'teachers ought to be kind to their students' carries quite different implications to 'you ought to dress smartly for this occasion'. The first statement is prescribing a particular mode of behaviour that is based on our opinion of how teachers ought to behave and so is a moral statement, while the second recommends a course of action on the basis of certain objective facts.

Ethical theory

Despite the problems of using ethical language, many ethical theories have emerged over the centuries that attempt to offer a means of resolving ethical and moral problems. An ethical theory is in a sense a tool. Ethical theories are based on different ways of defining what a good action might be and offer a means of applying that tool to different ethical situations. Ethical theories tend to be either relativist or absolutist. If they are relativist, they will not insist on the application of moral rules to determine the right action, but rather offer a principle that helps solve a range of different moral problems that may justify different responses. Absolutist theories propose what the right moral rules are in any given situation and allow little room for flexibility. Ethical theories develop because we face ethical and moral dilemmas. It is because we are reluctant to lay aside moral rules, and yet are both afraid and attracted by the consequences of our actions, that moral dilemmas are just that: dilemmas. If we knew for certain what to do every time we were faced with a moral dilemma there would be no need for debates about ethical theories; they grow out of the need to find answers to questions and dilemmas that are not immediately self-evident. There is no guarantee that ethical theories will solve ethical problems, but they offer a way of attempting to analyse profoundly difficult moral situations and to reach a conclusion regarding the right moral action.

In *What Does it All Mean?* (Oxford University Press, 1987), Thomas Nagel exposed the problem of applying ethical theory to moral dilemmas: ethical theories involve rational processes, reasoning and analysis of a situation in order to reach a balanced conclusion. Moral dilemmas are personal, subjective and emotive; to apply reason to them is not a natural step. To apply an ethical theory to a moral dilemma we need to remain emotionally removed from the dilemma itself, which takes considerable effort. We need to be aware from the start that the way in which ethical theory may help resolve moral dilemmas is limited. This is particularly challenging when many ethical dilemmas deal with issues that are extremely personal and that lead to great conflict. Ultimately, when faced with resolving an abortion dilemma in practice, or even attempting to reach a theoretical position on homosexuality, it is not likely that an individual, unless they can remain emotionally removed from the personal implications of their dilemma, will resort to an ethical theory to resolve it.

Nevertheless, ethical theories have been highly influential, even to the extent of affecting public policy and decision making. We shall examine them in detail in the next chapter.

Applied ethics

Ethical theories are really only of value when they are applied. **Applied ethics** is the study of areas of human moral behaviour that are open to moral debate and that raise moral questions. Applied ethics deals with

---

Taking it further...

The ethical theories you will study for AS (utilitarianism and situation ethics) are essentially **relativist**, although when you consider the relationship between religion and morality you will have to consider the possible role of **absolutism** in ethics, as some religious believers claim that all morality derives directly from God.

issues of moral and ethical concern and examines them, not only in relation to ethical theory, but by identifying the more general moral problems that arise. Some issues of applied ethics are enormous and affect almost everyone. For example, if a government makes a decision to go to war, everyone is affected in some way, even if they are not engaged in direct conflict. Hence the morality of warfare is a universal concern, and it will not simply be a matter of using an ethical theory to see if it is right to go to war, but will involve examining a range of moral issues, the sanctity of life, whether it is ever right to kill, the justifications for going to war and conduct in war, and how to deal with the environmental and economic effects of war.

In the modern world the range of issues that require us to apply ethics is ever increasing. But ethicists have always been interested in applied ethical matters. The Greek philosophers were concerned with how to live and die in a moral way, the medievalists with abortion and war. Hume wrote an essay on the morality of suicide (advocating it as the right of a free human agent), and Kant was concerned with exploring how to establish universal peace. The utilitarians perhaps most of all were concerned with the real ethics of society and not just theory.

In the modern world several branches of applied ethics have acquired independent academic status: bioethics, business ethics and the moral status of animals are of particular interest in the 21st century, while issues of sexual ethics, which never went away, have been given a new lease of life. It is very easy to find material about applied ethical issues because these issues are being debated every day in the news, on television and through other forms of media. They are also often the themes of novels and films, which provide tremendous stimulus for discussion.

For the religious believer, the question of how morality should be linked with religious faith is vital, and many approaches to ethics have aimed to clarify this debate. Many issues of applied ethics are fuelled by controversy between religious believers and secularists (those who do not analyse matters from a religious perspective) and, in some cases at least, if the religious dimension was not present an ethical code would be easier to establish.

In the following sections we shall examine this important issue, as well as analysing the key features of **utilitarianism** and **situation ethics**, two ethical theories that particularly reflect the time in which they emerged. In the next chapter we will explore two perennial areas of applied ethics, **sexual ethics** and the **ethics of war and peace**.

Taking it further...

There are many films that you can study from the perspective of the ethical dilemmas they raise. Four you could try are *Gattaca*, *Priest*, *The Bridges of Madison County* and *Brokeback Mountain*.

3.2 The relationship between morality and religion

Key Ideas

- ■ The reasons to make connections between religion and morality

- ■ Divine command ethics: God as the source of moral authority

- ■ Moral arguments for the existence of God

- ■ The nature and origin of conscience

- ■ Critiques of the link between religion and morality

Are morality and religion connected?

Ethical obligations (moral duties or requirements) are often thought of as commands with authority behind them. However, what is the source of that authority? Is it sufficient to say that the sole ground for them being moral obligations is that they have been commanded by God?

The nature of the relationship between religion and morality, indeed whether there is one at all, is a vital issue for religious believers to resolve. If at least part of what it means to believe in God is to live in obedience to his will and his law, then the way in which God makes moral commands is crucial to understanding how believers should respond to them. R. B. Braithwaite claims that to be religious and to make religious claims is to be committed to a set of moral values, and uses the instance of religious conversion, which includes a reorientation of the will, to illustrate this point. Much religious language is the language of morality, and religious believers have committed themselves to particular ways of behaving. This includes refraining from some actions and fulfilling others. However, how do we know what believers are committed to? Furthermore, is the connection between religion and morality and God and morality the same? Is it conceivable that religious morality may be far removed from the moral commands of God, or is it possible to be obedient to the commands of God without being part of a religious moral community?

Religious believers may argue that even if a person gets away with the most outrageous crimes on earth, he or she will be punished by God in the afterlife (as those who have resisted the temptation to do wrong will be rewarded), and so even if it is possible to avoid earthly punishment it is not in their **eschatological** interest to do so.

On the other hand, an **existentialist** view maintains that if there is no God to support the demands of the moral law, then there is no threat of punishment or promise of reward, and so morality is meaningless. Effectively, without God everything is permitted. In this case, God acts as the guardian of

Taking it further...

Eschatology is a study of the end times, heaven, hell, death and judgement. There is a close connection between issues of religious morality and eschatology because hell is traditionally associated with punishment for wrong doing and heaven with reward for goodness, although most Christians would argue that entrance to heaven is not achieved simply by doing good works.

morality, saving humans from falling into moral chaos. Dostoevsky thought of God as the lynchpin of order and morality in society. Without God all hierarchy collapses and everything could be permitted. He was troubled by suffering but unable to reject belief in God because God is necessary for morality.

The relationship between religion and morality

The relationship between religion and morality is highly ambiguous and there are several approaches that may be taken when attempting to work out how it may be connected. There are three broad views, that morality:

- depends on religion
- is independent of religion
- is opposed to religion.

The view that morality depends on religion maintains that without religion there would be no morality because moral codes are derived from religion, and moral opinions are judged against the standards set by religious teaching. The scope of religious moral teaching is wide and comes from more than one possible source of authority. Hence, whether moral behaviour conforms to or contradicts the teaching of God, religious texts, religious leaders or religious tradition will determine whether it is considered to be right or wrong. Some religious groups will place more emphasis on one source of authority over another. For example, Evangelical Christians will emphasise the authority of the teaching of the Bible, Muslims the Qur'an, and Roman Catholic morality will be influenced by the doctrines of the Church and Papal teaching. The same point applies, however: morality depends on a religious source of authority. Other sources of moral teaching are unreliable and may even be false.

Interestingly, the secular world often adopts or is influenced by religious moral teaching, and frequently looks to religion to make a moral stand on important issues such as abortion and war. Even if religious moral positions are not ultimately accepted by the secular world, the expectation that religion has something valuable to say about moral issues suggests that there is at least a strong perception that religion and morality are connected in a positive way.

In a similar way, religious leaders and believers are often expected to have high standards of morality and are called to account more readily if they fail to demonstrate them. The media is quick to expose religious leaders who have extramarital affairs, are caught out in financial irregularities or appear to be acting hypocritically. Overall, despite secularism (non-religious views of the world and society), the media often appeals to religion as having a beneficial effect on social morality.

Religious believers have also historically stood out against moral outrages and have resisted moral change if it appears not to be in the best interests of society. Pressure groups such as the UK organisation CARE (Christian Action for Research and Education) consistently lobby for a reduction in the time limit for legal abortions (typically to 18 weeks) and against the growing swell of public opinion in favour of legalising assisted suicide. In the USA, the influential organisation Focus on the Family is run by Dr James Dobson,

Taking it further...

Perhaps God does not have to actually exist for him to be the source of morality and the means of controlling moral behaviour: the idea of God is enough to keep moral order. This is an **authoritarian** view, imposing the notion that God will punish immorality and that the incentive for moral goodness is to avoid God's anger.

Religious authority for Catholics derives from the Pope

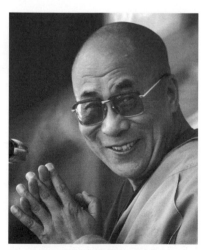

The Dalai Lama is a figure of authority for Tibetan Buddhists

a conservative Evangelical close to the White House. He has written numerous books on family life, parenting, marriage, sexual relationships and medical ethics. Dobson's radio commentaries are heard by more than 220 million people every day and he is seen on around 70 television stations in the USA.

Religious groups are often quick to stand up against moral outrages in secular society. 'A Connecticut abortion rights group has angered some conservative Christian groups by selling condom key chains that include an image of Michelangelo's Sistine Chapel with God handing Adam a condom. "It's an example of depraved morals and contempt for the sensibility of Catholics everywhere", said C. J. Doyle of the Catholic Action League of Massachusetts. The key chains, sold by Planned Parenthood of Connecticut on its web site, come in 28 designs. Judy Tabar, Planned Parenthood of Connecticut's president and chief executive, said 100,000 visitors swamped the site after Internet columnist Matt Drudge posted a statement by a conservative Christian group condemning the key chains as "blasphemous". Kristian Mineau, president of the conservative Massachusetts Family Institute, said, "This does nothing to deal with the horrific promiscuity rate we have among teenagers. We believe the real approach particularly to the young people that this is targeted at is abstinence before marriage"'. (*Yahoo News*, 14 January 2006.)

Divine command ethics

Generally those who accept **divine command ethics** look to sacred texts to provide moral standards, such as the Decalogue found in Exodus 20 in the Bible. A religious view of life gives us guidance in a complex world in which we tend to lose our way. The first Surah of the Qur'an expresses this very well: 'guide us along the straight path'. According to divine command ethics, God's will alone decides what is right and wrong and human reason can play no part in legitimising basic moral rules: human reason has no authority, God has absolute authority. All humans can do is accept and respond to God's revelation of what is right and wrong. Indeed, the need for moral guidance is often overwhelming, and God would appear to some to be the most reliable source of that guidance, as long as humans are able to establish what God's moral will is. A consequence of these claims is that if there is no God, then nothing is forbidden and nothing is obligatory either. Everything is equally morally permitted.

The view that without God nothing would be morally impermissible is, of course, very difficult to sustain, because it does not require a belief in divine command ethics to support the view that there are clear moral prohibitions in every society and moral actions that are deemed particularly praiseworthy. Nevertheless, divine command ethics has a long history. The Old Testament and the Qur'an are both full of teachings that consist of God asserting his moral law, and in the gospels Jesus teaches in the form of moral commands: 'love your neighbour as yourself', 'do not resist an evil doer', 'blessed are those who hear the word of God and obey it'.

The 'religions of the book' (Judaism, Christianity and Islam) offer good reasons why God's commands should be recognised as authoritative and why they should be obeyed. A. G. Grayling observes: 'Sin is disobedience to the

Taking it further...

In the Middle Ages, divine command ethics was championed by William of Ockham: 'God cannot be obligated to any act. With Him a thing becomes right solely because He wants it so'.

The handing down of the Ten Commandments is a classic example of divine command ethics

Taking it further...

Millar Burrows observes: 'What is right is not so because God commands it; he commands it because it is right, and it is right because it is good for man. This may be true even of what we may call strictly religious rather than moral requirements such as the observance of the Sabbath' (*An Outline of Biblical Theology*, The Westminster Press, 1946).

commands of god; virtue is obedience to them or, in the more graphic conception of Islam, submission' (*What is Good?*, Phoenix, 2003). He comments that the Old Testament offers a compelling reason to be obedient in the story of the expulsion from Eden (Genesis 2–3) and the punishments that followed it. Punishment is the chief reason, he suggests, that proponents of divine command ethics argue that it is good to obey God's commands.

However, there are clear problems with this. If humans obey God's moral commands simply because they fear punishment, they are acting prudently out of self-preservation rather than morally. Despite offering a moral argument for the existence of God, Kant maintained that fear of punishment or hope of reward should not be the motivation for moral goodness: 'Morality must not lower herself. Her own nature must be her recommendation. All else, even divine reward, is nothing else beside her' (*Lectures on Ethics*, Hackett, 1930).

Furthermore, if 'morally good' means 'what God has commanded' we end up with a circular, and trivial claim: 'what God commands is right and good' means 'what God commands is what God commands'. This means that there is no separate and distinct character to morality that humans are competent to recognise and that requires further authentication as morally good.

If a divine command emanates from a supremely powerful being, how can humans even conceive of being able to assess whether it is morally good or not? Worship of such a being and obedience to his commands would be merely passive and there would be little scope for a personal relationship with him. Such a being must also be omniscient and know the consequences of our actions and choices in a way that we never can. This requires us to take on trust that such a God really does will what is best for us and what will bring that about.

Finally, if obedience to divine commands is to be rewarded in the afterlife, there seems to be a dangerous inequality. Many apparently godly people are amply rewarded with material riches and happy lives in this world, while others endure great earthly suffering whilst waiting for their eschatological reward. The danger here is that believers will fall back on the qualifier 'God moves in mysterious ways'. This argument is employed when there seems to be no rational justification for God's actions, but it leads believers into making what Basil Mitchell calls 'vacuous statements' (*The Philosophy of Religion*, Oxford University Press, 1971): statements that have no real meaning because they fail to offer a real solution to the problem of why bad things happen to good people.

Aquinas and Kant

The dependency of morality on religion can, of course, be understood as a dependency on the existence of God. In his Fourth Way in the *Summa Theologica*, Aquinas argued that the gradation to be found in things pointed irrefutably to the existence of God: 'Among beings there are some more and some less good, true, noble and the like. But more and less are predicated of different things according as they resemble in their different ways something which is the maximum... so that there is something which is truest, something best, something noblest... Therefore there must also be something which is to all beings the cause of their being, goodness, and every other perfection, and this we call God' (cited in *The Existence of God*, edited by John Hick, Macmillan, 1964).

Aquinas's arguments were based on Plato's eternal forms, or **archetypes**, claiming that the contingent realities of which the human mind is aware are merely pale copies of a greater, unseen, reality. In this case, the goodness found in human beings and in the contingent world is a reflection of the supreme goodness of God, to whom contingent beings owe their lesser goodness. God, being perfect in goodness, is also perfect in his very being or existence. The 20th-century philosopher F. C. Copleston, in discussion with Bertrand Russell, claimed: 'I do think that all goodness reflects God in some way and proceeds from him, so that in a sense the man who loves what is truly good, loves God even if he doesn't advert to God' (cited in *The Existence of God*, edited by John Hick, Macmillan, 1964).

Obviously it is also possible to question whether good can only be measured by reference to the divine. Copleston maintained that it was necessary to refer to God in order to be able to distinguish between good and evil, whilst Russell argued: 'I love the things that I think are good, and I hate the things that I think are bad… I don't say these things are good because they participate in the divine goodness' (cited in *The Existence of God*, edited by John Hick, Macmillan, 1964).

In *The Critique of Practical Reason* (Cambridge University Press, 1997), Kant offered an argument for the existence of God based on the existence of morality. Kant maintained that all humans by use of reason could discern a moral law evident in the universe and they had a duty, or a categorical imperative, to seek the highest form of the good, which he coined the *summum bonum* (the state of pure virtue crowned with perfect happiness). In this argument he does not conclude that the existence of God is the only reason to be moral, but he maintains that for morality and its goal, the *summum bonum*, to be meaningful God must be a 'necessary postulate' of morality.

Nevertheless, Kant observed that the moral law would never be satisfied in this life. Hence, if humans would never be capable of achieving the *summum bonum* then the existence of God was necessary for the goal of morality to be realised.

Kant's proof for the existence of God led on to a proof of the absolute necessity of an afterlife, a *post mortem* existence, in which the achievement of the *summum bonum* would ultimately be accomplished. Kant observed how the moral law, while requiring happiness to be satisfied, did not itself guarantee that end, neither could human beings themselves ensure that virtue was rewarded and evil punished. Thus there had to be 'a holy Author of the world who makes possible the highest good':

'Hence, there is in us not merely the warrant but also the necessity, as a need connected with duty, to presuppose the possibility of this highest good, which, since it is possible only under the conditions of the existence of God, connects the presupposition of the existence of God inseparably with duty; that is, it is morally necessary to assume the existence of God' (Immanuel Kant, *Critique of Practical Reason*, Cambridge University Press, 1997).

Taking it further...

Aquinas's Fourth Way does not suggest how good can be defined. All we know is that God is the supreme source of it and it is his very essence to be perfectly good.

Taking it further...

A **categorical imperative** is an action that is pursued for its own sake, and not for any hypothetical imperative. A **hypothetical imperative** is an action that is motivated by extrinsic concerns, for example 'If I want to be well-liked, I must be kind'. The categorical imperative would simply be: 'be kind', because showing kindness is morally good in itself, not because it has a good outcome.

Kant maintained that morality and the postulate of a divine being that satisfied the moral law was known *a priori*. In other words, it was not our experience of the world that pointed to the existence of God, but that we know by reason that morality demands his existence. Moral behaviour *per se* would not be invalid if God did not exist, but Kant maintained that if the goal of morality was to be achieved, then God was demanded to bring it about. Kant argued that atheism interfered with the pursuit of the *summum bonum* because rationally it can only be achieved by God and yet atheists are compelled by duty to work towards its fulfilment, even though they do not believe in the God who is necessary to bring it about!

Conscience

Clearly, one way in which morality may be dependent on religion is through the **conscience**. The conscience may be understood as God-given, or even the voice of God, or it may be so informed by religious teaching that the demands of conscience cannot be separated. Conscience may be defined as 'the inner aspect of the life of the individual where a sense of what is right and wrong is developed' (*New Dictionary of Christian Ethics and Pastoral Theology*, IVP, 1995) or as the way in which people judge their own moral actions.

Joseph Butler (*Fifteen Sermons*, SPCK, 1970) wrote in the 18th century: 'That we have this moral approving and disapproving faculty, is certain from experiencing it in ourselves... whether called conscience, moral reason, or Divine reason'. For Butler the conscience directs us in accord with two principles, self-interest and concern for others; principles that, far from clashing, are entirely complementary. In *Gaudium et Spes*, a document of Vatican Two, the council wrote: 'Deep within his conscience man discovers a law which he has not laid upon himself but he must obey'. Cardinal J. H. Newman maintained that the conscience was the means by which we know about the existence and nature of God as a divine sovereign judge. In the conscience, he argued, we find a moral authority that is higher than any natural authority, so it must have a supernatural origin of ultimate moral goodness.

The New Testament view of conscience is as a guardian of believers' moral health, prompting them to respond to their moral code by stimulating feelings of guilt or well-being. Paul speaks of the conscience as:

- universal whether man believes in God or not, and is God given (Romans 2:12ff)
- affected by the fall and thus corrupted and imperfect (Genesis 3)
- capable of being redeemed by Jesus Christ (Romans 3:21–22).

The conscience needs to be instructed and trained, and the more right choices man makes the more he will be naturally inclined to make the right choice in the future without his freewill being limited. Aquinas associated conscience with **natural law** as the means that enables us to recognise rationally moral behaviour that will eventually lead humans to an acknowledgement of God's moral law. This would involve using logical reasoning and making judgements based on previous experience and on the

Taking it further...

Paul wrote of the role of the conscience as the judge, under God, of our behaviour, and the way in which it acts to control and interpret our actions, especially in the context of the church. But before this, Greek and Roman philosophy had already developed a strong view of conscience. Horace wrote 'have nothing on your conscience, no guilt to make you turn pale', and Cicero claimed that 'If conscience goes, then everything collapses around us'.

teaching of scripture. For the believer, training the conscience must involve a continuous attempt to work out God's will and to act in the best interests of the believing community to, ultimately, everyone's benefit.

Some religious views of conscience tend to emphasise the negative role it plays, stimulating feelings of guilt and shame. This may be a useful function as long as it does not lead to imagined guilt, anxiety and depression. Conscience is not an infallible guide, but a relative measuring tool. J. V. Langmead Casserly writes: 'Nevertheless, a well trained conscience remains a factor of the utmost importance in the moral life' (*Handbook of Christian Theology*, Fontana, 1960).

There are strong arguments against associating conscience with religious belief or the moral teachings of God. Furthermore, there can be no assurance that conscience is universal; conflicts between society and the individual and between societies frequently occur over matters of conscience. Conscience is ultimately subject to man's interpretation and therefore it will inevitably make mistakes of judgement. Rather than understanding conscience as God given, Sigmund Freud, for example, understood the conscience as a moral policeman, the internalised super-ego, that controlled and socialised human moral behaviour but that was capable of doing great damage to mental health, particularly when it was confused with religion. Freud believed that the religious conscience frustrated genuine moral development by imposing rules that had no basis in reality but in a 'universal neurosis'.

Critiques of the link between morality and religion

Despite these several arguments, it is still possible to put forward a strong case for the argument that morality is not dependent on religion. There are many legitimate reasons for arguing for the independence of morality, many of which are based on simple human experience of high levels of moral behaviour outside the framework of religious belief or teaching.

- Moral teaching based on scripture is unreliable because sacred texts are culturally relative and era dependent. The moral teaching they offer is not intended to offer eternal moral values and treating them as such leads to problems of interpretation.

- If religious believers are morally good only in the hope of receiving divine reward and avoiding punishment, is this genuine goodness?

- Religious moral teachings derive from secular moral values, not the other way round. They are given religious significance to add to their authority.

- Too much pressure is put on religious believers to live up to unrealistic standards of goodness.

- The demands of religious morality are sometimes counterintuitive.

- Society only appeals to religious morality in times of crisis, not for guidance on daily moral living.

- Resisting moral change in the name of religion can prevent moral progress.

However, perhaps the most developed challenge to the relationship between religion and morality was posed by Plato in the Euthyphro Dilemma: 'Do the gods love that which is holy, or is it holy because it is loved by the gods?'. In classical theistic terms this can be phrased 'Does God command X (where X is a moral command) because it is good, or is X good because God commands it?'. Both positions highlight problems for the relationship between God and morality and particularly for divine command ethics. Let us take the first position.

Does God command X because it is good?

In this case goodness exists as something separate from God, and to which God needs access in order to make a moral command. It can be illustrated as:

- Goodness → God → Man

God is the means by which man receives moral knowledge, but that knowledge has not come directly from God's morally good nature. Rather, that knowledge, while communicated by God, comes from outside his nature; he is not wholly good, although he may conform to that standard of goodness he receives and passes to man. Clearly in this case, God is not the guarantor of moral goodness and in some way his nature is qualified. He cannot bring goodness into being apart from that goodness he accesses from outside himself. This is surely not, therefore, the God of classical theism. Does the second position fare any better?

Is X good because God commands it?

In this case, there is no doubt that God is the direct source of moral knowledge. The chain of command can be illustrated this way:

- God → Good → Man

In this model, God's commands establish what is good, and nothing can be good unless God commands it. The answer to the question 'What is good?' has to be 'What God commands'. However, if this is the case, then the answer to the question 'Why is God good?' has to be 'Because he obeys his own commands', which seems a rather limited understanding of God's goodness because saying 'God is good' is essentially the same as saying 'God does what he commands'. We still have not learned much about God because he could effectively command anything he liked and it would, by virtue of his command, be good, and he would be good if he obeyed it.

This leads us to another issue, which may be even more challenging. If X is good because God commands it, then does it really mean that anything God commanded would be good by definition? If this is the case, there is no limit to what God can command and yet by virtue of his command it would be deemed good. The problems this raises can lead to the view that morality is not simply independent of religion but that religion is actually opposed to morality.

The command to sacrifice Isaac

'After these things, God tested Abraham. He said to him, "Abraham!" And he said, "Here I am". He said, "Take your son, your only son, Isaac, whom you love, and go to the land of Moriah, and offer him as a burnt offering on one of the mountains that I shall show you" (Genesis 22:1–2).

Taking it further...

Not everyone agrees that these positions raise such crucial problems. Some philosophers suggest that it is wrong to assume that the measure of goodness can be outside God. Some suggest that it is false to believe that we cannot trust God to love what we think of as good even though he is not logically compelled to do so.

God's command to sacrifice Isaac appears to go against universal understanding of morality

If you are not familiar with this story, then it is important to know that Abraham and his wife Sarah had waited a long time to have Isaac. God had promised them a child in their old age, against all the odds, who would carry the promises of many future generations. And yet God asks Abraham to sacrifice him! Even if it did not raise formidable moral questions, it is at least counterintuitive. But Abraham does not falter. He takes Isaac as commanded and it is not until Abraham raises the knife to kill his son that God intervenes. Abraham's willingness to kill Isaac has been enough for God to know that the patriarch would not 'withhold his only son' from him. A ram is conveniently found in a thicket and offered in Isaac's place.

The Danish philosopher Søren Kierkegaard struggled with this story in the book *Fear and Trembling* (Penguin, 2005). Was it ever reasonable for man to be asked to abandon what he understands to be intrinsically good in order to fulfil the demands of faith? Kierkegaard reached the conclusion that it was, because faith is the highest virtue, exemplified in Abraham's willingness to sacrifice his son for what must have seemed at best a capricious God, at worst a malevolent one. Nevertheless, John Habgood exposes the 'nagging doubt' that remains. 'If morality is supposed to be universal, can it really be discounted, even under such extreme pressure from God?' (*Varieties of Unbelief*, DLT, 2000).

Interestingly, the biblical writers offer no further comment on this episode, although many others have done so. The feminist theologian Daphne Hampson proposed a reading of the narrative from the perspective of Sarah who immediately recognises that God does not intend that Abraham should blindly obey his command to kill Isaac, but instead is offering him a stimulus for moral debate. 'What kind of God do you think you're dealing with? What kind of God would want you to kill your own son to prove how religious you are? Don't be so stupid! She's trying to teach you something: that you must challenge even the highest authority on questions of right and wrong' (cited in *Varieties of Unbelief*, John Habgood, DLT, 2000). Abraham will not listen, however, and Sarah is obliged to advise God to send an angel to intervene to prevent a tragic outcome!

Jephthah and Job

Interestingly, there is another, less often cited, story in the Old Testament that has a similarly horrific ring to it. In Judges 11:30, Jephthah the Gileadite vows to God that if he gives him victory that day over the Ammonites, he will sacrifice 'whoever comes out of the doors of my house to meet me when I return victorious... to be offered up by me as a burnt offering'. Unfortunately, it is Jephthah's daughter who greets him on his return. Astonishingly for the modern reader, she fully accepts that her father must fulfil his obligation to God, asking only for 2 months recreation with her friends before the act is carried out. John Gray (*Joshua, Judges, Ruth*, Marshall Pickering, 1986) suggests that the story is only an **aetiological** legend (a story that explains why some long-standing tradition has come about) to explain an annual rite of mourning in the fertility cult. Nevertheless, that such a legend could be adopted suggests an unthinking acceptance of the morality of the tale: it is not unreasonable of the God of Israel to expect Jephthah to go through with his vow even though he could never have anticipated what it would entail.

> **Taking it further...**
>
> In *God Jokes* (Slim Volumes, 2003), Philip Tyler speaks of Abraham interpreting the horror of God's command as a joke: what else could it be? 'God moves in very mysterious ways; strange almost … God jokes, it's well known … strange jokes sometimes, but he always knows the joke best and laughs the longest … In the fullness of time Isaac was born … I blessed God for my good fortune. But then came the day. Oh! Then came the day my God commanded that I should sacrifice my beloved son upon a pyre. How could I refuse? All that I had and all that I had known flowed from God. My son was the gift of God. His to bestow and his to take away.'

Another sufferer, apparently at the hands of God, is Job. A righteous and wealthy man, he is an easy target for Satan: 'Does Job fear God for nothing? Have you not put a fence around him and his house and all that he has… But stretch out your hand now, and touch all that he has, and he will curse you to your face' (Job 1:10–11). Incredibly, it seems, God permits Satan to do his worst, stopping short only of killing the man. Job's sufferings are all the more anguished because ultimately he realises he has no one to plead to but the God his friends assure him he must have offended to be faced with such grief. 'For now my witness is in heaven; there is One on high ready to answer for me. My appeal will come before God, while my eyes turn anxiously to him. If only there were one to arbitrate between man and God, as between a man and his neighbour!' (Job 16:19–21). John Habgood observes that Job's situation is resolved, as is Abraham's, by a new encounter with God. God's right to put Abraham under such severe conditions of testing, and to summarily hand his servant Job over to Satan, is justified by his subsequent graciousness: 'The fact that God answered at all, even though he said nothing new, was what made the difference' (*Varieties of Unbelief*, DLT, 2000).

A moral case against the existence of God

John Habgood resolves Job's and Abraham's situations by arguing that they were ultimately satisfied with hearing from God directly. However, does not God still face some serious moral questioning? Is it enough for us to 'not merely (morally and wrongly) to tempt but also (logically and rightly) to entitle us to say "God does not love us" or even "God does not exist"?' (Anthony Flew, *Theology and Falsification*, 1950, cited in *The Philosophy of Religoni*, edited by Basil Mitchell, Oxford University Press, 1971).

Even if it is not, then there are other moral arguments that pose serious problems for the God of classical theism. R. A. Sharpe puts forward a strong 'moral case against religious belief' in his book of that title (*Moral Case Against Religious Belief*, SCM, 1997), challenging what he claims to be a misconception that if more people believed in God there would be less immorality. 'We are predisposed to think of religion and morality as intimately connected', he writes, 'and are reluctant to condemn as immoral even moral views which are confused, inconsistent and which cause human suffering'. Sharpe makes a particular case for the Roman Catholic prohibition on contraception: 'Is it remotely conceivable that God should be interested in whether people use a condom rather than the rhythm method of contraception?', he asks.

Put this way, it does seem absurd, and there are many other, perhaps more serious, issues that could lead to similar questions. One of the most alarming examples of so-called religious morality that plays straight into the hands of the atheist is to be found on the web site hosted by the Westboro Baptist Church, bizarrely entitled www.godhatesfags.com. 'Thank God for 18 more dead troops, we wish it 18,000' one such headline declares. The abuse the web site heaps on the homosexual community of the USA, George W Bush and American society as a whole for supporting homosexuality is astonishing and it does not require an atheist to claim that the web site, which argues that it preaches 'Gospel truth', runs radically counter not only to secular

Taking it further...

The relationship between religion, God, and morality takes us very close to questions that are raised by the problem of evil, a classical puzzle in the philosophy of religion. If religious believers are to confront the problem of evil, they need to resolve the question of whether an omnibenevolent God is logically compelled to refrain from any action that humans perceive as immoral because of the suffering it causes, even if there may be good reasons for it, or if good consequences result.

morality but to most religious moral teaching. It seems counterintuitive to argue that God teaches hate, as the Westboro Baptist Church maintains. If this were so, then many religious believers might feel compelled to reconsider their commitment to God.

Another common challenge posed by opponents of religious morality is the limitation on human freedom it appears to impose. Nietzsche rejected Christianity and belief in God because it encouraged a 'slave morality' by which suffering and weakness were admired, while believers were discouraged from avenging wrong and instead showed forgiveness. Rather, Nietzsche believed that the 'autonomous man' will have 'developed his own, independent, long-range will, which dares to make promises; he has a sense of power and freedom, of absolute accomplishment' (cited in *Varieties of Unbelief*, John Habgood, DLT, 2000). One reason, perhaps, for this lack of moral assertiveness is that religion encourages its followers to have one eye on the next life where all injustice will be dealt with, taking away some of the impetus to set about restoring justice on earth. On the other hand, Charles Taylor observes: 'The moment one loses confidence in God or immortality, one becomes more self reliant, more courageous, and the more solicitous to aid where only human aid is possible' (cited in *Moral Case Against Religious Belief*, R. A. Sharpe, SCM, 1997).

Interestingly, in those atheist societies that drove faith underground when it could not suppress it altogether, religious belief was quick to rise again when the atheist system proved fallible. John Habgood cites the appeal of the Soviet prime minister before the fall of the Berlin wall, pleading with churches to step into the moral vacuum that would emerge as national life collapsed. 'Even atheists', Habgood writes, 'when faced with a crisis of confidence, may see the need for something more than instinct, custom and social convention' (*Varieties of Unbelief*, DLT, 2000).

Religious morality and modern society

Although we live in a multi-cultural world that is, in many ways, highly secular, religious morality has not gone away, and for many believers the only good reason to perform a morally good action or to refrain from a morally wrong action is because in doing so they conform to the will of God. We are now far more aware of the diversity of religious traditions and their accompanying moralities and we can see virtually at first hand how powerfully religious morality affects actions that have global significance.

However, A. C. Grayling puts forward an argument for the irrelevance of religion to contemporary morality. 'There is a widespread supposition that a religious ethic … has to be good for individuals and society because it is inherently more likely to make them good. This view is troubling because it is false: religion is precisely the wrong resource for thinking about moral issues in the contemporary world, and indeed subverts moral debate' (*What is Good?*, Phoenix, 2003). Grayling suggests that modern society values freedom, achievement, saving money, insuring against the future and being rewarded for success, while Christian morality in particular values the opposite. 'It tells people to take no thought for tomorrow, to give their possessions to the poor, and to be aware that a well-off person will find heaven unwelcoming.'

Taking it further...

The parable of the good Samaritan in Luke 10 may be read as an attack on religious morality. The two men who passed by on the other side were religious men, a priest and a levite, and were concerned to avoid being made ritually unclean by contact with the possibly dying man. The Samaritan had no such religious scruples and was able to offer 'aid where only human aid was possible'. Although he did not reject it altogether, Jesus did not hesitate to show up the weaknesses of religious morality when it failed to take into account the needs of the vulnerable and unhappy.

Grayling also observes that the preoccupations of modern morality include a great concern for the welfare and rights of people, animals and the environment, not because of a divine threat but because these things are intrinsically valuable in themselves. The secular view of morality, that people have intrinsic worth, is, he suggests, the only true source of morality.

A secular ethicist may argue that humans are more likely to be morally responsible in the absence of God. If there is no afterlife, then this life is what really counts and the way we behave has real implications, not for eschatological reward or punishment but because people have a limited life span and should be treated well. There is no making up for it later.

However, it cannot be denied that religion has played a significant part in moral education. Even if human beings can arrive at some understanding of morality for themselves, this does not mean that they do not need to be taught some, perhaps many, things. Religion clearly offers an enormous amount in that respect, whether or not religious moral commands come from God.

3.3 Utilitarianism

Key Ideas

■ The key characteristics of teleological ethics

■ Jeremy Bentham and universal ethical hedonism

■ The social and intellectual background to utilitarianism

■ J. S. Mill's adaptation of the theory

■ Modern applications of utilitarianism and its overall success or failure

Teleological ethics

'Some years ago, newspapers reported an accident… A family had gone away… and had left their keys with their neighbour… A few hours before they were due to arrive home… the neighbour thought he would do them a favour and make sure they would come home to a nice toasty house. He went in and turned on the furnace… The house burned down and the family came home to a burned-out lot… Suppose it had been reported by a classical utilitarian. Then the article might have ended up like this: "This neighbour will have to answer for the consequences of this terrible deed"' (Nina Rosenstand, *The Moral of the Story*, Mayfield, 2000).

Of course, burning down the neighbour's house is a frivolous example, and it is worth bearing in mind that ethical theories are not intended to solve this kind of moral dilemma. In an exam essay avoid using case studies that imply that ethical theories are concerned with trivial cases or are intended to justify moral action that any rational person would recognise as inherently wrong, such as cold blooded murder, abuse and torture.

Although Rosenstand's case study may appear to be a facetious example, it illustrates the nature of a society in which only the consequences of our actions matter, i.e. one in which all actions would be judged according to **teleological criteria**. How would we begin to calculate the rights and wrongs of any given situation? Would it be simple or complex? Would it work practically? Above all, would it enable us to make reliable moral decisions?

A **teleological ethical theory** concerns the purpose, end, function and goal of an action. The basis for judging the morality of an action is the results or consequences it is likely to yield. Hence teleological theories are **consequentialist**, and whether an action is good or bad, right or wrong depends on the outcome. There are several immediate issues that arise from this. Under such a system of ethics there can be no moral absolutes, things that are always right or wrong whatever the circumstances. Moral goodness or badness would be judged according to how well it would bring about the intended results, not whether the action or intention was inherently right or wrong. According to this approach actions have only **instrumental** value, they can help us get something else that we want, rather than **intrinsic value**, something that we value purely for its own sake. Some things have both values, for example education, which is good in itself but also instrumental because it helps to gain employment, but the primary concern for the teleologist is that the action achieves its goal; any secondary benefit is incidental.

Inevitably, this approach to ethics is going to pose problems because of the difficulty of establishing what constitutes a good, moral consequence. The moral value of a consequence surely depends on the individual's personal preference, so how can a group of individuals reach a consensus on what is a good consequence? Then we need to consider how far-reaching consequences should be. Are we concerned with immediate or ultimate consequences and how can we judge the moral value of a consequence when there are so many conflicting factors?

Taking it further...

It is true to say that humans are forward-looking creatures, who tend to ask 'What would happen if ...?' We are compelled to act or refrain from acting depending on what we think will be the likely consequences. We weigh the various likely outcomes and discard some actions because the happiness or well-being of some may suffer even if that of others may be increased.

The principle of utility

Teleological ethical theories tend to rely on a **principle of utility**. This is the measure of the usefulness, or fittingness for purpose, that an action may have. We can propose any principle of utility we like. If we believe that the best or most moral action we can perform is one that will enable consequence X or Y to come about, then we must assess, using a principle of utility, how likely or effective action A or B will be in contributing to that consequence. Both **utilitarianism** and **situation ethics** establish a principle of utility for judging the morality of an action. For utilitarianism the principle of utility is **the greatest happiness of the greatest number**.

'What then could be more plausible than that the right is to promote the general good – that our actions and our rules, if we must have rules, are to be decided upon by determining which of them produces or may be expected to produce the greatest general balance of good over evil?' (William K. Frankena, *Ethics*, Prentice-Hall, 1973).

Happiness or pleasure

Making moral judgements according to a principle of utility is notoriously difficult because they are invariably subjective, even if they have been arrived at through a careful evaluation of what is important to human beings. However, if happiness is not the best criteria for judging the moral value of an action, what is better? Happiness is universally valued and desirable in itself. Yet it can be open to abuse, perhaps at the expense of justice. But would justice, prudence or duty be better criteria for determining the morality of an action? Maybe so if happiness seems dangerously emotive, but justice alone can be dangerously harsh.

Hedonistic ethical theories are committed to the view that pleasure or happiness can be equated with good on several possible grounds: **psychological hedonism**, where pleasure is the only object of desire, **evaluative hedonism**, where pleasure is what we ought to desire, and **rationalising hedonism**, where pleasure is the only outcome that makes it rational to pursue as an end. Utilitarianism was originally associated with the first of these categories.

Before utilitarianism as an approach to ethical decision-making was formalised, the principle of utility based on happiness and consequentialism itself had long been advocated as the better way of approaching human morality. In 1751, in his *Inquiry Concerning the Principles of Morals* (Oxford University Press, 1975), David Hume analysed the various ways in which humans make judgements about character and conduct, drawing the conclusion that virtue consists of those qualities that are most useful to ourselves and others. In its most general sense, this is what we mean by utility, that which is most useful, and it makes sense to ask why do something that is of no use to anyone, especially if it is simply to make a moral point.

But we also need to ask 'useful for what?'. Like Hume, Bentham equated utility with happiness, pleasure or avoidance of pain. In 1789, in *Principles of Morals and Legislation* (Kessinger, 2005), he wrote: 'Nature has placed mankind under the governance of two sovereign masters, pain and pleasure. It is for them alone to point out what we ought to do as well as what we shall do.'

It is, nevertheless, difficult to define happiness or to establish its relationship with the moral or good life. Aristotle saw no distinction between living well, flourishing and the morally good life. Well-being is a condition of the good life and what that good life achieves, but it need not be a life free from comfort and enjoyment. For Bentham, it was enough to equate happiness with pleasure and the absence of pain and he proposed that the likelihood of an action bringing about happiness could be calculated simply by adding up the amount of pleasure and subtracting the amount of pain. This he did by means of the **hedonic** or **felicific calculus**, a purely quantitative means of measuring seven factors:

Taking it further...

Although happiness does appear, at first glance, to be the most desirable outcome, nevertheless, in a world where we had the choice of gourmet dinners but no justice, or free tickets to premiership football games but no compassion, surely most rational people would choose the latter.

Taking it further...

By 'making a moral point' we mean doing something in order to be seen to be moral, or admired for taking a moral stand, even if the outcome is less than favourable.

- intensity, how deep or superficial the happiness is

- duration, how temporary or permanent the happiness is

- certainty, how sure the happiness is

- propinquity, how near or remote the happiness is

- fecundity, how likely the happiness is to recur or lead to further happiness

- purity, how free from pain the happiness is

- extent, how far the happiness-giving effects of action will spread.

The calculus is, obviously, flawed. Not only is it impossible for human goodness to be reduced to a sensation, arguably nothing more than a chemical reaction, the calculus does not allow for the fact that some pleasurable sensations are, for some, those which are surely universally bad, for example those of the sadist or rapist. Potentially, the calculus seems to leave room for any number of horrifically immoral acts to be justified in the cause of maximising the pleasure of the majority. Philip Pettit writes: 'So long as they promised the best consequences… It would forbid absolutely nothing: not rape, not torture, not even murder' (cited in *A Companion to Ethics*, P. Singer, Blackwell, 1991). However, this is perhaps a misjudgement of the theory. Pettit observes that surely it would only be in 'horrendous circumstances' that such a charge would be legitimate, circumstances under which there would be little doubt that although a moral dilemma did exist, the situation was sufficiently unusual to justify an unusual act: the torture of an individual to prevent hundreds from dying in a terrorist explosion, perhaps. As a tool its value may lie in the simplicity of its application to the issues with which utilitarianism was primarily concerned: those of the 'greatest number'.

Peter Vardy and Paul Grosch (*The Puzzle of Ethics*, Fount, 1994) cite the case of a young married woman who is planning a skiing trip but finds herself to be pregnant. She can use a hedonic calculus to work out what to do. If she chooses to abort the pregnancy in order to ski, the pleasure will be minor and temporary; if she chooses to abandon the holiday, the long-lasting and intense pleasure of having the child will outweigh her initial disappointment.

Social and intellectual background to utilitarianism

The consideration of the 'greatest number' in utilitarianism is significant when we consider it in relation to the background against which the ethical theory emerged. Originally used by Frances Hutcheson, Bentham had discovered the phrase 'greatest good of the greatest number' in Joseph Priestley's *Essay on Government*. Bentham was motivated by the desire to establish a universal theory that could be applied to all ethical situations, and his influence on 18th-century society and beyond was considerable as he sought a theory of ethics that would iron out the deep inequalities of his time.

In his article *Utility and the Good* (cited in *A Companion to Ethics*, P. Singer, Blackwell, 1991), Robert E. Goodin claims 'Utilitarianism of whatever stripe is, first and foremost, a standard for judging public action'. Indeed, although the theory may arguably be of some value when making moral decisions of a

A trader's card featuring Jeremy Bentham, the 18th century philosopher who advocated the 'greatest good for the greatest number'

William Hogarth's Gin Lane *highlighted the appalling social conditions faced by London's poor in the mid-18th century*

personal nature, it is in the public arena that it comes into its own. When Jeremy Bentham adapted the utilitarian thought of his predecessors its value in the public sphere was potentially one of its most attractive features. Eighteenth-century England was experiencing radical social changes that were to leave it forever transformed. The industrial revolution had brought thousands of working families to the towns from the country, but rather than finding the streets paved with gold they faced appalling working and living conditions, and discovered that they had exchanged the rural tyranny of landowners for the urban oppression of the factory owners. Homelessness, poverty, overcrowding, alcoholism, child labour, slum prisons and prostitution abounded, whilst the minority of wealthy industrialists and entrepreneurs enjoyed the fruits of their employees' labours. The concern for the majority that Bentham's classical **act utilitarianism** encouraged, met the needs of the working classes, and the philanthropic and social reforms that gradually began to take place reflected this: Elizabeth Fry's prison reform (Bentham himself had designed a star-shaped prison that could be watched over by a single guard in the middle of the building), the abolition of slavery and the factory acts are just a few obvious examples. The Reform Bill of 1832 and the Factory Acts of 1833 and 1847 laid the foundation for the statutory regulations that still govern conditions and hours in many branches of industry. G. M. Trevelyan observes: 'The factory system which at its first coming bade fair to destroy the health and happiness of the race, has been gradually converted into any instrument to level up to the average material conditions under which labour is carried on' (*English Social History*, Pelican, 1967).

The development of a postal system that allowed the lowliest member of society to post a letter without the approval of their father or workplace superior was a less obvious example of social improvement. Much of this took place after Bentham's death in 1832 but it owed a considerable amount to the utilitarian philosophy that he had advocated. The suffering majority, not the wealthy factory owners but the struggling factory workers, chimney sweeps and the desperately poor, were finally receiving the attention they needed.

Bentham bridged the 18th and 19th centuries with a tremendous reforming zeal that was both idealistic and realistic. He was committed to attempting to solve the problems of humanity through benevolent practicality (he was intent on overarching legal reform) but he rejected religion. His major objection to it was that the Evangelical Christians of the time preached that poverty was a God-ordained state that could not be changed, they had simply to submit to God. The kind of thinking he rejected, that God has determined that some people will be rich and others poor, lies behind the verse in the traditional hymn, *All Things Bright and Beautiful,* which is now not printed in modern hymn books: 'The rich man in his castle, The poor man at his gate, God made them high and lowly, And ordered their estate'.

Rather than this submissive approach, Bentham believed that the rational principle based on an observation of human nature was 'Seek the happiness of others; seek your own happiness in the happiness of others'. This clearly raises a problem for religious ethicists and believers who may argue that happiness is a rather dubious benefit, quite different to joy, peace, loving, kindness, patience and charity, which are the gifts of the Holy Spirit. Many religious believers have been motivated to endure pain and humiliation for a cause they believe to be true, and have not shirked it for an easier road to happiness. The biblical writers did not suggest that happiness should be the motivating factor behind all man's actions. They did not expect happiness. Paul wrote: 'Who shall separate us from the love of God? Shall tribulation, or distress, or persecution, or famine, or nakedness, or peril, or sword. As it is written, "For thy sake we are being killed all the day long". No in all these things we are more than conquerors through him who loved us' (Romans 8:35–36).

Nevertheless, there is no doubt that Bentham's utilitarianism was enormously influential at its time and any evaluation of its success as a theory needs to take this into account. Despite the reformulations of the theory that followed, the approach targeted the real social needs of the time and cannot possibly be dismissed as having failed in this respect.

J. S. Mill and the development of utilitarianism

Nevertheless, it was not long before Bentham's form of utilitarianism came under the scrutiny of J. S. Mill, the son of Bentham's colleague James Mill. J. S. Mill was given such a rigorous and precocious education by his father, he began to study Greek at the age of 3 and Aristotle's logic at 13, that he suffered a nervous breakdown by the time he was 20. His breakdown, which left him aware that he had no enthusiasm for the things he had been taught were good to pursue, led him to reassess Bentham's theory on which he had been brought up, so leading him to the conclusion that Bentham's comfortable life had given him a non-real basis on which to assess what was really important to humans. He said of Bentham: 'He never knew poverty and adversity, passion not satiety: he never had even the experience which sickness gives; he lived from childhood to eighty-five in boyish health. He knew no dejection or heaviness of heart' (cited in *What is Good?*, A. C. Grayling, Phoenix, 2003).

Mill felt that Bentham had made a fundamental error in his assessment of what human beings found desirable, observing: 'Human beings are not governed in all their actions by their worldly interests'. He did not dismiss Bentham's whole theory, he was as committed as Bentham had been to the progress of humanity and the improvement of society through maximising what is good and what increases well-being. However, he felt that the pleasure that Bentham's utilitarianism could be claimed to support failed to recognise the deeper levels of human experience: 'If [Bentham] thought at all of any of the deeper feelings of human nature, it was but as idiosyncrasies of taste' (cited in *Philosophy for AS and A2*, edited by Elizabeth Burns and Stephen Law, Routledge, 2004), Mill observed. He maintained that feelings other than happiness were necessary for the good life: honour, dignity and generosity. Mill argued that some ideals; justice, truth and love, for example, were surely good whether or not people desired them or were made happy by them, and argued that once the physical needs of humans were met then they would surely prefer what he called a higher pleasure over a lower one. The individual does need to be 'competently acquainted' with both levels of pleasure, and thereby be in a position to make an informed judgement, but, armed with this knowledge, they would surely choose quality of happiness over quantity.

Taking it further...

It was important to Mill that people were 'competently acquainted' with different types of pleasure, but he did not believe that this was a matter of luck or fortune. Rather, he believed that everyone could learn to cultivate the higher pleasures and live life in the best way, fully able to evaluate the qualitative difference between higher and lower pleasures. Although it was written much later in 1913, G. B. Shaw's play, *Pygmalion* tells the story of a social experiment to educate a flower girl to appreciate the higher pleasures of the upper classes. It is less optimistic about the outcome than Mill would have been.

John Stuart Mill would have encouraged the upper class opera goers to educate the lower classes to enjoy higher pleasures of this kind

Taking it further...

Rule utilitarianism is essentially **deontological**, i.e. the moral value of the action is contained in obedience to the rule rather than the act itself or the outcome of that action. Deontological systems of ethics are in general intolerant of flexibility and change but recognise the intrinsic value of certain rules of moral behaviour.

John Stuart Mill (1806–1873), English philosopher and economist

Mill was concerned that human beings should achieve their highest potential, and famously observed that 'it is better to be a man dissatisfied than a pig satisfied'. The point that Mill wanted to make was that surely 'Few human creatures would consent to be changed into any of the lower animals, for a promise of the fullest allowance of a beast's pleasures... no person of feeling and conscience would be selfish and base, even though they should be persuaded that the fool... is better satisfied with his lot than they are with theirs' (cited in *What is Good?*, A. C. Grayling, Phoenix, 2003).

Mill maintained that happiness is 'much too complex and indefinite' to be the measure of the moral worth of an action. In general, happiness is a very unspecific term that can cover a range of satisfaction that a person might get from a particular activity. If it is not specifically locatable or identifiable it becomes a rather fragile tool for the utilitarian. Neither is it necessary, as Bentham inferred, to apply a calculus. Rather, Mill suggested, humans have worked out through trial and error those actions that lead best to human happiness, which they promote through moral rules, which he termed secondary principles: 'do not lie', 'protect the weak', 'keep your promises'. This is essentially **rule utilitarianism**, a more sophisticated application of Bentham's theory. Rather than claiming that we should always perform that action that promotes the greatest happiness, rule utilitarians suggest that our actions should be guided by rules that, if everyone followed them, would lead to the greatest overall happiness. Human experience has shown us that there are certain rules that tend to promote happiness, for example the keeping of promises and refraining from stealing, killing and lying. History reveals that it is better not to imprison the innocent because ultimately respect for the law would be undermined.

Rule utilitarianism proposes that we consider the practical consequences of an action before carrying it out, not to assess each situation as if it were new but to follow rules that have been established according to the principle of utility. The rules might not always be inherently and absolutely true, but they are useful tools for evaluating actions, they have instrumental value in themselves. This approach is subdivided into **strong** and **weak** rule utilitarianism. The former claims that certain rules that we agree have instrumental value should always be kept, while the latter acknowledges that there will be circumstances in which it would be better to allow for exceptions.

Nevertheless, although this goes some way to addressing the problems of Bentham's act utilitarianism – an action is morally good only if it produces a greater balance of pleasure over pain – we need to be careful with the application of these rules. We may agree that in general a rule regarding truthfulness is more likely to maximise happiness than one regarding dishonesty, but what about those occasions in which telling the truth will cause unhappiness? When do we accept we are dealing with an exceptional case and can justify dishonesty? More calculations are required. Nevertheless, rule utilitarianism does seem to satisfy human intuitions about morality more than act utilitarianism because it can never justify any action purely on the grounds that it produces more pleasure for more people.

Furthermore, Mill observed that the happiness different people derive from different actions cannot reasonably be compared, and yet the ideals that he favoured are surely universally desirable even if they do not immediately rank alongside more physical pleasures. Essentially, Mill saw happiness as intrinsically related to the whole sum of human experiences because even though it is true to say that humans pursue happiness, it is not to the exclusion of other goals, such as education, artistic talents and moral goodness, that are intrinsically, not simply instrumentally, valuable.

J. S. Mill was critical of 18th-century utilitarianism in so far as it did not appreciate how important it is for humans to work together in a stable social framework and as a result it did not place sufficient value on justice. Mill maintained that justice was 'a name for certain classes of moral rules, which concern the essentials of human wellbeing more nearly, are therefore a more absolute obligation than any other rules for the guidance of life'. He was also concerned with maintaining the human freedom that is essential for humans to develop those talents and interests that are the hallmark of higher pleasures. Only a society that values diversity can allow individual talents to flourish, and Mill was aware that the rule of the majority can frustrate this. The institutions of society must allow free thought and experimentation to take place. To this end, Mill contributed the **harm principle** in answer to the question of how much pressure the majority was allowed to exert on the minority. He wrote: 'That principle is, that the sole end for which mankind are warranted, individually or collectively, in interfering with the liberty of action of any of their number, is self-protection. That the only purpose for which power can be rightfully exercised over any member of a civilised community, against his will, is to prevent harm to others' (cited in *The Moral of the Story*, Nina Rosenstand, Mayfield, 2000).

Nina Rosenstand observes that the harm principle is at the foundation of the principle of civil liberties: that citizens have their right to privacy, to do whatever they wish as long as it does no harm. She asks, however, how would we evaluate the case of a suicidal teenager? Would society have no right to interfere because she was harming no one but herself? Mill would argue that she is causing harm to others, not least her grieving family and to other teenagers who might be encouraged to follow her example. This latter is indirect harm, however, and Mill did not allow for the majority to interfere on the grounds that other adults might imitate the actions of others.

Modern applications of utilitarianism

In recent times act and rule utilitarianism have given way to a considerable degree to **preference utilitarianism**: the satisfaction of people's preferences rather than aiming to achieve the greatest balance of pleasure over pain. This form is particularly associated with Peter Singer and R. M. Hare. It is undoubtedly easier to manage than classical utilitarianism, because while pleasure is enormously difficult to calculate people can express their preferences, including those which may have nothing to do with experiencing happiness or pleasure but which are none the less important to them. For example, a marathon runner may exercise his preference to run under conditions of great physical agony to achieve a personal best, or a prisoner may rather face death than betray his comrades. Neither is achieving happiness in the crudely hedonic sense, but they are acting on preferences or ideals that are more important to them than mere happiness. Horner and Westacott (*Thinking through Philosophy*, Cambridge University Press, 2000) observe: 'Imagine the case of Joan of Arc. It seems unlikely that her campaign

Taking it further...

Values such as justice can have no place in utilitarianism, because the majority may not support that which is just. Similarly, the rights of an individual or group can be ignored if it is not in the interests of the majority, and Bentham was known to remark that all talk of rights was 'nonsense on stilts'.

to rid France of the English was motivated entirely or even mainly by the search for pleasure. It is hardly credible that she was experiencing pleasure as she stood at the stake and the flames began to rise around her body... It seems more plausible that she... was experiencing pain for the sake of something she valued more highly than pleasure.'

Preference utilitarianism does not require any experience either because people can express their preference, for example not to be tortured, without having ever experienced torture. They know without prior experience that it would not increase their overall well-being and would only result in negative effects.

Sometimes preferences may be exercised as duties, for example the duty the prisoner feels to his comrades to save them from death leads him to prefer torture to betrayal, and we begin to creep closer to **deontology**. Is the solider who prefers to protect his comrades acting under a genuine preference or is he bound by duty, identified by that supreme deontologist, Immanuel Kant, as the only thing of moral worth? Is he keeping his moral hands clean, or is he making a choice where others were genuinely available and which could legitimately lead to a better personal outcome? The trouble we have with duty today is that is has negative overtones in a way it perhaps could not have done for Kant, and we feel we have so many choices and so many opportunities to act upon them that we despise and perhaps fear the call of duty.

Another recent formulation is **negative utilitarianism**, which seeks to promote the least amount of harm or pain, or to prevent the greatest harm to the greatest number. Proponents argue that this is a more effective approach because there are many more ways to do harm than to do good, and the greatest harms have more powerful consequences than the greatest goods, hence it is more valuable to seek to avoid them. It also promotes the reduction of pain as a greater moral obligation than increasing happiness. This may have some reasonable practical value in that, for example, a starving community would benefit more from a reduction in its suffering, by means of food and medical care, than being sent DVDs or invitations to a garden party.

However, some advocates of utilitarianism have suggested that the ultimate aim of negative utilitarianism would be to engender the quickest and least painful method of killing the greatest number of people to put them out of their misery, even to the extent of the whole of humanity! It also raises questions of how much suffering is too great and whether some pain is not valuable. To minimise suffering to the level of a pinprick would mean that the emotional baggage of suffering would be reduced, but perhaps there are some things that we value that would also be lost. There are some goods that cannot be experienced without some degree of suffering, for example to show compassion someone needs to be in pain, so the reduction of all pain to a minimum would reduce the opportunity for human growth, responsibility and participation in the development of the world as a good place to live.

Utilitarianism and *prima facie* obligations

A key feature of utilitarianism is that it demands an impartial or impersonal view. In general, morality allows for the fact that certain relationships tend to lead to certain obligations and that the individual is somehow entitled to

---

Taking it further...

Humans generally value acts that encourage loyalty and friendship, yet they are not always intrinsically pleasing or happiness giving. G. E. Moore proposed **ideal utilitarianism**, which involves tallying any consequence that we intuitively recognise as good or bad (and not simply as pleasurable or painful).

favour themselves, their family or others with whom they have a *prima facie* relationship. This is a relationship that is of primary importance to us and takes precedence over our relationships with strangers and those we know at second hand. Everyday morality tends to be 'agent relative', i.e. we can legitimately favour some rather than others. However, utilitarianism demands that if we can bring about greater benefit for strangers than for those close to us, we should do so.

Furthermore, because some forms of utilitarianism justify an action by the ends, not the means, it may make it morally obligatory to kill or injure some in order to prevent a greater number of overall deaths. The utilitarian needs to defend this position against those who argue that people should always be treated as ends in themselves and not as a means to an end.

Utilitarianism: a success or failure?

Overall, we may defend utilitarianism on the grounds that the evaluation of moral choices may be unreliable if there is no consideration of consequences and, while motives may be good or bad, only consequences have a real effect on human well-being. The principle encourages a democratic approach to decision making. The majority's interest is always considered, and a dangerous minority is not allowed to dominate. Present circumstances can be judged without reference to precedents and it is an approach that asks us to consider no more than the greatest good of the greatest number. It does not rest on any controversial or unverifiable theological or metaphysical claims or principles.

However, its practical application requires the ability to predict the long-term consequences of an action, and to predict those consequences with unfailing accuracy. Past experience, can, to some extent, guide future experience, but we know that there is no guarantee that circumstances will turn out exactly the same.

People may suffer second or third hand, even if the immediate consequences of an action fulfilled the conditions of the principle. Furthermore, the theory gives no credit to motivation. Not every action done out of good will is going to result in good consequences, but the attitude with which it is performed should be worthy of some credit. Instead, the theory relies on a single principle by which we make moral decisions. This is too simplistic. We cannot solve every dilemma by reference to one ethical theory, because every ethical dilemma is multifaceted and unique in some way.

Ultimately, however, utilitarianism served to formulate an approach to ethical decision-making that was unified. It offered a means of approaching ethics in a systematic way that was simple to understand and apply. Nevertheless, we can all think of situations in which preferences, duties and happiness overlap sufficiently for us to wonder whether the distinction made between consequentialist and non-consequentialist ethics reflects the reality of our moral choices as accurately as we may be led to believe. And this applies just as much in the social arena as the private, as Robert E. Goodin observes: 'In legislating for the more common, standard sort of case, the public policy makers will very much more often than not find that the requirements of the utility principle and those of Ten Commandment deontologists will dovetail nicely' (cited in *A Companion to Ethics*, P. Singer, Blackwell, 1991).

A *son giving his father a back massage in an Indian slum. Where would this rank on J.S. Mill's hierarchy of pleasure?*

Taking it further...

Bentham recognised the weakness of utilitarianism with respect to guaranteed happiness and saw that there can only be a reasonable expectation of happiness, not certainty. He further claimed that the aim of the calculus was to identify that which has the 'tendency' to maximise happiness: a reasonable level of expectation of happiness is all that is required.

3.4 Situation ethics

Key Ideas

- The social and intellectual background of the 1960s and its influence on situation ethics

- The change in theological perspective and the new morality

- *Agapé* love and Joseph Fletcher's situation ethics

- Challenges to situation ethics

- Evaluating the success of situation ethics

The social and intellectual background

In our discussion of divine command ethics, we saw that for some religious believers morality consists of obeying the commands of God as directly revealed by him through scripture and the Church. The consequence of such an approach is that the believer is committed to following those rules without exception because they define what is good. To be good is to follow God's commands, or God's commands as interpreted by the Church or Christian community, and it is impossible to be good if acting in a way that contradicts or otherwise opposes them. Kant's deontological approach to ethics went some way to defend this view. Moral rules are good in themselves and should be obeyed irrespective of the consequences, and they comprise moral duties and obligations that are binding to humans.

However, although Christian ethics has traditionally followed this line, an alternative approach emerged in the 1960s that could also be used more widely in secular ethical decision-making. Nevertheless, its Christian ethos is absolutely vital for understanding the theory and evaluating how effective it was in providing a genuinely religious ethic for an era when the moral foundations seemed to have dramatically shifted for everyone.

Situation ethics, most commonly associated with Joseph Fletcher and J. A. T. Robinson, emerged at time when society and the Church were facing drastic and permanent change. When Fletcher wrote *Situation Ethics* (SCM) in 1966, both the USA and the UK had witnessed a series of highly significant events that had changed the shape and direction of the latter half of the 20th century. Women occupied an increasingly prominent place in the work force, initially necessitated by the absence of men from the home front during the Second World War. Disenchantment with the USA's involvement in Vietnam and the devastating shock of Kennedy's assassination lead to a distrust of government and a deep disappointment in the fulfilment of the American Dream. What was the point of sacrificing life and youth in patriotic obedience to a country that could not deliver and that rejected its heroes on their return from the battlefield? Martin Luther King's legacy remained, and though it was to be many years (if ever) before the divisive pre-civil rights attitudes and laws were truly shaken off, the scene was set for a radical shift in the social power base.

The sexual revolution of the 1960s was the icing on a far more complex cake than might be assumed. As the post-war generation threw off the shackles of paternalism, authority, law and government, freely available, reliable contraception allowed them to express their new individualism and liberty in the form of non-marital sex as their parents and grandparents could not. Fashion, music, politics, mixed-race relationships, religion, drugs and all forms of social activity were affected. Between the end of the Second World War and the end of the 1960s, western Europe and North America (predominantly the northern states) were socially, culturally and morally transformed.

The rapidity with which moral perspectives changed in the 20th century cannot be underestimated. There are many other factors that could be included here: the emergence of the teenager as a social group with their own tastes in music, fashion, politics and even food; the rebellious spirit of rock and roll culture and the growing power of the student movement also contributed to the change in the moral climate.

Teenage culture was a key feature of cultural change after World War II

The advent of the pill transformed sexual morality

The Church's reaction

This change was not attractive to everyone. In 1964 the British Council of Churches (BCC), on the advice of its Advisory Group on Sex, Marriage and the Family, appointed a Working Party that set out to: 'Prepare a Statement of the Christian case for abstinence from sexual intercourse before marriage and faithfulness within marriage… and to suggest means whereby the Christian position may be effectively presented to the various sections of the community' (*Sex and Morality*, SCM, 1966). The BCC wanted to convey 'a sane and responsible attitude towards love and marriage in the face of the misleading suggestions conveyed by much popular literature, entertainment and advertising' (*Sex and Morality*, SCM, 1966). The 'misleading suggestions' that concerned them the most were, naturally, those that related to sexual behaviour. They observed 'a widespread feeling, especially among Christian people, that recent years have witnessed a general lowering of moral standards, and that this is particularly evident in the realm of sexual behaviour' (*Sex and Morality*, SCM, 1966). The BCC made extensive use of the Schofield Report (*The Sexual Behaviour of Young People*, Michael Schofield, prepared by the Central Council for Health Education, 1965), which identified the influences to which young people in the 1960s were exposed: 'greater independence; more money in their pockets and purses; the weakening of family bonds and religious influences; the development of earlier maturity, physically, emotionally and mentally; the impact of modern books, television [and] periodicals' (*Sex and Morality*, SCM, 1966). In the light of these influences, the BCC wanted to reassess where Christian moral truth lay, and this was a task that many theologians and ethicists were aware was an urgent task.

A change in perspective

In 1963, when J. A. T. Robinson published his highly controversial book *Honest to God* (SCM), the Church was thrown into disarray and disagreement. It may seem incredible to us now that a theology book could be the cause of such controversy, but it is not an exaggeration to say it shook

Taking it further...

In his introduction to *Honest to God* (Robinson, SCM, 1963) the Bishop of Woolwich observes: 'For I suspect we stand on the brink of a period in which it is going to become increasingly difficult to know what the true defence of Christian truth requires'.

the traditional church at its roots. Robinson challenged the traditional, conservative view of God as an objectively real being 'up there' at the top of a three-storied universe and, in line with Paul Tillich, suggested that God be understood as 'the ground of our being', of ultimate significance, but not a *deus ex machina*, a supernatural being who intervenes in the world from outside it.

If this was not enough, Robinson also supported the 'new morality'. Joseph Fletcher had not yet written *Situation Ethics* but he had written an article in the *Harvard Divinity Bulletin* entitled 'The New Look at Christian Ethics'. 'Christian ethics', Fletcher had written 'is not a scheme of codified conduct. It is a purposive effort to relate love to a world of relativities through a casuistry obedient to love' (cited in *Honest to God*, Robinson, SCM, 1963). In other words, the new Christian morality for 'man come of age' (Dietrich Bonhoeffer's phrase) was not based on law, or rather, perhaps, on one law only: the law of love.

The Bishop of Woolwich, writing in 1963 (his introduction to *Honest to God*, Robinson, SCM), anticipated that this change in moral perspective would lead to an increasing rift between Christians: 'I am inclined to think that the gulf must grow wider before it is bridged and that there will be an increasing alienation, both within the ranks of the Church and outside it'.

Soon after, the Working Party of the BCC came to the conclusion that 'the Christian position is not so easily defined as many imagine. Underlying much of our modern confusion there is a real uncertainty about what is the proper basis for Christian moral judgement.' The way forward was not going to be easy, but Robinson was to argue that 'Dr Fletcher's approach is the only ethic for "man come of age". To resist his approach in the name of religion will not stop it, it will only ensure the form it takes will be anti-Christian' (*Honest to God*, SCM, 1963).

The law of love

Fletcher and Robinson used New Testament dialogues between Jesus and the Pharisees as an illustration of old versus new morality. Jesus, they claimed, was an advocate, albeit 2000 years previously, of new morality, the Pharisees of the old. Whilst the Pharisees elaborated the Torah to accommodate every possible situation, Jesus went back to first principles. When asked about divorce law, Jesus referred people back to creation (Mark 10:1–12), rather than the Law of Moses, which was designed to accommodate man's sinful nature. Hence, Jesus declared the Sabbath to be made for man, not man for the Sabbath; he touched and healed lepers; he received an anointing from a woman of dubious reputation; he saved an allegedly adulterous woman from stoning, inviting her accusers instead to consider whether they were truly in a position to judge her sins. The story of the woman caught in adultery shows Jesus adopting a classic situationist approach (John 8:2–11), demonstrating love, compassion and integrity and showing the weakness of using absolute laws as a means of judging individual moral cases.

Joseph Fletcher observed that 'Bultmann was correct in saying that Jesus had no ethics if we accept, as I do not, that his definition of ethics was a system of values and rules "intelligible for all men". Yet the point is not so much that there is no such universal ethic... but that no ethic needs to be systematic and Jesus's ethic most certainly was not' (*Situation Ethics*, SCM, 1966). (Rudolph Bultmann was an influential early 20th-century German theologian.)

Fletcher and Robinson were aware that the move from a **supranaturalist** view of ethics, where right and wrong is derived directly from God through commandments and laws that are eternally valid for human life and behaviour, to a **situationalist** or **existential** ethic, was not going to be universally popular. As early as 1956, Pope Pius XII had seen the shape of things to come and had banned the view from all seminaries. Protestant reactions were equally suspicious because, at its heart, situation ethics declares that nothing can be labelled as 'wrong' or 'bad'. However, Robinson, argued, the only way in which people, rather than laws, could be truly valued, was to respond to them 'situationally, not prescriptively' (*Honest to God*, SCM, 1963). 'Whatever the pointers of the law to the demands of love, there can for the Christian be no "packaged" moral judgements – for persons are more important even than standards' (*Honest to God*, SCM, 1963).

Situation ethics and divorce law

Robinson argued that the ideals of situation ethics could be applied far more effectively to the then hotly debated issue of divorce law than the application of a pre-packaged moral judgement that divorce was 'always wrong'. Robinson questioned the conservative view that marriage created a supernatural bond that was impossible to break, based on the belief that behind earthly, human relationships lay quite independent, invisible structures that could not be questioned. Hence, although it may appear that marriage is about two human beings signing a legal contract, in reality 'something' happens in the metaphysical realm that binds those two people together in a relationship that is beyond the legal contract between them. The legal contract cannot be dissolved like a contract of employment, because it represents a far more binding union that has been made, witnessed, and ratified in the heavenly realms. 'It is not a question of "Those whom God hath joined together let no man put asunder": no man could if he tried. For marriage is not merely indissoluble: it is indelible' (*Honest to God*, SCM, 1963).

Robinson believed that this kind of thinking was out-dated and potentially damaging. Rather, it was time for humans to enter into their maturity and seek liberty from such supranaturalist thinking and, while allowing past experience to guide them, be ready to leave behind the restrictions of the old moral law if love was best served by so doing. The precise nature of love for the situationists is important, however. Fletcher and Robinson identified *agapé* love as the only intrinsically good thing. William Barclay defined it as: 'unconquerable good will; it is the determination to seek the other man's highest good, no matter what he does to you. Insult, injury, indifference – it does not matter; nothing but good will. It has been defined as purpose, not passion. It is an attitude to the other person' (*Ethics in a Permissive Society*, Collins, 1971).

This kind of love is highly demanding or, as Barclay suggested, 'a highly intelligent thing' (*Ethics in a Permissive Society*, Collins, 1971). It is not random, fatalistic, romantic love that cannot be demanded. Rather, *agapé*

Taking it further...

Significantly, the divorce law was reformed to allow more flexibility in the grounds for divorce in 1967, only 4 years after the publication of *Honest to God*. Robinson had not underestimated the spirit of the decade. Change was inevitable. Abortion law was also reformed in the same year and by the end of the 1960s family planning was the norm and the reality of sex before marriage could no longer be ignored.

love is required of one human being to another, and demands that the whole personality be involved in a deliberate directing of the will, heart and mind. Employing *agapé* situationally may demand that laws are put aside, a choice that leaves many legalists and supranaturalists without a reliable foundation on which to maintain their position of moral superiority. 'If the emotional and spiritual welfare of both parents and children in a particular family can be served best by a divorce, wrong and cheapjack as divorce commonly is, then love requires it' wrote Fletcher (cited in *Honest to God*, Robinson, SCM, 1963). Note that Fletcher emphasises 'particular family'. He is not advocating divorce for all, but rather observing that situationally, for some families, love is better served by allowing them the freedom to divorce.

Joseph Fletcher

Fletcher identified three approaches to morality.

- **Legalism**, a conservative rule-based morality, like that of the Pharisees: 'Solutions are preset, and you can look them up in a book – a Bible or a confessor's manual' (*Situation Ethics*, SCM, 1966).

- **Antinomianism**, the polar opposite to legalism. No rules or maxims can be applied to a moral situation, rather 'in every existential moment or unique situation… one must rely on the situation itself, then and there, to provide its ethical solution' (*Situation Ethics*, SCM, 1966).

- **Situationism**, a midway between the two other positions. 'The situationist enters into every decision-making situation fully armed with the ethical maxims of his community and its heritage, and he treats them with respect… Just the same he is prepared in any situation to compromise them or set them aside in the situation if love seems better served by doing so' (*Situation Ethics*, SCM, 1966).

The middle way always lay in the application of *agapé*, the love that Jesus commanded. 'You shall love the Lord your God with all your heart, and with all your soul, and with all your strength and with all your mind; and your neighbour as yourself' (Luke 10:27). 'Greater love has no man than this, that a man lay down his life for his friends' (John 15:13). 'And this is his commandment, that we should believe in the name of his Son Jesus Christ and love one another, just as he has commanded us' (1 John 3:23). Ultimately, of course, Jesus demonstrated love through his sacrificial death on the cross for the sake of sinful humanity.

Like utilitarianism, therefore, situation ethics is based on a single principle that enables man to enter every situation armed with the experience and precedents of past situations, but willing to lay them aside if the principle of love, *agapé*, is better served by so doing, and will enable us better to bring about the greatest good.

Take great care in exams when comparing **utilitarianism** with **situation ethics**. Although they share similarities of approach, rejecting absolute rules and allowing situations to be judged relatively according to a principle of utility, the principle of happiness and *agapé* are quite different. Only weak candidates fall into the trap of suggesting that situation ethics is utilitarianism adapted. The best candidates identify the highly distinctive nature of both theories.

Taking it further...

Fletcher called situationism 'principled relativism'. Maxims or general rules could illuminate a situation, but they would not prescribe an action. He observed: 'Situation ethics calls upon us to keep law in a subservient place, so that only love and reason really count when the chips are down' (*Situation Ethics*, SCM, 1966).

Principles and presuppositions

Furthermore, Fletcher proposed four presuppositions of situation ethics.

- **Pragmatism** demands that a proposed course of action should work, and that its success or failure should be judged according to the principle. Fletcher quoted William James: 'A pragmatist turns toward concreteness and adequacy, toward facts, toward actions, and toward power' (cited in *Situation Ethics*, SCM, 1966).

- **Relativism** rejects such absolutes as 'never', 'always', 'perfect' and 'complete'. Fletcher observed: 'This concept… cries "Relativity!" in the face of all smug pretensions to truth and righteousness. Christians cannot go on trying to lay down the law' (*Situation Ethics*, SCM, 1966).

- **Positivism** recognises that love is the most important criterion of all expressed in the teaching of 1 John 4:7–12: ' Beloved, let us love one another, because love is from God; everyone who loves is born of God and knows God'.

- **Personalism** demands that people should be put first. Fletcher emphasised the fact that ethics deals with human relations and should therefore put people at the centre. The legalist, he observed, asks 'what is the law?' while the situationist asks 'who is to be helped?'.

Additionally, Fletcher was detailed in explaining how *agapé* should be understood and how it applied to the theory of situation ethics.

• Love only is always good
This means that there is no action or moral rule that is good in itself. An action is good only in so far as it brings about *agapé*.

• Love is the only norm
Fletcher understood a norm to be a rule and appealed to Jesus's teaching in Mark 12:33 that the most important commandment is to love God and love your neighbour. He did allow that some rules might be useful, such as the Decalogue, but in cases of dispute love should decide what should be done.

• Love and justice are the same, and love is justice distributed
This idea was unique to Fletcher, who claimed that justice is the giving to every person what is their due, and that as the one thing due to everyone is love, then love and justice are the same. Justice settles how love is to be applied to every person in every situation and in particular cases. Justice cannot be distributed through the application of laws and principles that never change, as love without justice is sentimentality, and justice without love is rigidity. Love, therefore, needs to be calculating, with an eye to the intended outcome of the action.

• Love is not liking and always wills the neighbour's good
As *agapé* was not an emotion, it did not need to encompass liking. Because agapé involves sacrifice people should give love without expecting a return and irrespective of how they feel about others.

• Love is the only means
Situation ethics is a teleological theory that identifies the ends or the outcome of the action as the means of assessing its moral worth. In this case, it suggests that anything might be done if it brings about the most loving outcome.

Taking it further…

A teacher may not like a student, but he will still do what is good for them, and while it may not be pleasant to force them to work and sit an exam, it may be the most loving thing to do.

● Love decides there and then

Because there is no way of knowing in advance whether something is right or wrong because every situation is different, the situationist has to be prepared to make every moral decision afresh. There are no predetermined right or wrong answers to moral questions and it would be meaningless to discuss in advance whether certain actions were good or bad. Only when a real situation presents itself is it worth discussing what is right.

Unique situations

Fletcher developed his theory by drawing on a wide range of cases that could not be resolved by applying fixed rules and principles. Examples include the burning house and time to save only one person; your father or a doctor with the formulae for a cure for a killer disease in his head alone; the woman who kills her crying baby to save a party from massacre by Indians on the Wilderness Trail; the military nurse who deliberately treated her patients harshly so they would be determined to get fit and able to leave the hospital; the famous case of Mrs Bergmeier who deliberately asked a Russian prison camp guard to make her pregnant so she could be released to return to her family in Germany (an act that Fletcher called **sacrificial adultery**).

Fletcher also drew on situations that he had experienced first hand. In the course of his work he was asked to visit a man with stomach cancer who would die in 6 months without treatment that would cost $40 every 3 days. He would have to give up work and borrow on his life insurance to survive for 3 years if he followed this course of action. However, if he refused treatment he would die with his life insurance valid, providing his family with $100,000 after his death. If he refused treatment it would be tantamount to suicide, but if he accepted it his family would be heavily in debt after his death. What should he do? What is the loving thing in terms of his intention and the consequences for others?

Fletcher also cited the case of a patient in a mental hospital in 1962 who was raped by a fellow patient. The father requested that an abortion be performed, but the hospital refused to do so arguing that abortion was against the law in such a case. He argued 'Is it not the most loving thing possible (the right thing) and in this case a responsible decision to terminate the pregnancy? What think ye?' (*Situation Ethics*, SCM, 1966).

Fletcher borrowed examples from literature and history: the rainmaker in Nash's play of the same title, who makes love to an unmarried woman to save her from being 'spinsterised'; T. E. Lawrence's killing of an Arab who had murdered one of the Arab's fellow countrymen in order to prevent a drawn-out blood feud between their families. Still fresh in many people's memories was the bombing of Hiroshima and Nagasaki. When the Americans were attempting to decide whether to drop the atomic bomb on Hiroshima and Nagasaki, the committee responsible for advising President Truman was divided. Some were totally opposed. Others felt that the Japanese should be warned about the bomb's potential by dropping it first on an uninhabited part of the country. Others still felt that the dropping of the bomb was the only way to ensure the end of the war. In the event, the bomb was dropped on civilian and military targets. Was this right?

Hiroshima - civilians wounded in the world's first atomic bomb, August 1945. President Harry S. Truman said the United States had dropped the bomb 'in order to shorten the agony of war, in order to save the lives of thousands and thousands of young Americans'. About 80,000 people died instantly in the bombing; virtually every building in Hiroshima was destroyed or damaged

The evidence for the need for situationist ethics mounted and Fletcher's theory seemed to be based on sufficient evidence of the need for moral decision making to be flexible, and for humans to be prepared to act in challenging ways if the interests of love were best served by so doing.

Challenges to situation ethics

This all sounds well and good, admirable even. However, it's weaknesses were fiercely exposed by its opponents. Professor Gordon Dunstan wrote of Fletcher's theory: 'It is possible, though not easy, to forgive Professor Fletcher for writing this book, for he is a generous and loveable man. It is harder to forgive the SCM Press for publishing it' (cited in *Advanced Religious Studies*, Sarah K. Tyler and Gordon Reid, Philip Allan Updates, 2002). In *The Honest to God* debate, Glyn Simon wrote 'A false spirituality of this kind has always haunted the thinking of clever men' (cited in *Scandalous Risks*, Susan Howatch, HarperCollins, 1990). Perhaps most impressively of all, William Barclay outlined a carefully considered critique of the theory in his *Baird Lectures* in 1971, subsequently developed in *Ethics in a Permissive Society* (Fount, 1971). Barclay's lectures were an attempt to examine the nature of Christian ethics in the last quarter of the 20th century, aware of the drastic challenge to Christian ethics that had been posed over the previous 30 years. 'Thirty years ago no one ever really questioned the Christian ethic … No one ever doubted that divorce was disgraceful; that illegitimate babies were a disaster; that chastity was a good thing' (*Ethics in a Permissive Society,* Fount, 1971).

Barclay adopted a conservative view on Christian ethics, and challenged Fletcher's new morality on several grounds. Firstly, he correctly observes that Fletcher's cases are extreme ones. How often are we going to make the kind of life and death choices on which he bases situation ethics? Rarely, if ever. 'It is much easier to agree that extraordinary situations need extraordinary measures than to think that there are no laws for ordinary everyday life' (*Ethics in a Permissive Society,* Fount, 1971). Secondly, he suggests that Fletcher overestimates the value of being free from rules and the constant decision-making processes that this forces humans into. If it were the case that *agapé* could always be fairly and accurately dealt out, then laws would be redundant. As it is, there are no such guarantees, and so a degree of law is necessary for human survival.

The law, Barclay, observes, has several vital functions, which we would be ill advised to do away with: it clarifies experience; it is the means by which society determines what a reasonable life is; it defines crime; it has a deterrent value; and it protects society. Furthermore, he argues that Fletcher is unrealistic about the degree to which humans are truly free to make choices without the guidance and control of law. There are so many impositions on human freedom, including environment, upbringing and education, but also the past choices that we have made that define future choices, that freedom is virtually an illusion. Above all, Barclay, suggests, law ensures that humans do not make an artificial distinction between public and private morality: 'A man can live his own life, but when he begins deliberately to alter the lives of others, then a real problem arises, on which we cannot simply turn our backs, and in which there is a

Taking it further...

'It remains true … that a man must in the moment of decision do what he thinks is right. He cannot do otherwise. This does not mean that what he does will be right or even that he will not be worthy of blame or punishment. He simply has no choice, for he cannot at that moment see any discrepancy between what is right and what he thinks is right' (William K. Frankena, *Ethics*, Prentice Hall, 1973).

place for law an the encourager of morality' (*Ethics in a Permissive Society*, Fount, 1971).

Essentially, Barclay's criticisms suggest that Fletcher was overly optimistic about the capacity of human beings to make morally correct choices and not to be influenced by personal preferences. Human beings need the guidelines offered by rules to avoid moral chaos. Furthermore, how can we arbitrate a case in which two people reach different conclusions about an action, yet both claim to be acting in the interests of love? Are our actions as independent and flexible as Fletcher assumes? If we act in discrete ways in apparently similar circumstances, our actions would tend to appear to be unfair rather than moral. People like to be treated with a degree of consistency, and situation ethics permits inconsistency, even unreliability, in personal relationships.

Scandalous risks

In Susan Howatch's novel *Scandalous Risks* (HarperCollins, 1990), she describes an ecclesiastical community in 1963, the year J. A. T. Robinson wrote *Honest to God*. Howatch puts her characters in a moral dilemma that they attempt to examine from the position of situation ethics.

> *'Well, you see it's like this... I seem to have got myself into rather a peculiar situation with a clergyman...'*

> *'Oh, I'm very used to clergymen in peculiar situations', said Father Darrow.*

> *'We're madly in love, but it's all very confusing.'*

> *'There's a wife, I daresay, in the background', suggested Father Darrow helpfully.*

> *'Yes, but we've both accepted that there can be no divorce... The real problem is what sort of relationship we can have. You see, he believes – and he's terribly modern in his outlook – he believes there are no hard and fast rules any more when it comes to dealing with ethical situations; all you have to do is act with love... The catch is that you have to act with the very best kind of love, pure and noble. So if a man loves a girl and says to himself 'Do I take her to bed?' the answer's not yes, it's no, because if he really loves her he won't want to use her to satisfy himself in that way.'*

> *'This sounds like the New Morality outlined by Bishop Robinson in* Honest to God.*'*

> *'So you know all about that... What do you think of it?'*

> *'The important question is what you think of it.'*

> *'I just don't know any more, I'm so confused. My clergyman, following the New Morality, says that even though he's married we're allowed a romantic friendship so long as we truly love each other, because... we'll be high-minded enough to abstain from anything... that would hurt either us or other people... Well, that's fine... but the deeper I get into*

this relationship the less sense that seems to make… I mean, if you love someone you do want to go to bed with them…'

'You're saying that the gap between Dr Robinson's idealism and your experience of reality has now become intolerably wide…'.

In this scene Venetia has sought Father Darrow's help to understand the way in which her romantic friend rationalises and conducts their relationship along the lines of situation ethics. He will not fully consummate their relationship because in so doing he is showing true *agapé*, whilst not recognising any moral absolutes that would forbid him, as a married clergyman, to engage in any sort of intimate relationship with her. Venetia makes clear that attempting to conduct this relationship within the parameters of situation ethics has simply led to confusion. Her objection is that it is counterintuitive: the concept of love espoused by New Morality does not appear to bear any relation to reality, but only to theory. Venetia implies that she would feel less confused about her relationship with her clergyman if he simply said, 'I can't go to bed with you because I am a married clergyman and it would be wrong'. Instead, he muddies the waters.

Arguably, there is a moral absolute still at work, 'show pure, noble love', but the characters seem to conclude that all that is going on is a lot of self-deception. Ultimately, it seems that ethical theories such as situation ethics are **idealistic**; moral dilemmas are **realistic**. Rarely do our real-life situations conform to the neat solutions that would apparently be available to us if we applied the principles of ethical theory.

Is there any hope for situation ethics?

There is no doubt that situation ethics does have some clear advantages, particularly in that individual cases are judged on their own merits, irrespective of what has been done in similar situations in the past. This allows for compassionate use of reason and ensures that inappropriate judgements are not made. Flexibility is built into most democratic legal systems and most human relationships allow for a certain degree of leeway even in the most challenging moral dilemmas. The sacrifice demanded by true *agapé* is laudable and it is clearly praiseworthy to seek the well-being of others even if the course of action is not one of preference. Furthermore, situation ethics makes a genuine attempt to offer an ethic modelled on the teaching of Jesus, and so it could be considered a truly Christian ethic.

There is no doubt too, that the theory responded to the character and needs of the time. Since then, liberal Christians have attempted to live by the spirit rather than the letter of law, as illustrated by those who battle to protect the rights of homosexuals to enjoy Christian fellowship and even to be ordained, and who permit divorcees to remarry in church services, welcome 'sinners' into the Christian community and refuse to act as moral judge and jury. The Working Party of the BCC was less convinced in 1966. While acknowledging the social and relational changes that had occurred, it was persistently drawn back to the notion of love as being characterised best by loyalty that

> ### Taking it further...
>
> The principles of love were also espoused by the Old Testament writers. In Hosea 6:6 the prophet writes that God desires 'steadfast love, not sacrifice, knowledge of God rather than burnt offerings'. Amos 5:24 expresses similar sentiments: 'Let justice roll down like waters, and righteousness like an ever flowing stream'.

transcends sexual desire or desirability and that places trust at the heart of the family. They draw a daringly harsh conclusion on the dangers of family break-up: 'Children in their early years are so vulnerable that they need loving marriages and secure homes for their development, and a person who is responsible for a child's lack of this environment sin against it as seriously as a stranger who assaults it in a park' (*Sex and Morality*, SCM, 1966). Tough stuff indeed.

Overall, the jury seems to have delivered a verdict of 'unsound' on Robinson's and Fletcher's approach to moral decision-making, but situation ethics has not gone away. We strive daily for the freedom to make choices situationally, whether or not it be within the framework of *agapé*, but are constrained not only by law but also by the moral judgements of others. Most tellingly, perhaps, in an era when we might suppose that secularism and liberalism would have an even stronger hold on religions, morality organisations such as Silver Ring Thing and True Love Waits are encouraging young Christians to take vows of celibacy, urging a return to traditional Christian sexual ethics, and in the USA the religious right argue vociferously for a repeal in abortion law. Perhaps the reality that situation ethics exposes is not that moral judgements should be made situationally but that sometimes we wish they could.

CHAPTER 4
Ethical dilemmas

4.1 Sexual ethics

Key Ideas

■ The nature of sexual ethics and the relationship with religion and morality

■ Marriage and divorce: issues of religion, morality and situation ethics

■ Controversial issues: pornography, homosexuality and schisms within the Christian Church

The nature of sexual ethics

Sexual ethics covers a wide variety of issues, including marriage, divorce, homosexuality and pornography. Much of the controversy concerning them stems from religious attitudes to these issues, which have their roots in ancient times.

Sexual ethics in ancient times

The ancient Greeks, particularly the philosopher Pythagoras and the Stoics, believed that the ideal human life was one where a person abstained from physical pleasures and lived in quiet contemplation. For them, the world was divided into the physical and the spiritual; a position called **dualism**. They believed that a person's soul was imprisoned in the body and that it had to free itself from the temporary physical side in order to enter the everlasting spiritual side. Physical sex inhibited this because it made a person lose control and act on animal instinct. Sex was therefore considered unholy.

Modern sexual ethics

In the 21st century there are widely differing attitudes within sexual ethics, not just amongst religious believers but also in the media, parliament, law and moral philosophy. Today, sexual pleasure is often encouraged because it offers immediate physical pleasure. Notions of monogamy, faithfulness, commitment and love are often not assumed. The notion of the freedom of the individual to choose means that sexual activity is about mutual consent rather than long-term commitment, and marriage is no longer a prerequisite. Sexual ethics is a complex area, and legal and moral attitudes meet in a distinctive way. For example, adultery is considered by many to be immoral and it provides legal grounds for a divorce, yet it is not a crime. In the same way many people think that sex with many partners is promiscuous and immoral, while others argue that sexual activities between consenting adults,

Taking it further...

The ancient Hebrews, living in Old Testament times, had a marginally more positive attitude towards sex but it was confined within certain rules and regulations. It essentially restricted sexual intercourse to the marriage relationship between husband and wife.

married or unmarried, heterosexual or homosexual, are not a matter of morality at all. In *Law, Liberty and Morality* (Oxford University Press, 1986), H. L. A. Hart drew the important distinction between what is, and is not, sexually immoral: 'Sexual intercourse between husband and wife is not immoral, but if it takes place in public it is an affront to human decency'. He argues that a private sexual act could not harm anyone except 'a few neurotic… persons who are literally "made ill" by the thought of it'.

Western culture has found itself in a paradox: on the one hand encouraging sexual freedom, yet on the other facing steep rises in sexual crimes, teenage pregnancy rates, abortions and sexually transmitted diseases. This has led some people to blame the decline in religious values and the undermining of family values for this situation, while others blame these very same values for preventing a true realisation of sexual identity.

Christianity and sexuality

In the distant past, Christian writers such as Augustine portrayed sex in a negative light, teaching that it was sinful except for the purposes of reproduction. For many early Christians, the fact that Jesus did not marry led them to think that not having sexual relationships, **celibacy**, was a more holy way of living. Other believers were influenced by Paul's view that celibacy was preferable but, for those who find their sexual passions difficult to control, it was better to be married: 'But if they cannot control themselves, they should marry, for it is better to marry than to burn with passion' (1 Corinthians 7:9).

Much of this attitude still exists today: most Christian monks and nuns must remain celibate, as must Roman Catholic priests. However, the Protestant churches do not hold this position and priests are often actively encouraged to marry and have children. Interestingly, Evangelical Christian organisations such as True love Waits and Silver Ring Thing have begun to campaign for celibacy amongst teenagers, encouraging them to take chastity pledges vowing to abstain from sex until married.

Today, Christianity still teaches that marriage is the relationship that God has established for sexual relationships and many Christians continue to express their disquiet at other sexual activities, such as sex outside marriage, adultery and homosexuality. The relationship between sex, marriage and procreation is still asserted strongly by some Christians, particularly the Roman Catholic Church and Evangelicals, not least on the grounds that because children require a stable family environment, it follows that sexual relationships and reproduction should only take place within marriage.

In recent times, the Christian Church has placed a greater emphasis on the link between sex and love and the recognition of sex as a unifying and affirming part of the relationship between husband and wife. The Church of England's consultative document *Marriage and the Church's Task* (1978) states: 'love finds expression in the lovers' bodily union… It is an act of personal commitment which spans past, present and future. It is celebration, healing, renewal, pledge and future. Above all it communicates the affirmation of mutual belonging.' In *Pastoral Constitution* (1965) the Roman Catholic Church stated: 'This love is uniquely expressed and perfected through the marital act… these actions signify and promote the mutual self-giving by which spouses enrich each other with a joyful and thankful will'.

Conservative Christians continue to be opposed to same sex marriages

Taking it further...

Aquinas took the view of natural law, that sex led to reproduction. As that was the purpose of the sexual organs, they should not be used for anything other than reproduction. Sexual activities that did not lead to reproduction, such as masturbation and homosexuality, should therefore be forbidden.

Libertarianism and sexuality

The **libertarian** view is that sexual relationships are morally permissible if both parties are over the legal age limit and consent. Freewill is an important factor: libertarians do not permit sexual crimes such as rape, where there is no consent, and sex with children, who are not mature enough to consent. Nor is sex involving any kind of deception permitted because free choices cannot be made if one partner is unaware of all the issues.

Libertarians often adopt the **Harm Principle**, associated with J. S. Mill, which is that no harm must be done to the other party or to third parties. It follows the notion that people are free to do as they please, as long as they do not harm others or take away their freedom. This would, for example, mean that adultery would not be permitted if the betrayed spouse or children would be harmed, but adultery is not wrong purely on principle.

The advantage of libertarianism is that it allows consenting adults to do as they please and seems to offer a more tolerant and permissive lifestyle. However, the main weakness of the libertarian approach is that, if there is an imbalance in the relationship, then freewill and consent are often limited. For example someone may reluctantly agree to have sex in exchange for money or to get a job.

Utilitarianism and sexuality

Most **utilitarians** would probably support the view that sexual relations are acceptable as long as they take place in private among consenting adults. This means nobody is offended and the partners are able to increase their own happiness. In fact most moral arguments about the importance of safe sex are utilitarian. Having safe sex decreases the risk of infection and greater harm to society. At the same time, sexual relationships that cause emotional harm or deceit should be avoided as they lead to more harm than good.

Feminism and sexuality

Feminist critics have argued that Christian attitudes to sexual relationships are based on traditional and outdated notions of women as child-bearers, homemakers and submissive companions. Sexual behaviour assumes male dominance and women are definitely secondary. Socially constructed sexual roles make it very difficult for women to identify their own sexual desires. Women will only be equal when they are free from male sexual dominance. Moreover, most sexual crimes are committed by men. In *The Subjection of Women* (Hackett, 1988), J. S. Mill wrote: 'The principle which regulates the existing social relations between the two sexes – the legal subordination of one sex to the other – is wrong in itself… it ought to be replaced by a principle of perfect equality, admitting no power or privilege on the one side, nor disability on the other'. Liberal views of sexuality are also criticised because they assume that men and women have equal status in sexual relationships, which does not reflect underlying male dominance.

Computers and sex

It is said that with any new technology sex and gossip are the first things to take the most advantage of its possibilities, and it is clear that modern technology is increasingly affecting sexual behaviour. It is now possible, with the aid of computers, for people to have intimate relationships and never

Taking it further...

The libertarian view is sometimes called **contractarian**. Sex is not exclusively linked to the marriage relationship or reproduction. The most important principles are human freedom and autonomy.

Taking it further...

The feminist writer Catharine Mackinnon in *Feminism Unmodified* (Harvard University Press, 1988) argues for a complete rethinking of society's values regarding sexuality, to reflect the true status of men and women.

actually meet in person, for example through cybersex, online pornography, computerised sex toys and chat rooms. The moral issue here is that people are no longer seen as real, flesh and blood individuals, but simply as sexual objects, a view rejected by Christians as against the spirit of the teaching of Jesus: 'everyone who looks at another lustfully has already committed adultery in their heart' (Matthew 5: 28).

Marriage and divorce: the Christian perspective

'Marriage is a total troth communion which can be broken by any kind of prolonged infidelity, whether through the squandering of monies, unwillingness to share of self, breaking of confidences or other betrayals of trust' (*New Dictionary of Christian Ethics and Pastoral Theology*, edited by David Atkinson and David Field, IVP, 1995). The Christian view of marriage is that it is ordained by God, and is where a man and a woman make a commitment to an exclusive and binding relationship that will last until the death of one of the partners: 'a man will leave his father and mother and be united to his wife, and they will become one flesh' (Genesis 2:24). A conservative reading of this teaching is that all non-marital sexual relationships are therefore wrong in the eyes of God, because they undermine the trust and protection that marriage offers to both partners.

The purpose of Christian marriage is fidelity (*fides*) to one another, procreation (*proles*) and the union of man and woman (*sacramentum*). Many Christians teach that within marriage there is a natural **hierarchy** that reflects the relationship of Christ as the groom and the Church as the bride. The husband is the head of the wife and must love and honour her: 'as Christ loved the church and gave himself up for her' (Ephesians 5:25). In turn, she must love and respect him: 'each one of you also must love his wife as he loves himself, and the wife must respect her husband' (Ephesians 5:33).

The notion of a hierarchy in the marriage relationship has caused much controversy because it seems that there is little equality between the two: 'Wives, in the same way be submissive to your husband… Husbands, in the same way be considerate as you live with your wives, and treat them with respect' (1 Peter 3:1, 7).

However, Christians argue that the relationship is based upon Christ's headship over the church and is about love and sacrifice, not domination and power. Such love involves the man in making sure that the needs of his wife are met and the wife in showing respect for her husband, not because she is inferior to him, but out of love for him.

Divorce

There is some dispute among Christians concerning the interpretation of the teachings in the New Testament regarding divorce. The marriage relationship is a holy one and divorce is not favoured by God: 'Therefore what God has joined together, let man not separate' (Matthew 19:6). This seems to be supported by Jesus, who, in Mark's gospel, said that the Jewish law provided for divorce only as a concession to humanity's hardness of heart. Jesus then seems to forbid divorce: 'Anyone who divorces his wife and marries another woman commits adultery. And if she divorces her husband and marries another man, she commits adultery' (Mark 10:11–12). However, in Matthew's gospel there is something of an anomaly, because Jesus appears to allow divorce for unfaithfulness: 'anyone who divorces his wife, except for marital unfaithfulness, and marries another woman commits adultery' (Matthew 19:9).

Some Christians argue that this makes divorce permissible because adultery breaks the exclusive marriage relationship and commitment beyond repair. That said, it may provide permissible grounds for divorce but it does not mean there must always be a divorce. Selwyn Hughes, in *Marriage as God Intended* (Kingsway, 1983), argues that divorce need not be the inevitable end to marriage but rather that the Christian ought to forgive and seek reconciliation. However, if adultery is the only permissible grounds for divorce, then a Christian who seeks a divorce for any other reason, including cruelty, could be said to be acting immorally.

The major Christian denominations agree that, ideally, marriage should be for life, but they vary in how rigorously they apply biblical teaching. The Roman Catholic Church forbids divorce. In other churches, decisions concerning, for example, whether divorced Christians may marry again in church, will often be matters of conscience or the opinion of an individual priest.

Secular ethicists argue that there are many ways in which the marital bond of trust and commitment can be broken, and that it is unreasonable to refuse to allow a person suffering from, for example, severe physical abuse from their partner, to be prevented from obtaining a divorce.

John Robinson and situation ethics

In his controversial book *Honest to God* (SCM, 1963), which was influenced by the existential Christian thinking of Paul Tillich, Dietrich Bonheoffer and Joseph Fletcher, John A. T. Robinson argued that Christian moral teaching needed to change. He felt that Christianity was associated with traditional morality and that, although it had appeared to work in the past, it needed to adapt itself to the demands of the modern age. Robinson claimed that Christian morality was based on laws apparently handed down by God that were assumed to be eternally valid for human behaviour. These laws said that certain things were always wrong (sins) while others were always right. He highlighted this in the example of marriage: 'There is, for instance, a deep division on the interpretation of the "indissolubility" of marriage. There are those who say that "indissoluble" means "ought not to be dissolved" ought **never** to be dissolved. There are others who take it to mean "cannot be dissolved".'

Robinson argued that the Christian view of marriage was based on the absolute command of God. Yet this was an unrealistic position, which most people could not match up to and that, in reality 'it is a position that men honour much more in the breach than the observance'. Robinson believed that the moral and ethical teachings of Jesus were not intended to 'be understood legalistically, as prescribing what all Christians must do, whatever the circumstances... they are illustrations of what love may at any moment require of anyone'. He said that Jesus' teaching on marriage was not a law that stated: 'that divorce is always and in every case the greater of two evils...

Taking it further...

John Robinson claimed that the views of conservative religious morality were based on the belief that marriage is some kind of metaphysical reality that survives independently of the actual physical relationship and that cannot be affected by events: 'It is not a question of "Those whom God has joined together let no man put asunder": no man could if he tried' (*Honest to God*, SCM, 1963).

it is saying that utterly unconditional love, admits of no accommodation; you cannot define in advance situations in which it can be satisfied with less than complete and unreserved self-giving'.

For Robinson, it was inappropriate to say that sexual relations before marriage or getting a divorce are inherently wrong or sinful. He believed that the truly wrong thing is a lack of love. He cited Joseph Fletcher: '"If the emotional and spiritual welfare of both parents and children in a **particular** family can be served best by divorce, wrong and cheapjack as divorce commonly is, then love requires it"… And this is the criterion for every form of behaviour, inside marriage or out of it, in sexual ethics or in any other field. For **nothing else** makes a thing right or wrong' (*Honest to God*, SCM, 1963).

Homosexuality

Homosexuality is a term that applies to both men and women who have sexual feelings towards members of the same sex and identify themselves as being homosexual. In the UK today there is a growing acceptance of homosexuality and, in legal terms, homosexuality in regarded the same as heterosexuality, as same-sex relationships between consenting adults (those over the age of 16) in private.

The international Aids charity 'Avert' estimates that about 9% of women and 5% of men in the UK have had a sexual experience with a partner of the same sex. The present legislation concerning the rights of homosexuals has its origins in the 1957 Wolfenden Committee report on homosexuality that resulted in the Sexual Offences Act 1957, which went a considerable way towards ending intolerance and inequality against homosexuals.

The Civil Partnership Act of 2004 changed life radically for many same-sex couples

Homosexuality is a human rights issue and for many years it was felt that gay and lesbian marriage should be permitted in the same way that heterosexual marriage is. To that end, the government passed the Civil Partnership Act 2004, which became law in December 2005, allowing same-sex couples to register their partnership legally in a civil ceremony. Civil partnerships give the partners the same legal rights as married couples regarding matters such as property, inheritance tax and pension benefits. In the same way as when a marriage breaks up and the couple must seek a divorce, so too the partners in a civil partnership must go through a formal court action to dissolve their union. However, despite such public moves to win acceptance for homosexual couples, there are still problems and many people hold very strongly to the view that homosexuality is immoral, while others are openly hostile, as attacks on homosexual individuals and organisations so graphically demonstrate.

The causes of homosexuality

The origin and causes of homosexuality are still not fully known. Sigmund Freud claimed that homosexuality is a personality disorder resulting from a person's failure to deal with repressed issues of sexuality from infancy and to develop fully into mature sexuality. He claimed to have traced the causes of homosexuality, and indeed all sexual dysfunctions, back to the relationship between a child and his or her parents. Such a view was supported by

Elizabeth Moberly, who, in *Homosexuality: A New Christian Ethic* (James Clark, 1983), wrote: 'A homosexual orientation does not depend on a genetic predisposition, hormonal imbalance, or abnormal learning processes, but on difficulties in the parent–child relationships, especially in the earlier years of life'.

More recently, many researchers believe that homosexuality may be the result of an imbalance of the hormones or a genetic predisposition. Scientists have attempted to identify a 'homosexual gene', which would go some way to proving that homosexuality is a natural condition for some people.

However, critics argue that the discovery of a homosexual gene may cause more ethical dilemmas because parents may want to 'screen' their children for homosexuality with the hope of finding a 'cure' if they tested positive. In *Sexual Deviation* (Penguin, 1964), psychiatrist Anthony Storr wrote that homosexuals 'have a vested interest in affirming that their condition is an inborn abnormality rather than the result of circumstances; for any other explanation is bound to imply a criticism of themselves or their families and usually of both'.

Christianity and homosexuality

Christians are, for many reasons, deeply divided over the issue of homosexuality. On a natural law basis, homosexual sex cannot lead to reproduction and, because homosexual marriage would be considered invalid, then all homosexual sexual relationships are sinful. For many, including the Roman Catholic Church, homosexuality is contrary to the will of God: 'In sacred scripture homosexual acts are condemned as a serious depravity and presented as a sad consequence of rejecting God' (Roman Catholic Church, *Declaration on Sexual Ethics*, 1975).

In the *Catechism of the Catholic Church* (paras 2357–2359), the Roman Catholic Church teaches that homosexuals should be treated with respect, compassion and sensitivity and discrimination must be avoided. Homosexual feelings are not wrong, but putting those feelings into practice is. It is the actions, not the inclinations, that are sinful. They are sinful because they are contrary to God's will and contrary to natural law because they do not allow for reproduction. Homosexuals are, therefore, encouraged to pray and seek the help and support of their church to live a life of chastity.

There are many critics of the Catholic Church's standpoint. In his article *Homosexuality, Morals and the Law of Nature* (1997), Burton Leiser argues that, taking the Catholic view to its logical conclusion, if the purpose of sex is reproduction, a marriage between elderly or infertile couples who cannot have children must also be wrong.

Kate Saunders and Peter Stamford, in their book *Catholics and Sex* (Heinemann, 1992), observe that some Catholic cardinals have expressed views about homosexuals that could be seen as intolerant and that the Church may act in a discriminatory way against homosexuals in matters such as teaching and adoption. Arcigay, an Italian gay rights organisation, has suggested that the Catholic Church's teaching may be a factor in violence and intolerance. It estimates that, each year, more than 150 gay men are murdered in Italy.

Taking it further...

A supporter of the view that homosexuality is genetic is Nina Rosenstand, who argues that if this were proved then the objections to homosexuality as a moral choice that goes against nature would no longer be valid. There would then be no reason to discriminate against homosexuals in the belief that they had made an immoral choice.

Taking it further...

Burton Leiser, in *Homosexuality, Morals and the Law of Nature* (Macmillan, 1997), suggests that sexual organs are not only for reproduction but also for providing pleasure in oneself and others and that the Church is wrong to condemn people who use sex for pleasure rather than reproduction. This is not incompatible with the teaching of Paul in 1 Corinthians 7:3: 'The husband should give to his wife her conjugal rights, and likewise the wife to her husband'.

Taking it further...

Many liberal Christians argue that the important thing in any relationship, homosexual or heterosexual, is the quality of the love between the partners. They say that, as everyone is made in the image of God, then, if God creates homosexuals, they must be in his image too, because God would not have created 'disordered' human beings.

For Christians from other denominations, homosexuality is sometimes regarded as the natural way some people have been created by God and that homosexuals should be as welcome in the Christian community as heterosexuals. The Church of England does not recommend the physical expression of homosexual orientation but does acknowledge that the Church must respect those who 'are conscientiously convinced that they have more hope of growing in love for God and neighbour with the help of a loving and faithful homophile partnership, in intention lifelong, where mutual self-giving includes the expression of their attachment' (*What the Churches Say*, 2nd edition, CEM, 1995). More liberal still, the Lesbian and Gay Christian Movement maintains that 'human sexuality in all its richness is a gift from God gladly to be accepted, enjoyed and honoured'. This view finds some support in the Methodist Church, which declares: 'For homosexual men and women permanent relationships characterised by love can be an appropriate and Christian way of expressing their sexuality'. In *The Body in Context: Sex and Catholicism* (Academi, 2001), Gareth Moore suggests that the Bible requires Christians to help and support those who are marginalised in society, which would include homosexuals: 'God chose the weak things of the world to shame the strong. He chose the lowly things of this world and the despised things' (1 Corinthians 1:28).

The official position of the Church of England was established at the 1998 Lambeth Conference of Bishops, which declared that there were four positions from which homosexuality could be viewed, ranging from the most conservative to most liberal.

- Homosexuality is a disorder from which the Christian can seek deliverance.

- Homosexual relationships should be celibate.

- Whilst exclusive homosexual relationships fall short of God's best for man, they are to be preferred over promiscuous ones.

- The Church should fully accept homosexual partnerships and welcome homosexuals into the priesthood.

Within the Church of England many high-ranking clergymen have admitted to being homosexual, although this has not always had a happy result. In July 2003, following an outcry from the evangelical wing of the Anglican Church, Canon Jeffrey John, an open homosexual although celibate priest, reluctantly withdrew his acceptance of the post of Bishop of Reading. He did this to avoid creating a worldwide split in the Anglican Church over homosexual priests. This caused great division in the Church. On one side, evangelicals were pleased, taking the view expressed by Dr Philip Giddings of Greyfriars Church, who argued that the appointment of Jeffrey John was wrong in the first place because: 'We are not free to discard what is said in the Bible, however unpopular'. On the other side this view dismayed many liberal members of the Church, including the Dean of Southwark, the Very Reverend Colin Slee, who, in support of Jeffrey John, said: 'Canon John has become the victim of appalling prejudice and abuse which has its main proponents within the Church of England... the news will hurt thousands of Christian people who are not gay but believe strongly in God's love and redemption for all his children equally'.

Caught in the middle, and anxious to avoid a division in the Church, the Archbishop of Canterbury, Dr Rowan Williams said: 'This has been a time of open and painful confrontation in which some of our bonds of mutual trust have been severely strained'.

Later in 2003, a schism did finally develop within the Anglican Church worldwide (the Anglican Communion). The split happened between the liberal churches of the West and the traditional churches in Africa, most notably Nigeria where homosexuality is illegal and where, in some areas, offenders are stoned to death. The Nigerian church, which has 17 million members, openly opposed the ordination of a gay bishop, Gene Robinson, in the USA. A few months later, President Oluisegun Obasanjo of Nigeria said of homosexuality: 'Such a tendency is clearly un-Biblical, unnatural and definitely unAfrican'.

The President was supported by his Information Minister Frank Nweke, who said: 'In most cultures in Nigeria, same sex relationships, sodomy and the likes of that, are regarded as abominable'.

In September 2005, Archbishop Peter Akinola announced that the Nigerian Church was to break away from the western churches (the see of Canterbury), because they had strayed too far away from biblical teachings concerning homosexuality. The man at the centre of the controversy, Bishop Gene Robinson said: 'I believe that the acceptance of gay and lesbian people into the life of the church is something that is going to happen... it will happen in God's time'.

Archbishops Rowan Williams and Peter Akinola

The Bible and homosexuality

There are several passages in the Bible that seem to condemn homosexual practices. The scriptures suggest that the only sexual relationship that God approves of is one between married heterosexual partners. The creation narratives describe woman as being created especially for man: 'a helper suitable for him' (Genesis 2:18). Moreover, the most important aspect of the marriage bond is the sexual relationship between partners, and the requirement to reproduce: 'Be fruitful and increase' (Genesis 9:1). Clearly a homosexual partnership does not have this potential and could be said to be, in the biblical sense, unnatural.

In several passages the biblical writers appear to condemn homosexual practices and, in Old Testament times, it carried the death penalty: 'If a man lies with a man as one lies with a woman, both of them have done what is detestable. They must be put to death' (Leviticus 20:13), and 'Do not lie with a man as one lies with a woman; that is detestable' (Leviticus 18:22). In *Homosexuality and the Western Christian Tradition* (Longmans, 1955), D. S. Bailey wrote: 'It is hardly open to doubt, that both the laws in Leviticus relate to ordinary homosexual acts between men'.

In the New Testament, Paul included homosexuality in his list of moral wrongdoing that could jeopardise a person's chances of eternal life: 'Do not be deceived: Neither the sexually immoral, nor idolaters, nor adulterers, nor male prostitutes nor homosexual offenders... will inherit the kingdom of God' (1 Corinthians 6:9–10).

While some scholars such as Bailey have suggested that the biblical views on homosexuality are based on ancient cultures and traditions and are not relevant today, nevertheless many Christians believe that there is a strong biblical argument against homosexuality. They argue (controversially) that homosexuality is sinful and can only be dealt with through repentance, forgiveness, prayer and healing.

Taking it further...

Paul seemed to believe that homosexuality was the result of sin and the Fall, after which: 'Men also abandoned natural relations with women and were inflamed with lust for one another. Men committed indecent acts with other me' (Romans 1:27).

The Westboro Baptist Church picket against homosexuality in the United States. The church members believe that because of homosexuals and America's rebellious and immoral conduct God has brought on acts of terrorism as a way of punishing society

Taking it further...

The British film *Priest* (1997) is very useful as a stimulus for debate about both homosexuality and the celibacy of the Roman Catholic priesthood. It can provide a helpful case study for considering the dilemma within sexual ethics and is worth watching.

This teaching is associated with strongly conservative evangelical Christians, the majority of whom are nevertheless compassionate in their approach to homosexual people. However, at the furthest end of the conservative spectrum is the highly controversial Westboro Baptist Church, which hosts the violently homophobic web site www.godhatesfags.com. Their teaching is the worst example of Christian intolerance to homosexuality and should not be seen to represent the norm. However, it makes interesting, if sobering, reading.

Homosexuality and morality

Some ethicists argue that, although homosexuality is an important issue for religious believers, nevertheless it may not be an issue of serious ethical concern. John Harris, in *The Value of Life* (Routledge, 1984), claimed that sexual activities are an issue of manners and etiquette rather than ethics. He maintained that because homosexuality does not cause harm to society as a whole, such sexual relationships should be private and free from moral and ethical judgments.

For many religious believers, the issue is not so much one of sexual orientation but of sexual activity; the former may not be a matter of choice, but the latter is. A person cannot choose to be a homosexual but can choose not to be sexually active. In *Homosexuality and the Bible* (Grove Books, 1996), Mark Bonnington and Bob Fyall suggest that the solution lies in loving, but non-genital, same-sex relationships: 'An important contribution can be made through the rehabilitation of friendships between persons of the same sex. Warm companionship without any sexual element is not something that should be regarded as odd by the Christian community. Rather, it is to be welcomed as a valuable way of developing affectionate bonds within the church and providing the human support and comfort that most of us find we need'.

Pornography

Pornography comes from the Greek *pornographos*, meaning 'the writing of harlots', and originally referred to descriptions by prostitutes of their activities in the ancient world, sometimes graphically in early works of art.

Today pornography is widely available through the media, including the internet and adult satellite television channels. Pornography is a widely profitable and growing industry around the world. In *Laid Bare: A Path Through the Pornography Maze* (Hodder, 1996), Claire Wilson-Thomas and Nigel Williams reported that the annual expenditure on pornography in the UK was at least £60 million. Moreover, sexual explicitness is increasing. Andrea Whittam Smith, the President of the British Board of Film Classification said: 'The amount of explicit sex we see in cinemas has gradually increased. In Britain… tolerance of sexual explicitness is increasing. We have no way of stopping cultural trends' (cited in *Laid Bare: A Path Through the Pornography Maze*, Hodder, 1996).

Religious believers are, in general, opposed to the production and use of pornographic material for a range of reasons:

- pornography is associated with violence
- pornography violates the status of human beings as made in the image of God
- pornography involves and encourages addiction and generates millions of pounds for those who produce it
- pornography encourages the subordination of women
- pornography demeans the nature of a loving sexual relationship between husband and wife
- the Christian call to holiness is undermined, encouraging Christians to adopt worldly views and conform to worldly standards
- pornography does nothing to further the Kingdom of God or man's relationship with him.

With pornographic material so easily accessible, attempts are being made to prevent its sale to minors, but this is very difficult, especially with respect to internet porn. The easy availability of pornography is becoming a serious concern. Some sociologists argue that there is a connection between pornography and violent crime. Ted Bundy, an American serial killer executed in 1989, admitted that pornography had played a decisive role in his life and his crimes. He claimed: 'I have lived in prison for a long time. And I've met a lot of men who were motivated to commit violence just like me. And without exception, every one of them was deeply involved in pornography' (cited in *Laid Bare: A Path Through the Pornography Maze*, Claire Wilson-Thomas and Nigel Williams, Hodder, 1996).

Christians believe that humanity was made in the image and likeness of God (Genesis 1:27) and as such is set apart for God's purposes. A person's life should reflect the uniqueness of their relationship with God. As all human beings are equal in value in the sight of God, then all are entitled to be treated with respect and dignity by their fellow human beings and must, in turn, respect others.

Human beings should not subject others to any acts that degrade their special status in the eyes of God. Acts of violence, humiliation and exploitation, all of which characterise pornography, are therefore wrong. Moreover, pornography can be addictive and this has a serious effect on those who have access to it.

Women and men who are involved in the production of pornography are also exploited. Very often those who become part of the pornography business do so out of financial need. Homelessness, poverty or dependence on drugs can make men and women desperate, and involvement in the pornography industry can appear to be a lucrative solution to their problems. The role of women in the pornography trade is also of concern, because pornography does not reflect love and respect for women. The marriage bond is concerned with mutual love, trust and commitment, but these are violated by the use of pornography. In *Laid Bare: A Path Through the Pornography Maze* (Hodder, 1996), Claire Wilson-Thomas and Nigel Williams offer this example: 'Sally had been happily married for ten years… when her husband started getting heavily involved with pornography… He was beginning to use violence to make her submit to his wishes. She felt less and less a person of worth and

Taking it further...

'Pornography consists in removing real or simulated sexual acts from the intimacy of the partners, in order to display them deliberately to third parties… It does grave injury to the dignity of the participants… It immerses all who are involved in the illusion of a fantasy world. It is a grave offence' (*Catechism of the Catholic Church*, 1994).

Taking it further...

In *Laid Bare: A Path Through the Pornography Maze* (Hodder, 1996), Claire Wilson-Thomas and Nigel Williams describe the experience of Mike, who was introduced to pornography by school friends: 'It did not take him long to be heavily involved with pornography: all he wanted was more porn. Soon that did not satisfy and he went to Soho to find some prostitutes so that he could experience for himself all the perversions he had been reading about… Mike is now able to look back… realising "how close I came to committing rape"'.

more and more a possession for sex ... For Sally, pornography had ruined her marriage and her life.'

Christians believe that they are required to have lives of holiness that honour and reflect the nature of God. Pornography cannot play any part in the life of a Christian who is committed to presenting him- or herself as holy and acceptable to God: 'Flee from sexual immorality... he who sins sexually sins against his own body. Do you not know that your body is a temple of the Holy Spirit, who is in you, whom you have received from God?... Therefore honour God with your body' (1 Corinthians 6:18–20).

4.2 War and peace

Key Ideas

- The changing nature of war

- How the scriptures affect religious believers' views on war

- The development of the Just War theory and its application in modern times

- The growth of the pacifist movement

- The development of the arms trade and the morality of warfare

The nature of war

The Vietnam War (1965–75) had a profound impact on the United States. Over 58,000 Americans died in the conflict. 'Let every nation know, whether, it wishes us well or ill, that we shall pay any price, bear any burden, meet any hardship, support any friend, oppose any foe, in order to assure the survival of liberty.'
President John F. Kennedy, 1961

War can be defined as armed hostilities between peoples. It is usually between peoples of different nations but can sometimes be between peoples within the same nation, **civil** war, or between one small group and the state, **guerrilla** war. The aim is usually for one group to win by inflicting as much damage as possible on the other while receiving the minimum damage itself. In the 20th century 187 million people died as a result of wars and there has been no time since 1914 when there was not a war being fought somewhere in the world. Yet the nature of war has changed. In the first half of the 20th century wars were fought between sovereign states and empires, using huge conscript armies and involving entire populations. However, increasingly, civilians, rather than military personnel, have suffered as a result of war. For example, in the First World War only 5% of those who died were civilians; in the Second World War nearly 60% of those who died were civilians. Today, nearly 80% of the victims of modern wars are civilians. In the war in the Sudan in 1998, 97% of the casualties were civilians.

Today, conflict is carried out not between massive armies but between small numbers of troops, often armed with high-tech weapons. There is no declaration of war and no formal act of surrender and declaration of peace. Indeed, there is often no obvious end in sight. Instead, in places like the

Middle East, Angola and Chechnya, war is over ideologies and beliefs. So instead of wars between nations, we have 'war on terrorism' and the enemy is not another country but the 'axis of evil'. The aim of the war is not the wholesale destruction of the enemy but the defeat of the armed forces, and the immobilizing of facilities, followed by the establishment of peace and order. Moreover, there is no effective global authority that has the power to settle disputes.

The world spends far more on arms than it does on education. Many feel that countries who sell arms to others should act in a morally responsible way. In 1994, the Church of England recommended to the UK government that there should be a 'refusal of arms transfers to countries engaged in, or likely to engage in, aggression… and countries guilty of grave and consistent patterns of human rights violations'.

The Bible and war

In the Old Testament, God engages in conflict with those who oppose him and his will for his covenant people. Rules laid down for warfare allowed married men to be exempted from military service (Deuteronomy 24:5) and it was also clear that if someone was not invited to take part in a war that they felt left out (Judges 8:1). War in those times was brutal and cruel and the armies of Israel would slaughter their enemies to the last man: 'Joshua spared no one, everyone was put to death. This was what the Lord God of Israel had commanded' (Joshua 10:40).

God's ultimate aim is to bring about a holy people who can carry out his purposes. Enemy nations are used as instruments of judgment on God's people, but then will face God's judgment themselves: 'When the Lord has finished all his work on Mount Zion and on Jerusalem he will punish the arrogant boasting of the King of Assyria and his haughty pride' (Isaiah 10:12). The people of God are warned of the dangers of relying on military strength and the dangers of engaging in international intrigue unless it is guided and directed by God: 'He will judge between the nations and will settle disputes for many peoples. They will beat their swords into ploughshares and their spears into pruning hooks. Nation will not take up sword against nation, nor will they train for war any more' (Isaiah 2:4).

The New Testament

In the New Testament warfare is seen as a spiritual battle against evil that will culminate in a final spiritual battle at the end of time, which will be lead by the Messiah and his heavenly armies: 'And when the thousand years are ended, Satan will be loosed from his prison and will come out to deceive the nations which are at the four corners of the earth… And they marched up over the broad earth and surrounded the camp of the saints and the beloved city, but fire came down from heaven and consumed them, and the devil who had deceived them was thrown into the lake of fire and sulphur where the beast and the false prophet were, and they will be tormented day and night for ever and ever' (Revelation 20:7–10).

Paul teaches that believers must prepare to engage in direct conflict not only against the forces of Satan in the spiritual world: 'Put on the full armour of God so that you can take your stand against the devil's schemes. For our

Taking it further...

The biblical writers were aware that war is rooted in human selfishness and greed. Rivalry over land and wealth, international and individual pride and status are more likely to result in war than conflicts emerging out of a genuine desire to fight evil with good.

struggle is not against flesh and blood, but against… the powers of this dark world and against the spiritual forces of evil in the heavenly realms' (Ephesians 6:11–12).

Jesus refused to use military power: 'Put your sword back into its place; for all who take the sword will perish by the sword. Do you think that I cannot appeal to my Father and he will at once send me more than twelve legions of angels? But how then should the scriptures be fulfilled?' (Matthew 26:52–54). Jesus taught ideals of righteousness and peace, to love enemies and resist revenge: 'Love your enemies, do good to those that hate you' (Luke 6:27). Jesus's opposition to violence, however, is not against the prevention of wrong, or protection of those in need, but against personal insult and threat: 'Do not resist an evil person. If someone strokes you on the right cheek, turn to him your other also' (Matthew 5:39).

Paul confirmed the same teaching in his letter to the Romans, a church which faced real issues of how to respond to persecution: 'Do not be overcome by evil, but overcome evil with good' (Romans 12:21). 'Everyone must submit himself to the governing authorities, for there is no authority except that which God has established' (Romans 13:1).

In *An Outline of Biblical Theology* (Westminster, 1946), Millar Burrows writes: 'Both Old and New Testaments offer ground for assurance that any people or nation, however sinful, may by repentance and reformation find mercy and redemption, and any nation may be brought to destruction by corruption and injustice… The destruction of the world's peace or of civilisation itself by nations which are ruled by hatred or greed and do not desire peace or justice must be prevented.' Burrows argues that all nations should guard against the growth of international distrust and suspicion and rely on the principle of love in their dealings with others.

John Stott, in *New Issues Facing Christians Today* (Marshall Pickering, 1999), argues that war may sometimes be the lesser of two evils but should only be resorted to with the greatest reluctance: 'the quest for peace is much more costly than appeasement. We admire the loyalty, self-sacrifice and courage of serving soldiers. Yet we must not glamorise or glorify war in itself… in some circumstances it may be defended as the lesser of two evils, but it could never be regarded by the Christian mind as more than a painful necessity in a fallen world.'

War and the religious believer

While the Bible speaks of war against evil, the problem for the religious believer is the growth in the power of humanity's ability to wage war with weapons of mass destruction. War involves whole civilisations and has the potential to lay waste to the entire planet.

In recent times, however, there has been a gradual change in the public's perception of war. Nina Rosenstand in *The Moral of the Story* (Mayfield, 2000), observes that the idea of war as fulfilling heroic values vanished with the end of the First World War. However, she maintains that the concept of honour in war is still important: 'Although war is, for most people, the last moral option for dealing with conflict (and no moral option at all for pacifists) we can still talk about the moral conduct of the soldier… Even in stories with an anti-war message, the honour, decency, and heroism of the characters are emphasised by being contrasted with the meaninglessness of war.'

Today, people are far more likely to question the legitimacy of going to war than they did in the past. There was a great deal of questioning in the USA following the war in Vietnam and, more recently, both the USA and UK governments were put under intense scrutiny over the issue of whether it was right for the USA and UK to invade Iraq in March 2003 and topple Saddam Hussein.

Questions have also been asked about NATO's bombing of Yugoslavia in 1999 and the failure to intervene militarily during the conflicts in Bosnia and Rwanda. The public has grown increasing concerned because modern methods of warfare affect civilians, for example the terrorist attacks on the World Trade Centre in September 2001 and the tube train bombings in London in July 2005.

The Allied bombing of Dresden in 1945 resulted in an horrific number of civilian deaths

The Just War

The Bible does not offer a clear answer to the question of whether or not a religious believer should participate in war, although the early Church took the teachings of Jesus literally and adopted the principal of non-retaliation and absolute pacifism.

Christianity became the state religion of the Roman Empire in 324 CE. When Rome was facing defeat by the Visigoths in 410 CE, many believed that the failure of Christians to fight was weakening Rome's defence. To resolve this situation, the Church turned away from total pacifism and accepted the use of armed force by the state in certain circumstances. Augustine put forward two conditions under which a war could justifiably be waged:

- it was declared by a legitimate authority
- there was a just cause.

From this slowly developed the Christian form of the **Doctrine of the Just War Theory**. Thomas Aquinas added a further condition, namely that there had to be a right intention, and the rest were added later. Today, the doctrine consists of nine principles, six concerned with the beginning of war and three with the conduct of the war, discussed below. The Just War Theory is based on the belief that, while life is sacred, it may, at times, be taken in order to maintain justice and to protect or defend the lives of others.

When it is right to go to war: *jus ad bellum*

1 War must be in a just cause
A war is only just if it is fought for a reason that is justified and that carries sufficient moral weight. The just cause is to put right a wrong or to prevent a wrong from happening, for example to save life or protect human rights; to secure justice or remedy injustice. It must be defensive, not aggressive. Just causes may include self-defence against an invader or assisting a friendly nation that is under attack.

Taking it further...

The principle of the Just War Theory is not to justify all wars, and there are times when the potential cost of war, in terms of lives lost and the long- and short-term effects on the community, may mean some injustices are left unremedied. Discretion still remains the better part of valour.

The Japanese attack on Pearl Harbour, 1941 was a shocking event that galvanized the United States into fighting in World War II

The concept of defensive war is problematic, however, because it can lead to the assumption that the defender is always right and the aggressor always wrong. Intervention in an unjust situation, for example Saddam Hussein's regime in Iraq, could be considered technically aggressive but justifiable: 'War is permissible only to confront a real and certain danger' (Catholic Bishops of America Pastoral Letter, *The Challenge of Peace; God's Promise and Our Response*, 1983).

2 War must be declared by a competent authority

Only a war declared by the government or ruler of the state with the legitimate authority to declare war can be a just war, although in the Islamic concept of *jihad*, the legitimate authority is that of a religious leader. The Japanese attack on Pearl Harbor in 1941 is a famous example of an attack made before the legitimate authority had declared war.

The Catholic Church's position can be summarised thus: 'In the Catholic tradition the right to use force has always been joined to the common good; war must be declared by those with responsibility for public order, not by private groups and individuals' (Catholic Bishops of America Pastoral Letter, *The Challenge of Peace; God's Promise and Our Response*, 1983).

In recent times many have argued that the only legitimate authority able to declare war should be the United Nations, rather than individual countries, because the United Nations is the highest authority in the world and, under Article 2.4 of the United Nations Charter, member nations are required to 'refrain in their international relations from the threat or use of force'. Critics, however, say that the United Nations does not have the authority to declare war, and that this authority still rests with individual nations and alliances such as NATO.

3 There must be just intention

The intention must be as just as the cause, i.e. a war should not be undertaken with the deliberate intention of assassinating a country's leader or in a spirit of hatred or revenge. Just intentions might include restoring peace, righting a wrong or assisting the innocent. Wars fought from bad motives often lead to an unjust peace that leads to further conflict, for example, the harsh settlement on Germany at the end of the First World War was one of the factors that caused the Second World War. Aquinas stipulated that a war must be fought only for: 'the advancement of good, or the avoidance of evil'.

4 There must be comparison of justice on both sides

Both sides of the conflict should be examined and compared and, in principle, both should have a just reason to take up arms.

5 War must be a last resort

War should only be resorted to after all negotiation, arbitration and non-military sanctions have failed.

6 There should be a reasonable likelihood of success

This stems from the idea that war is a great evil and that it is wrong to cause death, pain and suffering if there is no chance of success. There should be a realistic prospect of the outcome resulting in a better state of affairs than before the war. Peace and justice must be restored afterwards. However, it may be necessary, for example, to fight a larger force in order to protect innocent people. Moreover, it implies that weak nations should never wage war against bigger, more aggressive ones.

Taking it further...

In recent years, while the United Nations has not actually declared war, it has passed resolutions that have been regarded as lawful authorisation, for example for coalition forces to expel Iraqi invaders from Kuwait and to preserve no-fly zones in Bosnia. In this respect, the UK and the USA have been criticised for invading Iraq without the authority of the United Nations.

Taking it further...

Sometimes weaker nations may go on to win a war. For example, Britain stood alone in the early years of the Second World War against the apparently overwhelming might of Germany, yet went on, with her allies, to win.

7 Proportionality

There must be a proportionate response between the injustice that led to the war and the damage, suffering and death caused by the war itself. Excessive or disproportionate violence should be avoided: 'the damage to be inflicted and the costs incurred by war must be proportionate to the good expected by taking up arms' (Catholic Bishops of America Pastoral Letter, *The Challenge of Peace; God's Promise and Our Response*, 1983).

Conduct in war: *jus in bello*

1 There should be a reasonable proportion between the injustice being fought and the suffering inflicted by war

The cause of justice must not be upheld by unjust means. Robert Holmes in *On War and Morality* (Princeton University Press, 1992) wrote: 'Unless one can justify the actions necessary to waging war, one cannot justify the conduct of war'.

2 Proportionality must be exercised

The use of weapons must be proportional to the threat and only minimum force should be used.

3 Warfare must be discriminate

Civilians should not be direct targets. The principle is that the intentional killing of civilians is prohibited. The Geneva Convention lays down that civilians are not to be attacked, this includes direct attacks and indiscriminate attacks against civilian areas. To some extent, new weapons are often intended to avoid civilian casualties, for example in the 1991 Gulf War a number of high-tech weapons such as laser-guided bombs and cruise missiles were used on cities but aimed at specifically non-civilian targets. Success was, however, limited, and some civilians still died. This was made worse by the fact that many military installations were placed in civilian areas. However, it is difficult to make a precise distinction between combatants and non-combatants because many civilians work directly in support of the war effort, even while they may not be engaged in conflict. The use of nuclear warfare renders discrimination impossible.

Criticisms of the Just War

The principles of the Just War Theory have come under considerable criticism from those who maintain that:

- all war is unjust

- the theory is unrealistic and pointless because nations decide to fight wars on the basis of realism and strength, not ethical theory

- the theory carries no guarantee that it will be appropriately applied or that it will be applicable to all circumstances

- the theory could be applied to any war to make it appear to be just, however both sides will say that their claim to justice is legitimate and yet both claims cannot be equally valid

- the fact that there are conditions in which a just war can be fought means that the war is more likely to be fought

- terrorists are often uninterested in ethical and moral considerations and to follow a moral way would therefore put a nation at a disadvantage when fighting terrorists.

Taking it further...

The Vatican statement *Gaudium et Spes* (Article 80) says: 'an act of war aimed indiscriminately at the destruction of entire cities or of extensive areas along with their populations is a crime against God and man himself' (*Concise Guide to the Documents of the Second Vatican Council*, Adrian Hastings, Darton, Longman & Todd, 1968).

What arguments does Osama bin Laden employ to justify the killing of civilians?

Members of organisations such as the Campaign for Nuclear Disarmament (CND) argue that weapons of mass destruction make the Just War Theory unworkable. Nuclear weapons do not prevent wars, because wars still go on without them, all they do is threaten the annihilation of everything. Others, however, argue that nuclear weapons are so awful that, in fact, they are preventing conflict, because nobody is really prepared to use them. Moreover, the use of nuclear shelters would ensure that many people would survive. Some suggest that the tactical use of small nuclear weapons to destroy enemy bases may be permissible.

The existence of nuclear arms goes way beyond the conditions in warfare that were envisaged by Aquinas. In the nuclear age, religious believers may feel that they have no option but to revert to pacifism rather than risk such devastation.

Finally, critics of the Just War Theory argue that it sets a moral standard that is unrealistic. There may be reasons for waging war that cannot be 'just' reasons if justice is defined as meaning fairness and equality on both sides, because that is not the reality of war. War is, of itself, unjust. Peter Vardy noted: 'The strongest argument against just war theories is the high moral standards they assume by the parties to the potential war. To adhere to the just war conditions, a state has to maintain an almost impossibly high moral standard as any breach of the conditions lays the state open to the sort of challenge it itself is fighting against. The very fact that innocents may be killed in a conflict can infringe the rules of proportionality and discrimination' (*The Puzzle of Ethics*, Fount, 1994).

Pacifism

A **pacifist** is someone who is opposed to war and violence and believes that it is wrong to harm or kill other people. For them, killing is wrong and, therefore, war is wrong. Bertrand Russell, in a *History of Western Philosophy* (Routledge, 2004), said: 'Patriots always talk of dying for their country, but never of killing for their country'.

There are several types of pacifism:

- **absolute pacifism**, the belief that it is never right to take part in war because nothing can justify the killing of human beings
- **relative pacifism**, war is wrong but there may be circumstances when war is the lesser of two evils
- **selective/nuclear pacifism**, opposition to wars involving weapons of mass destruction because of the devastating consequences of such weapons and the fact that wars using such weapons are unwinnable
- **active pacifism**, actively engaging in political activity and campaigns to promote peace.

In time of war pacifists may become **conscientious objectors**. They may still play a part during a war, for example as emergency workers in hospitals or the fire service. Many pacifists served in both world wars, caring for wounded and dying soldiers on the battlefield, a job that required considerable courage. In peacetime, pacifists may campaign and demonstrate against warfare and work to change society by removing the causes of war, such as injustice, oppression and exploitation. Many pacifists believe that people must take more seriously their responsibility for less violence in the world and actively seek to form a more peaceful method of co-existence as human brothers and sisters together, sharing a world for the benefit of all. Christian pacifists believe that war is incompatible with Christian teachings regarding the need to love your enemies. Absolute or total pacifism requires that there is no military activity, even if it is apparently just.

Absolute pacifism is the official stance today of such Christian groups as the Quakers, whose founder, George Fox, believed in the 'Brotherhood of Man' and that God dwelt inside everyone. Quakers believe that war is contrary to the teachings of Jesus: 'the spirit of Christ, which leads us into all truth, will never move us to fight and war against any man' (Declaration of the Society of Friends (Quakers)).

For pacifists, war is cruel, immoral, unjust and a waste of life and resources. Instead, they claim, disputes should be solved in peaceful ways, for example the non-violent campaigns led by Gandhi and Martin Luther King.

The aim of non-violent conflict is to convert your opponent and to help them to change their mind away from aggression. An important element is to give them a face-saving way out, rather than humiliate them. Some techniques of peaceful protest include peaceful demonstrations and sit-ins, vigils, fasting and hunger strikes. At a speech in Harijan in 1936, Gandhi said: 'Non-violence is a power which can be wielded equally by all – children, young men and women or grown-up people, provided they have a living faith in the God of Love and have therefore accepted equal love for all mankind'. For Christians, pacifism comes from the teaching of Jesus in the Sermon on the Mount (Matthew 5:38–48), where he taught his followers not to resist an evil person but to turn the other cheek, love their enemies, pray for their persecutors, and give up their right to *lex talionis*, justifiable and limited retribution for injustice.

Mahatma Gandhi, 1869–1948 – the great pacifist and campaigner for social justice

Over the centuries, Christians have worked to change things, to create better conditions for social justice, to build loving, trusting and co-operative relationships between different peoples and nations and to campaign against massive expenditure on weapons. They follow the famous teaching of Jesus: 'Love your neighbour as yourself' (Matthew 22:39).

Jesus put this teaching into effect himself. He refused to rebel against the occupying Roman power, and did not advocate tax avoidance or civil disobedience. At his trial, he refused to fight back. He was the innocent martyr: 'led like the lamb to the slaughter and as a sheep before her shearers is silent, so he did not open his mouth' (Isaiah 53:7). On the cross he forgave those who crucified him: 'Father, forgive them, for they do not know what they are doing' (Luke 23:34) and in the Sermon on the Mount, Jesus promised blessings on those who seek peace: 'Blessed are the peacemakers' (Matthew 5:10). In Romans 13, Paul teaches that the state should be respected as the legitimate bearer of God's authority to rule and that rebellion against it is disobedience to God. He proposed that in dealings in general with the world, Christians should not meet their enemies with violence but with kindness, and so 'heap burning coals upon their heads', and yet respect the legitimacy of the ruling authority to punish evil doers.

Many Christians have tried to develop non-violent methods of resolving conflicts, through negotiation and compromise. Pope John Paul II declared: 'do not believe in violence, do not support violence. It is not the Christian way... Believe in peace and forgiveness and love, for they are in Christ.'

Christians who take the view that violent struggle for justice is, sometimes, legitimate, may adopt relative, selective or nuclear pacifism. They would argue that the Bible emphasises the importance of avoiding the 'shedding of innocent blood' (Genesis 9:4, Leviticus 17:11). The view is that the governmental authority that God has given to the legitimate rulers of the state must only be used to protect civilians and to bring about a just end by just means.

Discrimination and proportionality are crucial. The Second Vatican Council declared: 'Any act of war aimed indiscriminately at the destruction of entire cities or of extensive areas along with their population is a crime against God and man himself' (*Concise Guide to the Documents of the Second Vatican Council*, Adrian Hastings, Darton, Longman & Todd, 1968). In a similar vein, the Church of England's unofficial report, *The Church and the Bomb* (Hodder and Stoughton, 1982), concluded: 'the use of nuclear weapons cannot be justified. Such weapons cannot be used without harming non-combatants, and could never be proportionate to the just cause and aim of war... In our view the cause of right cannot be upheld by fighting a nuclear war.'

John Stott, in *Issues Facing Christians Today* (Marshall Pickering, 1999), said that Christian peacemakers should pray, set an example as 'a community of peace', promote public debate on issues of peace and war, and maintain a confident stance that peace is a realistic and desirable goal. 'As much as anything, they (Christians) are to live at peace with all, preach the good news of personal salvation, love their enemies, overcome evil with good, deeply respect God's creation and become ministers of reconciliation'.

One problem with pacifism is that if all warfare is rejected, this also means rejecting the possibility of fighting against a cruel aggressor in order to protect innocent civilians. For example, if Britain had not taken up arms against Hitler, then the country may have been conquered by the Nazis. Furthermore, pacifism cannot be a national policy because if a nation declares that it will never fight it leaves itself open to attack and invasion. Many argue that nations have a moral obligation to protect their citizens and pacifism does not work in the face of extreme evil.

Peter Vardy argues that the United Nations may be the right body to determine when and whether the Just War criteria apply. However, he warns that this could only work if the United Nations was: 'a truly unbiased body and not one that is dominated by the wealthy nations – as is sometimes the case at the moment'.

The morality of warfare

The international arms trade

One of the real moral dilemmas arising from the nature of modern warfare is the selling of weapons by one country to another: the **arms trade**. There are a number of viewpoints. Those in favour of the arms trade argue that the

---

Taking it further...

Reinhold Niebuhr argued that absolute pacifists were forgetting the equally important biblical principle of justice and over-emphasised peace and reconciliation. He argued that pacifists were sometimes guilty of accepting tyranny and oppression rather than fighting against evil.

selling of arms is a legitimate business practice. They argue that weapons are only tools and it is not the buying and selling of arms that is a moral issue, only using them to kill is. Arms are a form of technology and can be used properly or improperly. It is the people who use arms who are the moral or immoral agents, not the arms themselves.

If it is acceptable for one nation to own certain types of weapons, then it must be equally right for other nations to possess the same weapons. Possession of weapons is neither morally right nor morally wrong, it is value neutral.

The weapons industry creates trade and employment in Britain and elsewhere and, if the arms trade was stopped, these countries would face unemployment and a loss of trade. Moreover, if Britain did not make and sell arms, then other nations would. (This, however, was also the argument used by supporters of the slave trade in the 18th century.)

Many, including most Western nations, support the view that arms should only be sold to 'stable' or 'friendly nations' and not to potential enemies, and that these weapons should only be used in self-defence. Weapons of mass destruction, including nuclear weapons, should not be sold in order to control nuclear proliferation (too many nations having nuclear weapons).

Interestingly, it was the Western nations, including the UK, who sold huge amounts of modern weapons to Saddam Hussein before the Gulf War, making him a powerful aggressor and enemy.

Iraqi Kurd sisters walk through Halabja cemetery in northern Iraq where 5,000 people were buried following Saddam Hussein's chemical attack in 1988. The chemicals used were supplied by the United States

However, those against the arms trade argue that weapons should not be sold and that the arms trade is immoral. The view here is not only that weapons are sold to kill human beings but that the buying and selling of weapons can produce an **arms race**. This is where one country buys weapons, so its enemies buy weapons; the first county, in turn, buys even more, so its enemies buy even more; and so on. This was the case in the Cold War and, more recently, in Africa, where much of the poverty has been caused by African governments spending money on weapons, rather than on food and medicine.

The Catholic Church argues that weapons should only be sold in proportionality, i.e. just sufficient to deal with the issue. The American Bishops observed one particular issue of deep concern is that of nuclear weapons and the principle of proportionality. Many argue that such weapons cause such enormous damage and loss of life that they should never be bought and sold. Of great concern is the fact that nuclear weapons could fall into the hands of terrorists or fanatical tyrants who might use them to commit an act of atrocity against a civilian population. Of course, the problem is that nuclear weapons are here and cannot be 'dis-invented' and nuclear knowledge is part of the world. However, this does not mean that those with nuclear capability should sell such weapons to those who do not.

In the Middle East, in particular, there has been great fear, not only that Israel may have nuclear weapons, but that nations such as Iran and Syria may be developing them. Equally, in other parts of the world, such as India, Pakistan and North Korea, there has been anxiety that the possible development of nuclear weapons could lead to war.

However, nuclear weapons are not the only weapons of mass destruction. Chemical and biological weapons can be equally destructive and there are many calls for such weapons to be banned too. One of the reasons why the USA and UK invaded Iraq was because of the fear that Saddam Hussein had weapons of mass destruction that he might one day use on his enemies.

There is no easy answer to the problems raised by the arms trade. One answer might be to decommission weapons of mass destruction. Jonathan Schnell, in *The Gift of Time: The Case for Abolishing Nuclear Weapons* (Granta, 1998) quoted Robert MacNamara, an adviser to the USA government during the Cold War Arms Race, who now states: 'I think it's not only desirable but essential that we eliminate nuclear weapons. They have no military utility other than to deter one's opponents from using nuclear weapons. And if our opponent doesn't have nuclear weapons, we don't need them... using nuclear weapons against a nuclear-equipped opponent of any size at all is suicide and... using them against a non-nuclear opponent is, I think, immoral.'

Moral problems of the Just War

Some believe that nations do not have the right to wage war unless they are attacked; only the United Nations has the right to wage war. But what if the United Nations fails to act, as it failed to stop the rape, killing and genocide in Rwanda and Kosova, for example? Do individual nations have the right to wage war in that case?

In a similar way, how can the United Nations decide what a 'just cause' would be? In an article *Just War – War Against Iraq* (Dialogue, November 2002), Peter Vardy notes: 'One person's terrorist is another person's freedom fighter and deciding on justice is not easy'. Many Muslims in the Arab world thought that those who took part in the 9/11 attack on the World Trade Centre in 2001 were justified, whilst others in the West, saw them as ruthless terrorists. It seems that each side fails to understand the views of the other.

A further problem is the nature of the aggression itself. In times past, war normally meant the army of one nation physically attacking another. However, today there are different types of aggression. A nation may try to incite a minority in another nation to rise up in rebellion, or may use its economic power to impose its will on other nations. In this sense, some have argued that rich Western nations have used economic aggression to keep poor countries in a state of weakness. However, would this kind of 'aggression' give poor nations the right to wage war on rich ones?

There is also the difficult question of whether or not it is right to bomb water supplies and power stations, which affect not only the armed forces but civilians as well, particularly hospitals. The aim of such bombing is not necessarily to kill civilians, but to destroy the infrastructure of a country. Nevertheless civilians do die or suffer badly as a result. Equally, civilians suffer if a nation is subject to sanctions, with no medical supplies being allowed in, for example.

The attacks of 9/11 have changed the West's perspective of war radically

Bombing that aims to destroy the infrastructure of a nation is also morally questionable on the grounds that it seeks to destroy the society itself. This is contrary to the spirit of the Just War criteria of a proportionate response and the need to preserve the essential structures of a society.

Civilians suffered after the Gulf War in 1991 and around half a million children died as a result. In response to this, the American Secretary of State, Madeline Albright, said; 'I think this is a very hard choice, but… we think the price was worth it'.

Finally, there is the question of who is actually to blame for an unjust war. Peter Vardy argues that it is everyone who participates in it or does not protest against it. This includes politicians, the armed forces, the support staff, those who make the weapons and those who pay their taxes to finance the war effort and those who do not protest against it. In Vardy's view: 'those who remain silent and inactive in the face of injustice are morally culpable' (*The Puzzle of Ethics*, Fount, 1994).

The changing face of warfare

● Holy wars

A **holy war** is one in which religion is the driving force. It is not enough that the name of God is used in the campaign. Many wars have been fought that way, with armies believing that God was on their side, but these wars were not, strictly speaking, holy. For many people, the idea of a holy war seems to be a contradiction, because religions speak of the importance of life. Holy wars usually have three characteristics:

- the achievement of a religious goal
- authorisation by a spiritual leader
- a spiritual reward for those who take part.

The aim of a holy war, therefore, might be to spread the faith, convert the people of other nations, recover sacred places or avenge blasphemous acts. In ancient times, the authority to declare war was usually seen as God, but today it is usually regarded as the Church or the head of the religious institution concerned. In recent years, a number of Muslim groups and organisations, such as Al-Qaeda, have declared holy war or *jihad* against those they see as the enemies of Islam.

In *When God goes to War* (*The Guardian*, 29 December 2003), Karen Armstrong notes: 'The Qur'an reflects the brutal tribal warfare that afflicted Arabia during the early seventh century… The scriptures bear all the scars of their violent begetting, so it is easy for extremists to find texts that give them a seal of divine approval to hatred.'

The Qur'an teaches that Muslims should be prepared to struggle or strive in the way of Islam. The word 'strive' in Arabic is *jihad*. However, the most important aspect is the greater, or inner, *jihad*, which is a struggle that believers fight within themselves to become truly submitted to Allah. The lesser *jihad* is about the physical struggle against the enemies of Islam and there are circumstances in which Islam accepts the need for war, for example in self-defence or to fight against oppression. The Qur'an and the Hadith permit Muslims to fight if they are attacked, and Muhammad fought in wars. However, above all, Islam emphasises the ideals of justice, freedom and opposition to oppression. If there is a chance to avoid war, then this alternative, as long as it is reasonable, must be taken.

Islamic law (*shariah*) sets down very strict rules about the conduct of a military *jihad*. Self-defence is always the underlying cause, and it can only be fought to promote and protect Islam and Muslims and to put right a wrong. Quite specifically, a military *jihad* is invalid if its intention is to conquer other nations, seize territory for economic gain or force people to convert to Islam.

Today, holy wars may not be about religion at all, but about other things: capitalism, globalisation, poverty, oppression and inequality. This is reflected in the words of Osama Bin Laden after the attack on the World Trade Centre: 'Here is America struck by God Almighty in one of its vital organs so that its greatest buildings are destroyed... I swear by Almighty God... that neither the United States nor he who lives in the United States will enjoy security before... all the infidel armies leave the land of Muhammad.' Warfare does not solve the problems of greed and poverty in the world and finding peaceful solutions is the challenge that faces the leaders of all countries and all religions. In *Violence in God's Name; Religion in an Age of Conflict* (Orbis Books, 2003), Oliver McTernan wrote: 'Until each faith group is prepared to promote actively a respect for the gift of life above all other beliefs, dogmas and interests, religion will always have the power to be an exclusive, divisive and destructive force in the world'.

● War crimes

One of the moral issues to arise out of warfare is the notion that individuals can be held criminally responsible for their own actions and those of others. **War crimes** are regarded as among the worst crimes in international law.

In recent times, war crime charges have been brought against the late Serbian leader Slobodan Milosevic. He was charged with masterminding the 'ethnic cleansing' campaign that was carried out by Serbian forces during the break-up of Yugoslavia. Belgian journalist Georges Omar Ruggiu was sentenced to 12 years imprisonment for making radio broadcasts that helped to incite the attempted genocide of the Tutsi population in Rwanda.

War crimes are defined by the Geneva Convention and International Law. War crimes include:

- planning, initiating or waging a war of aggression
- committing atrocities against persons or property
- inhumane treatment, rape, extermination or enslavement of civilians
- murder of prisoners or hostages
- torture
- wanton destruction of cities, towns or villages.

The leader of a nation or group, for example an army commander, who plans, authorises or participates in such actions, is responsible for everything done by those carrying out the crimes. In addition, those who actually perform the crimes are responsible; they cannot just claim that they were obeying orders.

Taking it further...

War crimes are considered to be so serious that those who are charged with them are pursued for years, sometimes decades, and brought to justice. For example, many ex-Nazis were tried for war crimes more than 50 years after the end of the Second World War.

- **Genocide**

Perhaps the most serious war crime of all is **genocide**, which is the deliberate attempt to destroy a national, ethnic, racial or religious group. In recent times, famous examples of genocide have included:

- the Holocaust in the Second World War, in which millions of Jews, Gypsies and other groups were exterminated by the Nazis
- the massacre in Rwanda in 1994 of 800,000 Tutsis by the Hutus
- the 'ethnic cleansing' of different racial groups during the break-up of Yugoslavia between 1992 and 1995.

Holocaust survivor Rafael Lemkin described genocide as the: 'disintegration of the political and social institutions, of culture, language, national feelings, religion and the economic existence of national groups and the destruction of the personal security, liberty, dignity, and even the lives of the individuals belonging to such groups'.

CHAPTER 5
Exam guidance and sample questions

Understanding the assessment objectives

Edexcel sets out **two** assessment objectives (AO) that allow the value of work to be judged.

AO1 (28 marks for knowledge and understanding – 70% of the total marks)

You earn these marks by showing that you know the subject, understand what is relevant to the question, can present evidence and examples, and can use technical language appropriately. One of your study aims during the course should be to identify and learn the facts and vocabulary you need to know. If you do this well then you will have mastered both the relevant knowledge and the terminology and your AO1 material will be confident and convincing.

The demands of AO1 can only be met by solid learning. Under exam conditions you should be able to write 700 words to give you the best chance to fulfill the criteria. Relating your information directly to the question is vital in terms of maximizing your marks. Check the wording of the question to ensure that you use material in the right place and way, and do not just roll out a block of memorized notes without reference to what you are being asked to do with it. Using examples appropriately can boost your marks, but too much narrative, or use of ethical case studies, or incidental anecdote is not the best way to gain AO1 credit. Make sure the information you are presenting genuinely reveals you as an A level candidate, so avoid superficiality, general knowledge and repetition.

AO2 (12 marks for evaluation – 30% of the total marks)

You earn these marks by sustaining a critical line of argument and justifying a point of view.

This is the more subtle part of the question and these marks are the ones needed to push you over into the higher grade boundaries. Repetition of material from the AO1 part of the question cannot gain you further credit, so be sure that you don't reduce AO2 to learning a list of criticisms which don't reveal your ability to assess their strengths and weaknesses. Genuine evaluation grows out of an awareness of a range of views and an ability to assess which position is the stronger. Save something up for this part of the question too, perhaps a scholarly quotation or an idea which you feel is decisive for the topic. You are not expected to arrive at a definitive answer, or to come up with something original, but you must show that you are aware that there is a case to be answered, whatever your personal views on the matter. It is legitimate to refer to your own opinion, but that must be in direct response to, or supported by, scholarly opinion. The examiner is not otherwise in the slightest interested in your views!

Anything that you write which is relevant to the exam question and which meets the criteria for AO1 and AO2 will get you marks. You do not lose marks for work that fails to address the question because marking is not negative – you can only gain credit from zero upwards – but you may lose time and opportunities. For example, if you are writing about Utilitarianism, biographical details of J S Mill, however fascinating, are not going to gain credit. An understanding of his Utilitarian theory will do so. Blow by blow narrative accounts of parables will gain very little credit unless you use them to illustrate key elements of Jesus's teaching.

Don't worry if you include AO2 material in the AO1 part of the question – it will still be credited. Examiners appreciate that high level AO1 inevitably includes an evaluative element. However, if you provide AO1 material where AO2 is required you are not meeting the demands of the question. Make sure you practise applying AO2 to the material you have studied.

All of your study should be aimed at giving you the confidence and the competence to meet the two assessment objectives, so you must ask your teacher if you are not sure how to do this.

Trigger words in exam questions

Exam questions are built around trigger words which provide the instructions for how to answer the question.

	AS	A2
AO1	Describe Examine Identify Outline Select What How Illustrate For what reasons Give an account of In what ways	Analyse Clarify Compare and contrast Differentiate Distinguish between Define Examine Explain Comment critically
AO2	Comment on Consider How far To what extent Why	Assess Why Consider critically Criticise Discuss Evaluate Interpret Justify To what extent

Practise writing questions using these words and rewrite your teacher's questions using trigger words if they don't include them already. You need to be aware of the difference between 'giving an account of' and 'commenting on'. To give an account, you draw essentially on your knowledge, which you may then be required to develop through 'commenting on' it. Commenting on involves drawing conclusions about the significance and value of what you have learned. There are certain phrases which you may find useful to do this: 'This is important because...'; 'The most significant is...because'; 'However...'; 'On the other hand...'; It is likely that...because;' Therefore...'; Nevertheless...'; 'The implications of this are...'. As you work, keep asking yourself 'why is this relevant to my answer?' and 'what are the implications of this view/issue?'.

How to achieve high marks

The trigger words help to focus your answer so that you can demonstrate that you have fulfilled the overall aims of AS Religious Studies which are to:

Acquire knowledge and understanding of:
- key concepts within the chosen areas of study and how they are expressed in texts, writings, and practices
- the contribution of significant people, traditions and movements
- religious language and terminology
- major issues and questions arising
- the relationship between the areas of study and other specified aspects of human experience.

Develop the following skills:
- recall, select, and deploy knowledge
- identify, investigate and analyse questions and issues arising from it
- use appropriate and correct language and terminology
- interpret and evaluate relevant concepts
- communicate, using reasoned argument substantiated by evidence
- make connections between areas of study and other aspects of experience.

AO1

AO1 asks you to show relevant **knowledge** of what you have been studying. For example: *Outline how scholars have understood the term 'miracle'.*

This question is asking you to demonstrate an understanding of terminology and the debates that lie behind the use of that terminology. A strong answer may consider whether a miracle must be a break in the laws of nature or simply a surprising event. Some philosophers think that it is only a miracle if the laws of nature have been broken, since 'an extraordinary event' is only surprising if you do not know how the laws of nature led up to it. However, other philosophers question whether we can speak of natural laws at all, or if natural laws, by definition, cannot perform differently. You could raise issues such as coincidence miracles, or the need for a miracle to have religious significance ie. for God to be the only explanation for the event. Classic definitions of the term from Aquinas, Hume and other scholars will add to the credit you will gain for demonstrating well-learned knowledge. It is important to show that you understand how and why the term is not easily defined, and that the range of different definitions leads to different problems about whether miracles can occur and what they reveal.

As you study, look out for how new information fits into what you already know. Try not to leave a new set of facts or ideas without seeing how they relate to each other and what they add to your overall understanding of the subject. This means that you will need to review your notes and other materials each time so you can incorporate your new information in the right place. Don't shirk reorganizing your file on at least a weekly basis so that you always know if you are missing something and where material should go. Keep essays with the relevant topic rather than putting them in a separate file, as you should use them for revision.

AO2

AO2 is the skill of **evaluation** and it is the more difficult of the skills you have to demonstrate. AO2 skills are built on AO1: you can only evaluate when you have sound knowledge and understanding. AO2 breaks down into two: sustaining a critical line of argument and justifying a point of view. Each of the areas of study is based on some key questions about the area. None of these questions has ever been given an answer which satisfies all the experts in that area and this is why these questions are still addressed. A critical line of argument aims to provide a possible answer to one of these key questions. The evidence is examined, other arguments are discussed, and reasons for and against the argument being proposed are given. This cannot be done in a sentence or two, and this is why you are asked to **sustain** a critical line of argument.

When you are asked to evaluate, you are expected to have an **opinion** and to make a case for holding that opinion. This is not asking you to become a theologian or philosopher overnight. It is possible for an AS student to come up with original thinking on a topic, but your point of view can legitimately be that those experts who hold one particular answer to a question are right and that those who do not are wrong. Indeed, it is better to work on the assumption that evaluating a body of existing information is a safer ploy than making up your own evaluation, especially on the spur of the moment in the exam room. However, hopefully, over your course you and other students will have contributed to the body of information which you have all absorbed. This will certainly help you to remember it better than if you have never given it your stamp of individuality.

A typical AO2 question which would follow on from an AO1 question about the definition of the term miracle could be *'Comment on the view that miracles cannot happen today'.*

In this case, you need to recognise that you are not being asked to agree or disagree with the claim made – the examiner doesn't care what you personally think, just how well you can weigh up the opposing responses to this claim. You must offer evidence which supports the claim and which opposes it before coming to a conclusion as to which is the more convincing. For example, you might suggest that miracles cannot happen today because there appear to be very few – if any - cases of genuinely miraculous activity; that miracles by definition cannot occur (Hume's argument) and so not only can they not happen today, they have never happened; miracles belonged to an age in which God was communicating in a different way with his people and they do not happen today because God uses sacred texts and religious leaders to reveal his word and will to his people.

Then you need to offer reasons which oppose the claim. For example, that there are many occurrences of miracles worldwide, for which you may briefly cite supporting evidence; or that the definition of a miracle as a violation of a natural law which leads to the rejection of miracles as physically impossible is wrong – a miracle need not be a breaking of a natural law, but merely an event which is unexpected and which the person experiencing it interprets as God's action in the world. There is no reason to assume that God intended miracles to belong only to one age in history – there are several quotations from the gospels which would suggest otherwise.

Finally, you need to offer a reason why one view is stronger than the other, or, perhaps, to suggest that the view depends on how the speaker understands the term miracle. For example, if we take an anti-realist view of miracles, then a miracle is in the eye of the beholder and so if the person experiencing it believes they have experienced a miracle that is all that matters – hence, they can happen for as long as there are people who believe that God can perform miracles.

A key to meeting the AO2 objective is to learn what questions the experts are asking about the topic being studied and what some of the mainstream answers are. This should be clear from your teaching and reading. As soon as you notice that an opinion is being expressed, you should ask yourself what arguments and evidence are being put forward to support it.

Level descriptors

When an examiner marks your work, they will be looking for a number of key qualities that you need to demonstrate in order to achieve a particular grade:

AO1

- **Level Four – 23–28 marks**
  A full and well-structured account of the subject matter, with accurate and relevant detail, clearly identifying the most important features; using evidence to explain key ideas; expressed accurately and fluently, using a range of technical vocabulary.

- **Level Three – 15–22 marks**
  A range of accurate and relevant knowledge, presented within a recognisable and generally coherent structure, selecting significant features for emphasis and clarity, and dealing at a basic level with some key ideas and concepts; expressed clearly and accurately using some technical terms.

- **Level Two – 7–14 marks**
  Accurate and relevant information presented within a structure which shows a basic awareness of the issue raised, and expressed with a sufficient degree of accuracy to make the meaning clear.

- **Level One – 1–6 marks**
  A limited range of isolated facts which are accurate and relevant, but unstructured; a generalised presentation with little detail; imprecisely expressed.

AO2

- **Level Four – 9-12 marks**
  An attempt at the critical analysis of an issue by reference to an understanding of alternative viewpoints and balanced reasoning; expressed accurately, fluently and using a range of technical vocabulary.

- **Level Three – 5–8 marks**
  A clear attempt to sustain an argument, showing an awareness of alternative views and a limited attempt at a balanced conclusion, and expressed clearly and accurately using some technical terms.
- **Level Two – 3–4 marks**
  Clear argument(s) at a simple level to support a point of view on the basis of evidence; expressed clearly and communicated with a sufficient degree of accuracy to make the meaning clear.
- **Level One – 1–2 marks**
  A mainly descriptive response, but there is limited evidence of an attempt to argue the case, typically by reference to an appropriate source or comment by a scholar; imprecisely expressed.

Learning, revision and exam technique

As you prepare for your AS exam, there are stages which your teacher will directly help you with, and stages which you must be prepared to work on alone. In the end, your teacher cannot go into the exam and do it for you, and while they can give you information and guide you as to the best way of using it in the exam, you have to make sure you have learned it and developed an effective exam technique.

Lessons

Ask questions about the material you are given in class. Questions can help you to clarify what you have just heard, as well as clearing up misunderstandings. Ask questions about the implications of the material your teacher is covering and about how it relates to other aspects of the specification. Your lessons also give you the opportunity to practise the vital skill of evaluation. You will hear many views expressed which might be quite different from your own, which you can – in an empathetic (i.e. non-confrontational) way – evaluate: 'Am I right in thinking that you believe X to be right because of Y?'. Be prepared, in turn, for your views to be evaluated by others, and to explain why you hold them: 'I think that Z is wrong because if you take Y into consideration, the conclusion cannot be X'.

Homework

You must use homework tasks as an essential tool for refining your written skills. One of the most useful things you should be doing for homework is practising past questions which will enable you to be totally confident about the way Edexcel requires you to use the knowledge and understanding you have gained. Your teacher can explain to you how he or she has marked your work in accordance with the exam board's principles and so you can gain some insight into the way the system works.

You should plan an essay once you have read, understood and compared the appropriate range of sources dealing with the topic. Homework essays are different from the essays which you will be required to write in the exam, but they shouldn't be so different as to be of no use to you in revision. Your teacher may want you to write long essays during the course so that your awareness of the topic can be widely tested. But bear in mind that in the exam you will have only 40 minutes to write an essay. Make sure you write several timed essays during your course as practice, as well as at least two full mocks. When you do a timed essay you have to be selective about what you include from your source notes. Follow the pattern of the exam questions.

Independent learning and consolidation

Even the best teacher is not going to cover absolutely everything that is available about a topic in the class time available to them. The time you put in outside of the classroom will be decisive in the result you achieve. You may read an article that no one else in your class has seen, watch a television programme, or simply just go over your class notes one more time and in so doing finally understand a difficult area. There is no doubt that the top grades usually go to candidates who are prepared to do something extra.

Revision and the exam

It is never too early to start to revise. From the moment the first topic has been completed in class, you should be making concise revision notes, learning quotations, and making essay plans. If you leave it until the exams are looming, you will only have time to get it into your short-term memory, and you will feel far less able to deal with the unexpected or to spend time in the exam ensuring that your written style is the best you can offer on the day. Revision techniques do, and indeed should, vary. Everybody learns and remembers differently, so don't be led into thinking that you should be doing it exactly the same way as everybody else. Experiment with a range of strategies but make sure they are multi-sensory. This means that you should involve as many of the appropriate senses in the learning process as possible. If you are just reading through the notes in your file, you are using only one method - reading - and therefore only one channel to receive and process that information. Reading, making fresh notes, applying them to a question, writing it out again, repeating it orally to a friend – all these approaches contribute to the cumulative process of learning and establish the material more firmly in your memory.

Make sure that you are absolutely certain about key issues such as the day and time of the exam! Knowing dates well in advance enables you to make a revision plan, allocating specific tasks to each day as the exam approaches, so that your revision is never random or unplanned.

You also must be sure of what you will be required to do in the exam and how much time you have to do it in. This is why you must practise exam questions to time and not just under homework conditions. A top candidate can achieve a disappointing result because he or she didn't work to time, writing one or two long answers, but resorting to a plan, or notes for the third. If you have two hours to answer three questions, that means 40 minutes per question. Stick to this rule in all your timed work.

In the exam, keep in control and, even if the questions are not the ones you hoped would come up, think calmly and carefully and use the material you have learned to answer the questions that are there! Do what you are asked and nothing else. Don't panic and leave early, but think. Read what you have written and check it over for silly mistakes and mis-spellings.

Sample exam questions

1.2 The design argument

Sample essay question

(i) Outline the key ideas of the design argument. (20 marks)

(ii) For what reasons have some philosophers rejected the design argument? How far does the argument remain a convincing one? (20 marks)

Sample essay plan

For (i)

- Identify key ideas including the need for explanation; the features of the universe which may suggest order, purpose, benefit, providence.
- Describe analogical and inductive forms of the argument with relevant scholars and examples.
- Conclude with other forms of the argument, aesthetic argument and anthropic principle, for example.
- Don't spend all your time on one form or stress the contribution of one scholar over another too much.

For (ii)

- Identify key philosophers, particularly Hume and cover his criticisms in detail.
- Raise other criticisms offered, for example by Dawkins, or challenges to the aesthetic and anthropic principles.
- Consider the continuing appeal of the design argument, by reference perhaps to intelligent design, but also to the *a posteriori* nature of the argument which makes it accessible.
- Even scholars who ultimately rejected the argument (eg. Kant) recognised the power of its appeal to experience.
- However, modern science has served to fulfil the need for an explanation for the world and an atheist will not be convinced by the argument's assumptions.

1.3 The cosmological argument

Sample essay question

(i) Outline the cosmological argument for the existence of God. (20 marks)

(ii) What are the main criticisms of the cosmological argument? How far is it fair to say that the strengths of the argument outweigh its weaknesses? (20 marks)

Sample essay plan

For (i)

- Identify the key features of the cosmological argument, including its demand for an explanation of the universe, the need to find a first cause and mover, according to Aquinas's Five Ways and the Kalam Argument.
- You can include some reference to the early approaches to the argument in Greek philosophy.
- Move on to the search for a necessary being as an explanation for the existence of contingent beings, referring to Aquinas's Third Way and the ideas of F C Copleston.

For (ii)

- Outline the criticisms raised by David Hume and Bertrand Russell, focussing perhaps on the problems of looking for a cause for the whole and not just for parts.
- Is it reasonable to reject infinite regress and/or presume the existence of a necessary being?
- Identify some key strengths of the argument (reasons why it continues to be valid and attractive).
- Offer two or three clear reasons why these may be more convincing than the weaknesses, or vice versa.

2.1 The problem of evil

Sample essay question

(i) What is the problem of evil? (8 marks)
(ii) Examine any two theodicies and comment on how successful they are in solving the problem. (32 marks)

Sample essay plan

For (i)

- Discuss the nature of God and the qualities of omnipotence, omniscience and omnibenevolence.
- Discuss the inconstistent triad and the issue of how these qualities can be correct if evil exists.
- Put forward the views of scholars eg. Augustine and Aquinas.

For (ii)

- Outline the main points of Augustinian theodicy.
- Consider the strengths and weaknesses.
- Outline the main points of Irenaean theodicy or process theodicy.
- Consider the strengths and weaknesses.
- Comment on the views of scholars.
- Conclusion – evaluate the evidence.

2.2 Miracles

Sample essay question

(i) Outline the views of one scholar concerning the nature of miracles. (8 marks)
(ii) Examine and consider the views of scholars concerning the evidence for and against miracles. (32 marks)

Sample essay plan

For (i)

- Outline Aquinas's definition – it offers plenty of detail.
- Give his view on the three kinds of miracles.
- Compare Aquinas's definition briefly with another definition, such as David Hume's.

For (ii)

- Discuss the views of scholars who challenge the notion of miracles – eg. Davis and the 'interventionalist' God and Hick's challenge to the notion of natural law.

- Discuss the views of scholars who support miracles – eg. Swinburne – the religious significance of miracles and religious believers who see miracles as signs.
- Examine arguments concerning the moral grounds for miracles (Vardy and Wiles).
- Discuss Holland and Hare - the notion of coincidences and bliks.
- Provide an in-depth look at the criticisms of Hume and the problems raised for and against.
- Raise Swinburne's principles of testimony and credulity.
- Provide a conclusion, perhaps contrasting the views of an atheist and a religious believer.

3.2 Morality and religion

Sample essay question

(i) **Examine the views of scholars concerning the view that religion and morality are linked. (28 marks)**

(ii) **Comment on the view that religion and morality are not linked. (12 marks)**

Sample essay plan

For (i)

- Identify the key scholarly contributions in support of the link between religion and morality and the reason why there may be a relationship of dependency – for example: *Ethical obligations (moral duties or requirements) are often thought of as commands with authority behind them. However, what is the source of that authority? Is it sufficient to say that the sole reason for them being moral obligations is that they have been commanded by God?*
- Introduce divine command ethics – morality directly commanded by God.
- Discuss Aquinas's views – God as the source of morality and the ultimate good.
- Discuss Kant – a moral argument which identifies God as the necessary postulate of morality, although morality does stand alone.
- Put forward other reasons for linking religion and morality: tradition, teaching, authority of Church or religious leaders; religious influence on moral matters.

For (ii)

- Identify three key arguments against the link between religion and morality, for example:
  - the Euthyphro dilemma
  - examples of God commanding apparently immoral actions
  - religious morality encouraging moral standards which are opposed to modern or secular morality.
- Reassess whether the link between morality and religion is more sound than these critiques. Save up an evaluative comment, for example, that humans need moral guidance and it is as reasonable, if not more so, to rely on God to give it than on other human beings.
- Conclusion: come back to the critiques and identify one reason why they may be stronger than the arguments in support of the link between religion and morality.

3.3 Utilitarianism

Sample essay question

(i)   What are the main advantages of utilitarianism? (28 marks)
(ii) Identify the main problems of utilitarianism. To what extent do these make utilitarianism unacceptable? (12 marks)

Sample essay plan

For (i)
Identify the key features of utilitarianism in the form of strengths:

- Principle of utility, concern for majority and recognition of happiness as of intrinsic value to humans.
- Response to the social needs of the 18th century.
- Recognition of consequences as of particular value; realistic approach to moral decision making.
- Mill's adaptation resolved some difficulties with act utilitarianism – higher pleasures, ideals and desirable human qualities.
- Harm principle brings the power of the majority under control.

For (ii)
Identify the main problems of a consequentialist ethic:

- Too much emphasis on one factor – happiness/well being.
- Does not allow for *prima facie* relationships or agent relative moral decisions.
- Mill's form is too optimistic about human nature and inclines towards a rule-based morality.

However...

- Modern formulations of the theory show its perennial value: preference and negative utilitarianism.
- Formulates moral thought in a systematic way.
- It ultimately combines usefully with other ways of making moral decisions in the real world, in private and public.

3.4 Situation ethics

Sample essay question

(i)   Examine the key features of situation ethics. (20 marks)
(ii) Outline the main weaknesses of situation ethics. How far do they lead to a rejection of the theory? (20 marks)

Sample essay plan

For (i)

- Describe the background to situation ethics – social and moral change of perspective.
- Bring in the change in view on the traditional concept of God and of the role of religious morality.
- Discuss situation ethics as proposed by Fletcher and Robinson: *agape* as only norm; rejection of absolute laws and rules; presuppositions and principles of Fletcher's situation ethics.
- Bring in the new morality of Robinson, particularly in relation to divorce.
- Discuss Fletcher's use of case studies to illustrate the problems of absolutism.

For (ii)

- Outline Barclay's criticisms in detail.
- Outline the other weaknesses of situation ethics particularly as exemplified by Susan Howatch's characters.
- Comment on the comparative strengths of the theory: compassionate, flexible, consequentialist. It allows for careful reflection and mature reason, rather than slavish obedience to laws which may not be appropriate.
- Draw a balanced conclusion as to the success of situation ethics. Conceivably it reflects the need for moral flexibility, but does not recognise sufficiently the importance of moral guidelines.

4.1 Sexual ethics

Sample essay question

(i) Examine the differences in ethical and religious views concerning homosexuality. (28 marks)

(ii) To what extent may these differences reflect changes in social and cultural practices? (12 marks)

Sample essay plan

For (i)

- Look at ethical teachings concerning homosexuality – lowering age of consent, civil partnerships, equal rights and opportunities, tolerance.
- Examine religious teachings eg. Biblical view both pro and anti; Jesus's teaching on love and respect for all.
- Put forward the differing views on the nature and causes of homosexuality.
- Investigate views in society – tolerance, views of Roman Catholic Church and Church of England; ordination of Bishop Gene Robinson.

For (ii)

- Look at social and cultural changes – more awareness, tolerance, changes in the law.
- Changes in the Church – ordination of homosexual priests, division within the Church. Controversy with Bishop Jeffrey John. Schism with Nigerian Church.

4.2 War and peace

Sample essay question

(i) Examine the conditions laid down for the Just War Theory. (28 marks)

(ii) Comment on the view that these conditions can never justify war. (12 marks)

Sample essay plan

For (i)

- Outline what the Just War Theory is and what it aims to achieve.
- Examine the conditions concerning going to war (*jus ad bellum*).
- Examine the conditions for conduct in war (*jus in bello*).
- Highlight the religious basis of the theory – eg teachings of scriptures.

For (ii)

- Consider arguments for and against the Just War Theory.
- Comment on views of scholars and pacifists.
- Consider the arguments – may include reference to nuclear war, *jihad* and role of United Nations.
- Consider if war can ever be justified by the theory – arguments for and against. Look for examples eg. Gulf War, Rwanda genocide and Balkans conflict.

Index

Page numbers in *italics* are for 'Taking it further' notes in margins
Names prefixed by 'al-' are entered under the main element of the name, i.e. al-Ghazali is under 'G'